Unresolved Tensions in Papal-Episcopal Relations

Os Justi Studies in Catholic Tradition
General Editor: Peter A. Kwasniewski

1 • J. Joy, *Disputed Questions on Papal Infallibility*

2 • R.-M. Rivoire, *Does* Traditionis Custodes *Pass the Juridical Rationality Test?*

3 • J. Shaw, *The Liturgy, the Family, and the Crisis of Modernity*

4 • P. Kwasniewski (ed.), *Illusions of Reform*

5 • G. Steckler, *The Triumph of Romanticism*

6 • T. Crean, *"Letters from that City…": A Guide to Holy Scripture for Students of Theology*

7 • S. Lanzetta, *God's Abode with Man: The Mystery of Divine Grace*

8 • A. Fimister, *The Iron Sceptre of the Son of Man*

9 • S. Lanzetta, Super Hanc Petram: *The Pope and the Church at a Dramatic Moment in History*

10 • P. Kwasniewski (ed.), *Ultramontanism and Tradition*

11 • U. Hannon, *Thomistic Mystagogy*

12 • A. Thornton-Norris, *The Spiritual History of English*

13 • P. Kwasniewski (ed.), *Unresolved Tensions in the Papal-Episcopal Relationship*

Unresolved Tensions in Papal-Episcopal Relations

Essays Occasioned by the Deposition of Bishop Joseph Strickland

Edited by
Peter A. Kwasniewski

Foreword by
Joseph Shaw

Lincoln, Nebraska

Copyright © 2024 by individual authors of chapters
Anthology © 2024 by Os Justi Press

All rights reserved.

No part of this book may be reproduced, stored in a retrieval system, or transmitted in any form, or by any means, electronic, mechanical, photocopying, or otherwise, without the prior written permission of the publisher, except by a reviewer, who may quote brief passages in a review.

Os Justi Press
P.O. Box 21814
Lincoln, NE 68542
www.osjustipress.com

Send inquiries to
info@osjustipress.com

ISBN 978-1-960711-72-4 (paperback)
ISBN 978-1-960711-73-1 (hardcover)
ISBN 978-1-960711-74-8 (ebook)

Typesetting by Nora Malone
Cover design by Julian Kwasniewski
Painting of chair from *The Repository of Arts, Literature, Fashions &c.*, 3rd series, volume 6, July–December 1825 (public domain)

Contents

Foreword
JOSEPH SHAW vii

Preface. xv

1. On the Scope and Limits of Papal Power
   A FRIAR OF THE ORDER OF PREACHERS. 1

2. The Duty of the Bishop and the Jurisdiction of the Pope
   CARLOS A. CASANOVA 16

3. Why a Good Bishop Should Not Ignore but Obey
   His Unjust Deposition by a Pope
   JOSÉ ANTONIO URETA 27

4. On the Papal Deposition of Bishops
   JOHN LAMONT 35

5. It Is Churchmen Who Need Reform, Not the Church:
   In Defense of Papal Prerogatives
   JOSÉ ANTONIO URETA 80

6. In Defense of the Moderate Position on Papal Jurisdiction:
   A Reply to José Ureta
   JOHN LAMONT 110

7. Closing Remarks in My Debate with Dr. John Lamont
   JOSÉ ANTONIO URETA 132

8. Two Prelates Speak Out: Cardinal Müller and Bishop Schneider
   on Bishop Strickland 135

9. Pope Francis Has No Right to Dismiss Bishop Strickland Without Cause
   ANTONIO FRANCÉS 137

10. Bishop Strickland's Removal Was Against Canon Law
    GERALD E. MURRAY 140

11. Was Bishop Strickland's Termination Invalid?
    CARLOS ESTEBAN 143

12. The Pope May Not Depose Bishops Without Grave Cause
    ANTONIO FRANCÉS 146

13. The Removal of Strickland: An Act of the Arrogance of Power
    STEFANO FONTANA 151

14. May a Pope Fire a Bishop? What Is Bishop Strickland to Do?
    BRIAN M. MCCALL 154

15. In What Sense Is the Pope Above Canon Law?
    PHILLIP CAMPBELL 163

16. May a Bishop in Extraordinary Circumstances
    Ordain Another Bishop Without Papal Consent?
    ANTONIO FRANCÉS 171

17. The Responsibility of the Bishops for the Universal Church
    in a Time of Confusion
    PRO ECCLESIA UNIVERSALI 179

Epilogue 202

Appendix 1: Is the Pope the Vicar of Christ or CEO of Vatican, Inc.?
    PETER A. KWASNIEWSKI 203

Appendix 2: Why a Bishop Should Ignore His Unjust Deposition by a Pope
    PETER A. KWASNIEWSKI 208

Appendix 3: Do Not Go Gentle into That Good Retirement
    PETER A. KWASNIEWSKI 223

Latin and French Texts for Chapter 4 229

Works Cited 246

Index of Names . . . .

Foreword

Joseph Shaw

The Catholic Church, in addition to Word, sacrament, and creed, is also a community of law. Canon law orders Church life, harmonizes its institutions and procedures, and guarantees the rights of believers.[1]

These are the words of "Demos II," an anonymous cardinal who circulated a memorandum to members of the College of Cardinals regarding the principles that should guide them in a future conclave. They are a statement of the obvious, but this obvious truth is in danger of being forgotten by Catholics with a wide range of views on other matters. One might even say, in Aristotle's phrase, that it is evident in itself, but not evident to us.

The present collection of writings is an attempt to make this truth evident to Catholics once more, to reiterate and clarify its status as evident. We are grappling with a problem that has been creeping up on the Church for centuries, and yet has received inadequate attention from theologians: not just the relationship between the pope and bishops, but the relationship between the pope and law.

Until recently, it was commonplace to hear Catholic theologians and commentators who regard themselves as "progressive" dismiss the "hyperpapalism" of some historic theological schools and the ambitious claims of popes such as Innocent III, Pius V, and Pius X. On the old, progressive narrative, the Second Vatican Council rightly put an end to this self-aggrandizement, and having relinquished the papal tiara and gestatorial chair, popes must now accept that the bishops of the world are their co-workers in the vineyard of the Lord, with their own share in magisterial authority and a mandate directly from God. Only such a conception of the dignity of the "local church" (as they like to call each diocese) would be acceptable to their ecumenical "dialogue partners" among the Protestants and Orthodox. The next items on the liberal agenda for the relationship between pope and bishops were the restoration of some version of the ancient custom of bishops being elected by the clergy of a diocese—and perhaps by the laity as well—and the idea that the pope has a primacy not of monarchical power, but merely of respect and love.

---

[1] Demos II, "A profile of the next Pope, writes Cardinal," *Daily Compass*, February 29, 2024.

Unresolved Tensions in Papal-Episcopal Relations

There was always a tension in this position. Although progressives like to suggest that papal prerogatives had been exaggerated, in theory or in practice, by the Councils of Trent and Vatican I, Vatican II set in motion an exercise of papal power the like of which had never been seen before in the annals of the Church: a root and branch reform that left almost nothing untouched, from the position of the tabernacle in tens of thousands of churches to the formula to be used to bless a rosary, and from the dress of female religious to the relationship between Church and state in the constitutions of Catholic countries. *Some* kind of reform was mandated by the Council, certainly, but the Council's instructions were for the most part impressionistic, and it was clearly impractical for the Council as an institution to oversee their implementation. The sweeping reforms were actually carried out by commissions of "experts," of varying quality, appointed by and answerable to the pope, and their proposals were implemented by papal legislation. The postconciliar popes—for the reforms were far from complete at the death of Pope Paul VI in 1978—*remade* the Church, sometimes cleaving faithfully to Vatican II, sometimes going far beyond it, and occasionally directly contradicting it.

The most famous example of the last phenomenon concerns the place of Latin in the liturgy. The Council had declared that "the use of the Latin language is to be preserved,"[2] a statement that was explained in the course of the debate by the official "relator" as meaning that Mass could *never* be celebrated wholly in the vernacular; and, equipped with this understanding, the bishops voted in favor of the text.[3] This, however, as everyone quickly experienced, is not at all what happened. Bishops around the world felt helpless in the face of a new array of legislation—their only remaining discretion, to be exercised at a collective level, being the timing of when some of the changes would come into force. Even in this regard, Cardinal John Heenan of Westminster, England,[4] complained that delay was impossible: "Most of us would be content to delay changes but the mood of the Council compels us to act. Otherwise the attack from our own people would become ever more bitter."[5] This is the apotheosis of the model of a bishop as "the pope's vicar"—a model decisively rejected by the very Council in whose name the reforms were being carried out.

---

[2] Second Vatican Council, Constitution on the Sacred Liturgy *Sacrosanctum Concilium*, no. 36 § 1.
[3] Congregatio Generalis XLIII, *Relatio circa emendationes propositas. Acta Synodalia*, Volumen II, Periodus secunda, Pars II (Typis Polyglottis Vaticanis, 1972), 291. Discussed in Joseph Shaw, ed., *The Intellectuals and the Latin Mass: Petitions to Save the Ancient Mass from 1966 to 2007* (Waterloo, ON: Arouca Press, 2023), 93–95.
[4] He died in office in 1975.
[5] Letter to Evelyn Waugh in 1964: see Alcuin Reid, ed., *A Bitter Trial: Evelyn Waugh and John Carmel Cardinal Heenan on the Liturgical Changes* (San Francisco: Ignatius Press, 2011), 62.

Foreword

However, progressives balanced their ruthless use of papal authority with a large-scale campaign of disobedience to the Holy See, which started even before the liturgical reform was fully in place. The defiance of papal authority reached an early crescendo in response to Pope Paul VI's 1968 encyclical reaffirming the Church's bimillennial teaching on contraception, *Humanae Vitae*, but it extended far beyond that issue. As the decades passed, liberal bishops would boast that papal directives, such as those on liturgical abuses, didn't touch their desks on the way to the waste-paper basket. The long period during which the Code of Canon Law was being revised gave a new sense to the term "*vacatio legis*": it was as if the law had gone on holiday, since the old Code was clearly moot and no one could know what the new one would say. By the time the new Code finally emerged, in 1983, the idea of taking Canon Law seriously seemed like an attitude belonging to a long-dead age.

However, the antinomianism of the postconciliar period has not, in general, been to the advantage of bishops. On the contrary, their room for maneuver has been drastically reduced by a novel institution that was supposed to manifest their restored role in the life of the Church: the episcopal conference. Conferences quickly set up secretariats; its departments are headed by bishops, but bishops are busy men and much of their work inevitably devolves to committees, often composed of laity. I will never forget dealing with one such committee, of the Conference of England and Wales, whose lay members were clearly under the impression that for practical purposes they *were* the Conference: that their decisions were not mere advice to the bishops, but were actually decisions of the Conference, with all the weight this implied.

Bishops can fare little better than laity in dealing with this bureaucratic "blob." In 2007, Bishop Patrick O'Donahue of Lancaster in England[6] published a booklet for the many Catholic schools in his diocese, *Fit for Mission? Schools*. He was criticized for this on the basis that education was not his responsibility within the Bishops' Conference. Since every area of Catholic life has its own conference department, this clearly leaves no area in which a bishop can do more than meekly implement a policy decided by a committee, of which he is probably not a member. In this way, a bishop becomes not so much the vicar of the pope as a dogsbody commissioned to carry out the wishes of unaccountable administrators.

Conferences are sometimes given a decision to make (by a two-thirds majority) by the Holy See, but they are not institutions of divine law, and have no authority of themselves to make rules that bind their members. The President of a conference

---

[6] Retired 2009, died 2021.

may not act for its members if even one of them disagrees (see can. 455 §4). Bishop O'Donoghue could ignore these complaints, and did so, but he paid a price. He was identified as an outlier among the Catholic bishops, even a dissident. When he was criticized by a politician, not one of his brother bishops defended him.[7] The recommendations he made to his own schools, which ran counter both to the direction of government policy and to the attitude of the conference's educational organ, the Catholic Education Service, could be dismissed by the educational establishment as not representing the official Catholic position. This undermined his influence within his own diocese; his "lack of collegiality" might, if exhibited today, even mark him out as a target for removal from office.

The oscillation of the Catholic progressive tendency between anarchism and authoritarianism is not as surprising as it sounds. As Anne Roche Muggeridge noted, referring to James Hitchcock's *The Decline and Fall of Radical Catholicism*,[8] "to survive in power over a large number of unwilling subjects who still adhere to the older order, a revolution is forced to maintain a more rigid and punitive orthodoxy that the one it is trying to supplant."[9] The role of the bishops' conference exemplifies the fact that the structure of the Church established by her divine Founder, and elaborated by canon law and tradition—in short, law—is today *not* the source of real power in the Church. When law loses its proper role in ordering a society, it is replaced not by an increase of freedom held by individuals, but by the influence of people able to wield power deriving from other sources. In an institution like the Church, this comes down to things like the power of patronage and social networks. Annoy the wrong people and your life becomes very difficult, not because you have exceeded your legal prerogatives, but because no one will back you up or help you out, in public or behind the scenes. Instead, you will find people hindering, confusing, and undermining your plans. Cardinal Heenan was frightened of being publicly criticized by Catholic intellectuals; Bishop O'Donoghue experienced the loneliness of not being supported by his brother bishops.

Similarly, we hear anecdotally that the liturgical conservative Bishop William Gordon Wheeler of Leeds[10] is said to have remarked that the other bishops "rolled their eyes" whenever he spoke up in meetings. More recently, it is said that certain bishops at one time had to sit on their own at meals, at episcopal gatherings, because the other

---

[7] "Bishop O'Donoghue: I was baffled by lack of support from fellow bishops," *Catholic Herald*, April 2, 2015.
[8] James Hitchcock, *The Decline and Fall of Radical Catholicism* (New York: Herder and Herder, 1971).
[9] Anne Roche Muggeridge, *The Desolate City: Revolution in the City of God*, revised and expanded ed. (New York: HarperCollins, 1990), 174.
[10] Retired 1985, died 1996.

Foreword

bishops wouldn't sit next to them. Such things may seem trivial, but it becomes serious if a bishop's initiatives are publicly opposed by a small but noisy clique of laity and priests, with their brother bishops' quiet approval. The media and local public figures are unlikely to come to their rescue, and such bishops can look as though they have become incapable of governing their dioceses. If they then get a visit from the Nuncio to indicate that the pope would welcome a letter of resignation, this may seem to remove the last major element of moral support that they have. Their resignation becomes inevitable for reasons that are psychological, political, and social.

This kind of pressure has sometimes been employed to bring about good results, such as the removal of criminals from office; yet even in these cases it is problematic. Canonical trials can be somewhat opaque, but the alternative—a demand for a resignation which may or may not have been preceded by some kind of non-public investigation, visitation, or administrative procedure—hides the process completely not only from the public but from the accuser (in abuse cases, for example), and even from the accused. Nearly all the principles of natural justice are thereby ignored: the testing of witnesses; the accused having a genuine opportunity to defend himself; the making public of the evidence; even the revelation of the nature of the alleged crimes. The process results in a decision that may appear overly harsh or strangely lenient, but it is impossible for outsiders to tell how it really sits in relation to the facts. We are living in an age when it is almost unheard-of for justice to be seen to be done in the Church. It is some satisfaction, to be sure, to see criminal clerics departing the scene, on the occasions when this does happen, but such a process does not inspire confidence in the system.

There is another reason, in addition to justice and transparency, why the extra-legal use of power is problematic. Like the One Ring in Tolkien's epic, it tends to corrupt the user, thanks to the lack of checks, balances, and proper procedures. But even leaving that problem aside, it is also like the One Ring in that it is difficult to use this power for good. The reason for this has already been hinted at in my examples: however skilfully it may be wielded, the system of social pressure that has been substituted for legal process in the Church inevitably leans in a certain ideological direction. It is easy to bring social pressure to bear on a bishop (or a priest) not to oppose the convictions of an aggressively anti-Catholic secular elite. He can even be told that his positions are correct but that he has "gone about promoting them in the wrong way" and needs to step aside for the good of the Church. It is much more difficult to shame a bishop or priest into going quietly into retirement for downplaying the seriousness of the secular elite's favourite sins.

Unresolved Tensions in Papal-Episcopal Relations

This reality goes a long way towards explaining the extraordinary difficulty experienced by successive popes in dealing effectively with powerful heterodox bishops, sometimes even when serious effort is expended in the matter, from Archbishop Raymond Hunthausen of Seattle in the early 1980s to the ongoing case of former Cardinal McCarrick today. This problem is paralleled by the Holy See's difficulty in dealing with problems in American seminaries or female religious orders, investigations into which concluded in 1986 and 2014 respectively, and the failure to deal decisively with the Legionaries of Christ in 2019.

By contrast, Bishop Strickland is only the most recent case of the instant dismissal of an essentially conservative bishop, for misdemeanours that clearly don't rise to the level of canonical crime. Nor is this a phenomenon limited to the present pontificate. Due to the objections of local progressive Catholics, Bishop Wolfgang Haas of Chur, Switzerland, was moved sideways by Pope John Paul II in 1997, who created a new diocese in Vaduz, Liechtenstein, to receive him. Similarly, Gerhard Wagner, appointed auxiliary bishop of Linz in Austria in 2009 by Pope Benedict XVI, turned the post down only two weeks later, due to intense media pressure.

These dynamics need to be understood better by conservative Catholic defenders of arbitrary papal power. In the current state of the Church and the world, the Nuncio's tap on the shoulder is highly effective in getting rid of orthodox bishops who have run into opposition in their dioceses. With sufficient force of character, it can be made to work against bishops deeply implicated in clerical abuse or financial scandals, particularly if the press or the secular courts have become involved. It can be made to work after years of patient effort against outrageously heterodox bishops such as Bill Morris of Toowoomba, Australia, who called for the ordination of women in 2006, received an apostolic visitation in 2007, and resigned in 2011. But it is almost useless as a way of removing those who harm the Church by being too closely aligned with secular opinion on moral issues.

This may seem difficult to understand, as the claim that is being advanced by the more authoritarian conservatives is that the Nuncio's suggestion has real legal force, that it is not just a matter of social pressure. My point is not that it lacks legal validity—that argument will be made at length in the pages of this book—but simply that its *effectiveness* derives from social pressure. It will be obeyed by those vulnerable to this pressure, because of some combination of factors such as a personal feeling of obligation to the pope, ostracism by fellow bishops, or attacks in the local press or on social media. Those buoyed up by the support of liberal elites will be emboldened to resist it, and without recourse to proper legal procedure—which has, in the meantime, become almost unthinkable—a conservative pope may find he has no other cards left to play.

Foreword

This last point is worth underlining: that the use of proper legal procedures against bishops by the Holy See has become almost unthinkable. If the law of the Church is to function again, reforms are needed: the efficiency, stability, transparency, and impartiality of the law must be re-established; its institutions and personnel must be renewed; and mechanisms must be created to make the law useful, not only as a tool of control by the Holy See but as a way for subordinates, including the laity, to vindicate their rights. No such reforms will have credibility, however, unless the pope is seen not only as a legislator, but also as a subject of law. Though he cannot be judged, he should still feel the obligation that law lays upon him, and give law the respect it deserves for the good of the Church. (This point is brought out especially well in chapter 15 below.)

The extra-legal exercise of power is a constant temptation, and indeed informal methods may often be proportionate in bringing about good results. Nevertheless, for serious matters—and the deposition of a bishop is nothing if not serious—a fair and open canonical procedure, concluding with the condemnation and sentencing of the accused, is far more difficult to fabricate against the good, and far more difficult for the bad to resist.

Preface

The forcible removal of Bishop Joseph E. Strickland from his episcopal see of Tyler, Texas, by way of a sober notice in the Vatican's daily bulletin on November 11, 2023, was greeted around the world with a firestorm of protest. As more information emerged, Catholics learned that "America's bishop" had first been asked to resign, and refused to do so; this refusal was countered with unilateral deposition by Pope Francis, for unspecified reasons and accompanied by no canonical process.

The swiftness, secrecy, and irregularity of the move prompted speculation on all sides as to what the actual motives for the removal may have been, with Bishop Strickland himself opining it was for his outspoken proclamation of Catholic orthodoxy and his defense of the faithful entrusted to his care. Soon enough, modern Catholic discourse being what it is, two armies engaged in battle: on the one side, those who claim that a pope has an all but unlimited authority to appoint, control, and dismiss bishops as he pleases; on the other, those who claim that a pope, though he calls certain men to undertake the episcopal burden, must respect the office of the successors of the apostles whom Christ the Lord constitutes true shepherds in the Church. This debate naturally raised the further question of what Bishop Strickland (or, for that matter, any bishop similarly maltreated) should do or should have done when unjustly deposed.

The increasingly autocratic governance of Pope Francis has spurred theologians, canonists, and "vaticanists" to assess the nature and limits of a pope's jurisdictional authority over his brother bishops in the apostolic college. The best of such writing, to my knowledge, is gathered in the present volume, which I offer to the public as a triple resource: first, as a permanent historical record of the evils inflicted on the Church by her rulers in this present darkness; second, as a reflection on the ecclesiological realities involved, advancing substantive answers for vexing questions; third, as a source of strength and future resolution for those who have suffered abuse at the hands of superiors. I would draw the reader's attention to chapters 1 and 4 in particular: in the former, a Thomist friar of the Order of Preachers elegantly summarizes bimillennial Catholic teaching on the scope and limits of papal power, and in the latter, Dr. John Lamont masterfully analyzes the debated question of whether the pope has a *supreme* power of jurisdiction (the moderate view) or possesses the *whole* of that power in

Unresolved Tensions in Papal-Episcopal Relations

himself (the "strong" view), such that all episcopal authority derives immediately and personally from him. Much depends on which side is true. Lamont compellingly argues for the moderate view. In keeping with the Thomistic spirit of reasoned debate for love of the truth, this book contains José Antonio Ureta's extensive responses to Lamont (chapters 5 and 7) as well as Lamont's rejoinder (chapter 6). Lastly, we are pleased to give a wider diffusion to a document written by a Polish lay initiative called Pro Ecclesia Universali: "The Responsibility of the Bishops for the Universal Church in a Time of Confusion," which was first published online in February 2024 in seven languages, and whose authors kindly allowed us to include an edited version in the present anthology.

Four appendices close out the volume. The first three are chapters of mine that appeared in other books but are reprinted here both because they directly concern the subject-matter of *this* book and also because other authors herein reference them. The notes in these appendices replicate the notes with which the chapters were originally published, except that a few cross-references have been added to relevant chapters elsewhere in this book. The last appendix contains the original Latin and French texts for which Dr. Lamont provides a translation in chapter 4.

This work joins others of a similar character published recently by Os Justi Press: John P. Joy's *Disputed Questions on Papal Infallibility*; Fr Serafino Lanzetta's *Super Hanc Petram: The Pope and the Church at a Dramatic Moment in History*; and the anthology *Ultramontanism and Tradition: The Role of Papal Authority in the Catholic Faith*. As is true throughout Church history, so it is today: errors offer opportunities for articulating truths as yet implicit and for rediscovering old truths forgotten in the upheavals of time.

Translations from St. Thomas Aquinas's *Summa theologiae* are taken from the standard edition by the Fathers of the English Dominican Province, online at the New Advent website, which also supplies a number of Patristic quotations.

My thanks to all who gave permission for the inclusion of previously published material, and to Joseph Shaw for providing, as the Foreword, a splendid essay, which appears here for the first time.

Peter A. Kwasniewski
March 12, 2024
St. Gregory the Great

1

On the Scope and Limits of Papal Power

A Friar of the Order of Preachers

Fundamental truths

By "power" in this essay, I mean *legitimate* power, also called "authority." Authority may be defined as the right to oblige someone in view of some good end to be achieved. The person who possesses authority is called the superior, and those over whom he possesses it are called his subjects.

God Himself is the first superior and He has unlimited authority, not in the sense that He can oblige His rational creatures to do anything whatsoever, but in the sense that there is no one outside Himself who may limit His right of commanding His subjects for a good end. God cannot oblige His subjects to do anything whatsoever: for example, He cannot oblige human beings to hate themselves or to desire their neighbors to sin, since such actions do not tend to good and hence are not the sort of things to which anyone may be obliged. But God can appoint any good end for His rational creatures, and He can ordain the means by which they are to reach it, and no one has the right to gainsay or resist Him. "O man, who art thou that repliest against God," asks St. Paul (Rom 9:20).

The end which God has in fact appointed for mortal men is beatitude; and we are to reach this end by serving Him within His kingdom on earth, the mystical Body of His Son, the holy Catholic Church. Yet for as long as we remain "away from the Lord" (2 Cor 5:6), that is, until we reach heaven, most of us do not receive direct prophetic revelations from God to tell us more precisely in what our service of Him is to consist. Instead, He wills to govern us through intermediaries. As Pope Boniface VIII said in the bull *Unam Sanctam*: "According to the Blessed Dionysius, it is a law of the divinity that the lowest things reach the highest place by intermediaries." Hence, St. Paul instructs St. Timothy on the duties of laymen, laywomen, bishops, and deacons and bids him pass on this teaching, so that they "may know how one ought to behave in the household of God, which is the church of the living God" (1 Tim 3:15).

First published at the Substack *Tradition and Sanity*, February 22 and 29, 2024.

Unresolved Tensions in Papal-Episcopal Relations

Within the household of God there are various kinds of authority, which differ essentially and not simply insofar as they are exercised over more or fewer people. Thus, the authority of a husband over his wife is a different kind of thing from that of parents over their children. The authority of a baptized king or other temporal ruler over a baptized people, in the constitutional arrangement called Christendom, is a different kind of thing again. Above all these comes the spiritual authority which by the will of Christ is possessed by the pope and the other Catholic bishops.

Since this power, unlike the other kinds of authority just mentioned, does not derive from the natural end of man but is a result of God's having raised us to a supernatural end, we can only know the scope of this power by divine revelation. However, once we know that this spiritual authority of the pope and bishops exists to bring human beings to beatitude, we do know straightway that it cannot be used contrary to this end. Hence, St. Paul refers to "the power which the Lord hath given me unto edification, and not unto destruction" (2 Cor 13:10).

The exact nature of papal power

Within the Church on earth, the bishop of Rome or the pope has what is sometimes called a "plenitude or fullness of power," *plenitudo potestatis*. This does not mean that he can do anything at all, since as we have already seen, not even God Himself can command acts which are intrinsically wicked. It means that whatever can be done by any bearer of spiritual power within the Church can be done by the pope.

The present code of canon law, which dates from 1983, describes papal authority in the following way:

> Can. 331. The bishop of the Roman Church, in whom endures the office uniquely entrusted by the Lord to Peter to be passed on to his successors, is the head of the college of bishops, the vicar of Christ, and the shepherd of the universal Church on this earth. Thus, by virtue of his office, he enjoys supreme, full, immediate, universal, and ordinary power in the Church, which he can always freely exercise.

These five adjectives—supreme, full, immediate, universal, and ordinary—derive from earlier documents, in particular those of the First and Second Vatican Councils, and the 1917 code of canon law, but they are here brought together for the first time.

- ❖ "Supreme" means that the pope has no superior on earth, that is, no one who may claim to exercise authority over him. This is why, for example, one cannot appeal against a judgement of the pope to an ecumenical council.

❖ "Full" means that he exercises authority over the whole Church; thus while a diocesan bishop governs his diocese and a patriarch his patriarchate, the bishop of Rome governs the whole Church. We are all subjects of the pope. The First Vatican Council expressed this idea by saying that the "Roman Pontiff possesses primacy over the whole world (*in universum orbem tenere primatum*)."[11]

❖ "Immediate" means that the pope can exercise his authority on any of his subjects directly without needing to pass through their lower superiors: for example, if someone makes a private vow, such as a vow to say the rosary every day, that person's parish priest can dispense him from the vow if it proved too onerous; but if the person happened to be in Rome, then he could ask the pope to dispense him from it instead.

❖ "Universal" does not have a sense clearly distinct from "full," although the authoritative *New Commentary on the Code of Canon Law* considers that the word "universal" also evokes that papal power over temporal rulers which was exercised in the days of Christendom when popes declared that certain rulers had forfeited their right to rule because of heresy (hence, as good liberals, the authors of this *Commentary* apparently regret the inclusion of the word within the Code).

❖ Finally, "ordinary" in this context means a power which belongs to someone by virtue of the very fact that he possesses a certain office within the Church. Ordinary is contrasted with "delegated" power, which does not belong to someone simply in virtue of an office that he holds, but which has to be given to him, for example the faculty which a priest may receive to hear confessions. Since a pope has no superior on earth, it is obvious that the authority which he enjoys cannot be delegated to him, and therefore must be ordinary, belonging to him by virtue of his office.

This full and supreme authority of the pope relates, of course, only to the Church on earth. He does not have jurisdiction over the souls in purgatory, which is why, when he grants an indulgence to be gained for the holy souls, the indulgence is said to be applied to them "by way of suffrage," that is, as a specially powerful prayer, not as a guarantee that a given soul will be released from purgation by means of it. Likewise, he does not have any authority over the Church triumphant, though according to St. Thomas, piety inclines us to accept that if a pope canonizes someone, that is, places

---

[11] First Vatican Council, Dogmatic Constitution on the Church of Christ *Pastor Aeternus*, ch. 3.

that person's name into the liturgy properly belonging to the Roman church, his or her soul will indeed be in heaven.[12]

A basic distinction: magisterium vs. jurisdiction

The pope, like the other bishops, has received power from Our Lord to help us attain the happiness of heaven. To reach heaven it is necessary both to believe the truth and to act in accordance with it. "This is the work of God, that you believe in him whom he hath sent" (Jn 6:29); "Not everyone that saith to me, Lord, Lord, shall enter the kingdom of heaven: but he that doth the will of my Father that is in heaven, he shall enter the kingdom of heaven" (Mt 7:21).

For this reason, authority within the Church is twofold:
- the right to teach, also called *magisterium*, and
- the right to govern, sometimes called *jurisdiction*.

The latter authority, the power of governance or jurisdiction, is itself divided into legislative, judicial, and executive (can. 135); these three terms can be roughly defined as the right to make laws, the right to deal with alleged breaches of law, and the right to get things done. When a bishop ordains that the parish priests in his diocese shall make an annual retreat, he is exercising legislative power; when he tries a Catholic politician for heresy, he is exercising judicial power; when he uses diocesan funds to build a new school, he is exercising his executive power.

Since the pope's power in the Church is supreme, it must extend to matters both of governance and of teaching. The First Vatican Council defined both these matters in the dogmatic constitution *Pastor Aeternus*. With regard to the pope's right to govern the Church, having first explicitly rejected the ideas that an ecumenical council could have any authority over a pope or that temporal rulers might lawfully impede the communication between a pope and any of the faithful, the Council fathers defined the following dogma:

> If anyone, then, shall say that the Roman pontiff has the office merely of inspection or direction, and not the full and supreme power of jurisdiction over the universal Church, not only in things which belong to faith and morals, but also in those which relate to the discipline and government of the Church spread throughout the world; or assert that he possesses merely the principal part, and not all the fullness of this supreme power; or that this power which he enjoys

---

[12] Note the care with which this statement is articulated: if that person's name is placed "into the liturgy properly belonging to the Roman church," that is, the traditional Roman rite.

is not ordinary and immediate, both over each and all the Churches and over each and all the pastors and the faithful; let him be anathema.[13]

With regard to teaching, the same Council defined the following:

> The Roman pontiff, when he speaks *ex cathedra*—that is, when in discharge of the office of pastor and teacher of all Christians, by virtue of his supreme apostolic authority, he defines a doctrine regarding faith or morals to be held by the universal Church—is, by the divine assistance promised to him in blessed Peter, possessed of that infallibility with which the divine Redeemer willed that His Church should be endowed for defining doctrine regarding faith or morals: and . . . therefore such definitions of the Roman pontiff are irreformable of themselves, and not from the consent of the Church.[14]

Following this definition of papal infallibility, and in the course of the twentieth century, theologians have also given their attention to forms of papal teaching which do not meet all the conditions included in the definition, and hence are not guaranteed to be infallible. These lesser forms of teaching have come to be called "merely authentic" teachings. This means that they are statements about faith and morals made publicly by a pope but not issued *ex cathedra*. Such teachings, while not obliging us to accept them under pain of losing our faith, nevertheless of themselves call for a ready acceptance based on the piety which we rightly have toward him whom God has appointed shepherd of our souls (*obsequium religiosum*). I say that "of themselves" they call for this ready acceptance; for now, I do not consider the way in which unusual circumstances may modify this requirement.[15]

"Absolute monarch"

Given all this, should we refer to the pope as an "absolute monarch"?

First, we must define our terms. An absolute monarch differs from a tyrant. A tyrant is one who rules some society for his own good and not for the good of his subjects. Since this is contrary to the nature of authority, tyranny is always an evil, and hence our

---

[13] *Pastor Aeternus*, ch. 3.

[14] *Pastor Aeternus*, ch. 4.

[15] On such unusual circumstances, see John P. Joy, "Is There a Charism of Infallible Safety?" and Jeremy Holmes, "On Non-infallible Teachings of the Magisterium and the Meaning of *Obsequium Religiosum*" in Peter Kwasniewski, ed., *Ultramontanism and Tradition: The Role of Papal Authority in the Catholic Faith* (Lincoln, NE: Os Justi Press, 2024), 149–60; see also Edward Feser, "Refuting the Hyperpapalist Approach to Death Penalty Debate," ibid., 48–74.

Unresolved Tensions in Papal-Episcopal Relations

Lord cannot have made tyranny an element in His holy Church. An absolute monarch, by contrast, is one who in his government is constrained by nothing other than natural law and positive, that is, revealed, divine law, and not by any human law or person. It is sometimes said that the Russian czars were monarchs of this kind. It is not intrinsically wrong, though it will usually be very dangerous, to be an absolute monarch.

The pope, however, is *not* an absolute monarch, since he is bound not only by natural and divine law, but also by canon law, as we shall see. Moreover, divine law constrains him more closely than it constrains temporal rulers, since he, unlike them, deals directly with divine things. Let us examine in turn these three limits to papal authority: natural, canonical, and divine.

First, then, the pope is bound by natural law, both as a private person and as head of the Church on earth. As a private person, this is obvious: for example, he may not tell lies. As head of the Church, he is subject to those requirements of natural law to which all human rulers are subject. What are these requirements? According to St. Thomas, every ruler is naturally bound to have a care both for "divine good" and for "human good"; or as we might more commonly say today, by natural law the ruler must respect both the rights of God and the rights of men.[16] The rights of God mean that no ruler, and therefore no pope, may require someone to sin. Hence, a pope could not, for example, forbid us to honor our parents, or forbid us from rightly worshiping God.

How does a ruler respect human good, or, as we might say, the rights of men? Human good, Aquinas says, requires that acts of governance have a proper end, a proper form, and a proper author.

They have a proper end when the ruler is acting for some general benefit and not from private desire or vainglory. A law lacking a proper end, he adds, would be more like an act of violence than a law, and so would not bind the subjects under pain of sin. For example, if a pope taxed the faithful in order to build a fleet of luxury yachts for himself and all the cardinals, that would not seem to be a true law, and so one need not pay the tax.

Next, laws lack a proper form if they distribute some benefit or burden unequally over the community without a proper cause. Hence, a pope could not pass a law requiring that all brown-haired people fast on Christmas Eve, and that no one else need fast, since there is no connection between the color of our hair and the state of our soul.

Thirdly, a law must have a proper author, which means that the subject matter on which it bears must be one in which the lawgiver is competent. Hence, for example,

---

[16] *Summa theologiae* I-II, Q. 96, art. 4.

just as neither a king nor a president may pass a law requiring all families in his domain to eat dinner at a certain time, so neither could a pope; for by natural law each man's household is under his own sway.

The pope's subjection to canon law

Next, we may consider how a pope is subject to canon law. Canon law contains some provisions which belong to it not by human initiative but by divine revelation, for example, the canon stating that only a baptized man may be validly ordained. I am not now considering these provisions of canon law but rather those parts of it which are both of human origin and which are changeable. (I leave to the end of this paper the question of whether there are laws in the Church which, though instituted by man, are now unchangeable.)

Is the pope subject to canon law in its human and changeable aspect? Since the pope is himself in this case the legislator, it might seem impossible for him to be so bound. However, this claim—sometimes expressed in the saying that "the pope is above canon law"—is, at best, a half-truth. The relevant principles were elucidated by St. Thomas in his discussion of the more general question of whether a ruler (*princeps*) is subject to the laws of his realm. The Angelic Doctor writes as follows:

> The ruler is said to be "exempt from the law" [*solutus a lege*], as to its coercive power; since, properly speaking, no man is coerced by himself, and law has no coercive power save from the authority of the ruler. So it is in this way that the ruler is said to be exempt from the law, for none is competent to pass sentence on him, if he acts against it. Wherefore on Psalm 50:6, *To Thee only have I sinned*, a gloss says that "there is no man who can judge the deeds of a king." But as to the directive force of law, the ruler is subject to the law by means of his own will, according to the statement (*Extra*, De Constit. cap. Cum omnes) that "whatever law a man makes for another, he should keep himself." And a wise authority says: "Obey the law that thou makest thyself." Moreover, the Lord in Matthew 23 reproaches those who *say and do not*; and who *bind heavy burdens and lay them on men's shoulders, but with a finger of their own they will not move them*. Hence, in the judgement of God, the ruler is not exempt from the law, as to its directive force; but he must fulfil it voluntarily and not by constraint.[17]

In other words, just as the King of England must within his own domains drive on the left-hand side of the road, though no English court may punish him if he does not, so the

---

[17] *Summa theologiae* I-II, Q. 96, art. 5, ad 3.

bishop of Rome must follow the canon law of the Latin Church by which good order is maintained within it, though he is answerable only to God and not to man if he does not.

Thus, for example, he must say or assist at Mass on holy days of obligation and do penance on Fridays, and must not consecrate an eighteen-year-old man as a bishop. He can change at least certain elements of canon laws, for example by adding to or subtracting from the list of feasts of obligation, but he must do this by a public, legal act, and, until he has done so, he remains subject to the directive force of the existing law. Again, canon law recognizes that the pope, and in fact every diocesan bishop within his diocese, has a power to dispense from certain provisions of canon law, but it also states that there must be a *just and reasonable cause* for doing so, without which the dispensation would be illicit (can. 90).[18] So a pope could dispense the precept of Friday abstinence when a certain Friday was a day of celebration for a given country, but if he sought to dispense it just because he had a nephew who was a butcher and who wanted to sell more meat, his action would be unlawful. Again, canon law tells us that he cannot validly dispense from those provisions of law which constitute legal entities, for example, religious orders (can. 86); hence he couldn't allow someone to join a religious order without being bound by the vow of poverty.

How divine law limits the pope

We come now to the third set of limits on papal power, namely those placed upon him by divine law. By divine law we mean the law revealed by God in the New Testament, summed up near the beginning of the Gospel of St. Mark as the command to "repent and believe the gospel" (Mk 1:15). A pope has no power over divine law, just as he has no power over natural law, because in each case it is not he but God who is the law-giver. The pope, together with all the Catholics bishops, is the authoritative expositor of divine law, having the right to state what is included within it; but he has no power to *add* to it or to *subtract* from it. He is therefore *subject*, like all the faithful—and even more than they—to the threat uttered by Our Lord at the end of the Apocalypse:

> I testify to everyone that heareth the words of the prophecy of this book: if any man shall add to these things, God shall add unto him the plagues written in this book. If any man shall take away from the words of the book of this prophecy, God shall take away his part out of the book of life, and out of the holy city. (Rev 22:18–19)

---

[18] The same canon, however, states that the dispensation would still be valid. This is a matter of discussion among canonists.

This threat limits the way in which a pope may use that supreme power of teaching and governance which we have seen him to possess.

In regard to teaching, since public divine revelation ended with the death of St. John, the beloved and last apostle, the pope may not declare any new revelation to be binding on the faithful, for example, by claiming that God had revealed, to himself or to some prophet living since the apostles, the exact number of souls who will be in heaven, and saying that Catholics must believe this. As the First Vatican Council says:

> The Holy Spirit was promised to the successors of Peter not so that they might, by his revelation, make known some new doctrine, but that, by his assistance, they might religiously guard and faithfully expound the revelation or deposit of faith transmitted by the apostles.[19]

For the same reason, the pope cannot remove something from the deposit of divine revelation. This means in the first place that he may not suppress any part of Holy Scripture. It might seem unnecessary to say this, but some years ago a long-standing author in *The Tablet*, the English equivalent of *National Catholic Reporter*, proposed that the pope of the time (I think it was John Paul II) be petitioned to declare infallibly that John 8:44 is not a part of inspired Scripture. This is the verse in which Christ says to some of the Jews in Jerusalem, "You are of your father the devil." To adapt some words of the great Samuel Johnson: "Modernist ultramontanism is a very horrid thing."

Just as the pope's teaching power does not allow him to suppress any jot or tittle in God's written word, Holy Scripture, so neither does it allow him to suppress any part of God's unwritten word, Holy Tradition—by which I understand here the teachings which, whether or not they are also included in the Bible, the apostles passed on orally to the next generation. Since, by definition, there is no inspired, written list of these teachings, we learn them by the words of later witnesses to apostolic tradition, and among these, the Fathers of the Church enjoy a privileged place in virtue of their closeness to the source. Indeed, the Church teaches that it is not permitted to interpret Holy Scripture against the unanimous judgement of the Fathers.[20] Hence, a pope cannot declare someone to be a Father of the Church who does not meet the proper criteria (namely, orthodoxy, antiquity, and authorship) or declare someone not to be a Father who does meet these criteria, since he would thus risk falsifying the word of God.

---

[19] *Pastor Aeternus*, ch. 4.
[20] The pertinent passage from *Dei Filius* is quoted below on p. 23.

Unresolved Tensions in Papal-Episcopal Relations

Bound by prior definitive teaching

Just as the pope may not tamper with the word of God, but must rather guard it as a faithful steward against the day of the Lord's return, so also he must faithfully guard the teachings by which the Church declares what is contained in this revealed word.

Hence, he cannot revoke any of the dogmatic canons and anathemas of past ecumenical councils or any of the definitions of his predecessors, or claim that these canons and definitions fail adequately to express divine revelation. For the same reason, he cannot contradict or revoke any of those things which, without having yet been defined, have nevertheless been taught by what is called the ordinary and universal magisterium, for example the truth that Christ's tomb was empty on Easter Sunday, or that Our Lord worked true miracles, or that capital punishment is sometimes lawful.

The law of the Church also recognizes a category of teachings about faith and morals which, while they do not necessarily express truths which have been directly revealed, are nonetheless taught infallibly, as necessary for revelation to be safely preserved and lived out in a holy manner (can. 750 §2). Examples of such teachings might be that man's bodily senses are not generally illusory but give him true information about a world that exists independently of himself, or that bringing about conception by artificial means, such as *in vitro* fertilization, is a sin.

Hence, although a pope may not add to the deposit of faith, he may teach things of this kind which are necessary for the preservation of faith and holiness. However, he may not bind the faithful to give any kind of assent to things which are neither part of divine revelation nor necessary to preserve it—for example, that Mozart was a greater composer than Beethoven. Hence, he may not bind them to accept his opinions about subjects where discovering the truth requires either political prudence or a specialised human knowledge, for wrong opinions about such subjects are nonetheless compatible with faith and holiness. Thus, while a pope does well to remind political rulers of their general duty to harbour the harbourless or to be good stewards of creation, he cannot tell them *how many* immigrants they should permit to enter their country, or whether it is desirable or possible for them to seek to control the climate, or with what means they must do so.

If ever a pope, in the course of his public statements, should say something apparently contrary or injurious to divine revelation, then one should—if reasonably possible—interpret his words in a good sense; if this becomes impossible, one should note the error and, depending on one's rank and competence, one may and sometimes should petition him to correct it. It is the opinion of the great theologians and canonists who have discussed the question, including doctors of the Church such as St. Robert

On the Scope and Limits of Papal Power

Bellarmine and St. Francis de Sales, that if a pope should persist in public heresy, then divine law enables other bearers of spiritual power first to warn him and finally, if these formal warnings are ignored, even to declare that he has freely divested himself of the papacy. Hence, Pope Innocent III stated in a sermon on the consecration of the sovereign pontiff: "God alone is my judge for other sins; I can be judged by the Church only for sins committed against the faith." However, as Catholics we believe that the Holy Spirit will prevent a pope from ever teaching heresy *ex cathedra*, i.e., in a definitive and binding way that commits the full force of papal authority. As to what is possible up to that point, opinions vary, and experience will, sadly, be the best teacher.

Limits on papal governance

We come, finally, to limits placed by divine law on the pope's governance of the Church. Just as the pope may not, in his *teaching*, add to or subtract from the divine word (either in itself or in its past infallible expression by the Church), so too, he may not *govern* the Church contrary to the demands of God's word.

Hence, he may not invent new sacraments or suppress any of the sacraments or the sacrifice of the Mass. Nor may he suppress the divine office, since St. Clement, bishop of Rome at the end of the first century, declared that the Lord has decreed that religious services should be performed "not thoughtlessly or irregularly, but at the appointed times and hours."[21]

Again, he cannot suppress the universal episcopate, dismissing all the bishops and governing every diocese directly. When Otto von Bismarck, the anti-Catholic Chancellor of Germany at the end of the nineteenth century, asserted that the First Vatican Council's definition of the pope's immediate jurisdiction over all the baptized meant that such an abolition of the episcopacy was now conceivable, the German bishops rejected this interpretation, and Pope Pius IX confirmed the truth of their words.[22] The Second Vatican Council in its decree *Unitatis Redintegratio* specified that the Eastern churches, that is, the *Catholic* patriarchal churches outside the Roman patriarchate, have the right to govern themselves—a right which Pope John Paul II declared to belong to them by the law itself, without its having been *granted* to them as a privilege by any pope. It would follow that no pope can take away this right, or suppress the ancient patriarchal sees such as Antioch or Alexandria.

---

[21] *Epistle of Clement*, ch. 40.

[22] For the text of the bishops' letter together with Pius IX's *Mirabilis Illa Constantia*, see Denzinger, 43rd ed., nos. 3112–17; for commentary, see "Objections and Replies on *Pastor Aeternus*" in Peter Kwasniewski, *Bound by Truth: Authority, Obedience, Tradition, and the Common Good* (Brooklyn, NY: Angelico Press, 2023), 30–38.

Unresolved Tensions in Papal-Episcopal Relations

That the pope cannot suppress the Mass, the sacraments, or the episcopacy is, I hope, rather obvious. However, tradition appears to circumscribe his power of governance more closely still. We may say that there has always been, at least till the twentieth century, a strong sense among Catholics that both the liturgical rites and the discipline or canon law that have come down from ancient days are sacred by reason of their very antiquity and perpetuity and hence that the pope may not modify them except with the greatest caution and where the need is obvious or the gain sure.

Even by natural law, in fact, legislators have the duty to make no changes to the laws of their realm except where the advantage of the change will outweigh that weakening of the power of law as such over men's minds which any change in a body of laws will tend to produce. But in the case of the pope's duty toward tradition, the obligation to exercise caution is all the more intense, since the ancient discipline and ceremonial is a witness to Sacred Tradition, and so any changes to it risk obscuring the word of God that is transmitted by that means. We can also say that since the Church is ruled by the Spirit of God, we may presume that He will cause customs to grow up within her, customs whose divine origin will be manifested by the peaceful and universal acceptance of them by the faithful, and which therefore no human power may overturn. Hence St. Augustine declared:

> The customs of God's people and the institutions of our ancestors are to be considered as laws. And just as those who disobey the laws of God are liable to coercion, so also are those who throw contempt upon the customs of the Church.[23]

For this reason, the *Liber Diurnus Romanorum Pontificum*, a book apparently used from the late seventh or early eighth until the eleventh century, contained a profession of faith to be made by a newly-elected pope that included the promise "to keep inviolate the discipline and the liturgy of the Church as I have found them and as they were transmitted by my holy predecessors."[24]

In the year 787, the Second Council of Nicaea declared: "If anyone rejects any written or unwritten tradition of the Church, let him be anathema." The context of the anathema was the defense of sacred images against the iconoclasts. Pope Innocent III, about to discuss the ceremonies of the Roman Mass around the year 1200, describes

---

[23] *Epistle 36.*
[24] *PL* 105:9–188. On this important witness to tradition, see Peter Kwasniewski, "The Pope's Boundedness to Tradition as a Legislative Limit," in idem, ed., *From Benedict's Peace to Francis's War: Catholics Respond to the Motu Proprio* Traditionis Custodes *on the Latin Mass* (Brooklyn, NY: Angelico Press, 2021), 222–47.

the words, gestures, and vestments of the Mass as "full of divine things," and implies that the rite as a whole was included in the vision of perfect divine worship shown to Moses on the mountain.[25] When, in 1417, the Council of Constance proposed that a new pope should declare, among other things, "I will follow and observe in every way the rite handed down of the ecclesiastical sacraments of the Catholic Church" (Session 39), no one appeared to think the suggestion strange. In the mid-sixteenth century, the Council of Trent promulgated the following canon:

> If anyone says that the received and approved rites of the Catholic Church, accustomed to be used in the administration of the sacraments, may be despised or omitted by the ministers without sin and at their pleasure, or may be changed by any pastor of the churches to other new ones, let him be anathema.

Although the canon does not mention the pope, it is hard to see why it would not apply to him, the pastor of the churches *par excellence*. Indeed, in the following century, the great Jesuit theologian Francisco Suárez argued that one way in which a pope could actually commit the sin of schism would be "if he should wish to overturn all the ecclesiastical ceremonies which have been enforced by apostolic tradition."[26] In the nineteenth century, St. John Henry Newman rejoiced in the fact that the papacy had been the great conserving force within the Church:

> It is one of the reproaches urged against the Church of Rome that it has originated nothing, and has only served as a sort of *remora* or break in the development of doctrine. And it is an objection which I embrace as a truth; for such I conceive to be the main purpose of its extraordinary gift.[27]

Well known, also, is the reply of Bl. Pius IX to some who petitioned him to add the name of St. Joseph to the Roman Canon: "I cannot do this, I am only the pope!"

The Second Vatican Council's Constitution on the Sacred Liturgy *Sacrosanctum Concilium*, though doubtless a Janus-faced document, evokes this same tradition at least in its twenty-third paragraph, where it states that no liturgical modifications must be made "unless the good of the Church genuinely and certainly requires them." Likewise, the modern *Catechism of the Catholic Church*, in what may strike some people as a fine example of stable-door shutting, notes that the supreme authority within the

---

[25] *De sacro altaris mysterio*, prologue (PL 217:774).
[26] "si vellet omnes ecclesiasticas caeremonias apostolica traditione firmatas evertere" (*De caritate* disp. XII.1).
[27] *Apologia pro vita sua*, ch. 5. On this notion of the papal office as *remora*, see John Hunwicke, "Peter Says No," *First Things* online, February 7, 2017.

Unresolved Tensions in Papal-Episcopal Relations

Church—that is, the pope acting with or without the body of bishops—cannot change the liturgy as he pleases (*ad placitum*), but only "in the obedience of faith and with holy reverence (*religiosa observantia*)."[28]

What, in practice, does all this mean?

As examples, not a complete list, of the kinds of thing which the *Liber Diurnus* had in mind when it bade the pope promise to preserve the liturgy and discipline that he had received, I would mention the following:

- the principal seasons of the liturgical year;
- Sunday as the day when Christians must come together for worship;
- the building of churches toward the east, and the offering of worship in that direction;
- the distinct rites of the patriarchal churches (the Roman rite, the Byzantine rite, the Coptic rite, and so on);
- Lent as a time of bodily penance;
- the practice of perfect continence by those in major orders;
- the use of candles, sacred images, incense, and holy water in worship;
- fasting from midnight before receiving Holy Communion;
- solemn religious vows;
- offering the holy sacrifice of the Mass over the relics of saints;
- the practice of burial and not cremation;
- the non-admission of women to service at the altar;
- Friday penance; and, at least within the Latin church,
- the seven major and minor orders, and the observance of the Ember Days in the four seasons of the year.

It is presumably such things as these that St. Augustine had in mind when he distinguished the customs of the Church from the laws of God. Yet the law of God itself obliges us to esteem the customs of the Church.

It seems to be a mark of an ecclesiastical custom that, if it could ever become necessary to grant a temporary exemption from following it, a pope would have the power to do so; for example, by allowing cremation or absence from Sunday Mass during a time of plague—as, by contrast, he can never grant an exemption from the duty to be baptized or to be faithful to one's spouse. This is not to say that all exemptions and indults that have been

---

[28] *Catechism of the Catholic Church* [CCC], no. 1125.

granted have been wise or even lawful: one would have to consider each case separately. What we can say with confidence is that no pope may treat these things as unimportant, or as able to be suitably replaced by other customs; he should promote the ecclesiastical customs strenuously, and, where they have fallen into decay, seek to revive them.

The pope is the steward of God's house, ruling it until the Master returns. If the truths of faith are like the pillars or walls of that house, holy customs are its ornament and its splendour, over which also the divine law makes him the guard. Like all the other faithful and indeed more than all of them, the pope must be able to say: *Domine, dilexi decorem domus tuae, et locum habitationis gloriae tuae*; "O Lord, I have loved the beauty of thy house, and the place of the dwelling of thy glory."[29]

---

[29] Ps 25:8. Psalm 25:6–12 is recited by the celebrant during the washing of hands in the ancient Roman Rite.

2

The Duty of the Bishop and the Jurisdiction of the Pope

Carlos A. Casanova

We live at a time when Rome can credibly be said to abuse its power and authority over the bishops of the whole world. Bishops who wish to protect the rights of their subjects are forbidden to do so; their ability to grant reasonable dispensations is negated.[30] Orthodox bishops are removed without legal procedure and clearly for the wrong reasons. Moreover, precisely the *orthodoxy* of the bishops becomes the motive of their demotion. In these cases, should the demoted bishops accept such an arbitrary decision obediently? If they did, they would be acting on the basis of an ecclesiological mistake. The authority of the bishop does not come from the pope, but from God.[31] As *Lumen Gentium* teaches:

> *Bishops, as vicars and ambassadors of Christ, govern the particular churches entrusted to them* by their counsel, exhortations, example, and even by their authority and sacred power, which indeed they use only for the edification of their flock in truth and holiness, remembering that he who is greater should become as the lesser and he who is the chief become as the servant (cf. Lk 22:26–27). This power, which *they personally exercise in Christ's name, is proper, ordinary, and immediate*, although its exercise is ultimately regulated by the supreme authority of the Church, and can be circumscribed by certain limits, for the advantage of the Church or of the faithful. In virtue of this power, bishops have the sacred right and the duty before the Lord to make laws for their subjects, to pass judgment on them, and to moderate everything pertaining to the ordering of worship and the apostolate. *The pastoral office or the habitual and daily care of their sheep is entrusted to them completely; nor are they to be regarded as vicars of the Roman Pontiffs, for they exercise an authority that is proper to them, and are quite correctly called "prelates,"* heads of the people whom they govern. Their power, therefore,

---

First published at *OnePeterFive*, October 28, 2022. Edited for inclusion in this volume.

[30] See Réginald-Marie Rivoire, FSVF, *Does Traditionis Custodes Pass the Juridical Rationality Test?* (Lincoln, NE: Os Justi Press, 2022).

[31] See Second Vatican Council, Dogmatic Constitution on the Church *Lumen Gentium*—e.g., no. 22.

is not destroyed by the supreme and universal power, but on the contrary it is affirmed, strengthened, and vindicated by it, since the Holy Spirit unfailingly preserves the form of government established by Christ the Lord in His Church.[32]

If it is true that the pope has a universal jurisdiction, it is also true that that jurisdiction has as its end service to the Church's Faith and the good of souls. For this reason, it may not and cannot be used tyrannically as if the pope were the vicar of Satan instead of Christ.

In order to provide arguments for the faithful bishops, with the hope of serving the defense of Christ's Bride in these times of the Enemy's turbulent attacks, I have written these pages, gathering ancient witnesses and the principles proclaimed by the Magisterium of the Church. I know that it is Christ who protects His Church, but I also know that He does so as the First Cause who makes use of secondary causes. We must be His instruments, by His grace.

Catena of ancient texts

One of the *Apostolic Canons* contains the following teaching:

> The bishops of every nation are bound to acknowledge the principal among them, and to count him as a head, and to do nothing extraordinary without his advice, but to do those things alone individually which relate to the diocese of each respectively and its towns. He, in turn, must not act without the advice of all.[33]

According to John Henry Newman, when even heretics concur on a certain point with the unanimous teaching of the Fathers and received usage, we can be the more certain we are dealing with a view truly apostolic.[34] The Synod of Antioch, although tainted with Arian tendencies, received this apostolic canon and adapted it in the fourth century:

> The bishops in each province are bound to acknowledge the bishop ruling in the metropolitan see, and that he has the care of the whole province, because all who have business have recourse from every quarter to the metropolis. Whence it has seemed good that he should be first in honor also, and that the other bishops should do nothing extraordinary without him (according to that most ancient canon which has been in force from our fathers' time), or such

---

[32] *Lumen Gentium*, no. 27, emphasis added.
[33] John Henry Newman, *The Church of the Fathers* (London and New York: John Cane, 1900), 243.
[34] See Newman, 229.

Unresolved Tensions in Papal-Episcopal Relations

things only as relate to the diocese of each and the places under it. For each bishop has power over his own diocese to administer it according to his own conscience, and to provide for the whole territory subject to his own city, so as to ordain presbyters and deacons, and to dispose all things with consideration, but to attempt no proceedings beyond this without the metropolitan bishop; and he, in turn, must not act without the advice of the rest.[35]

From all this, Newman concludes that "no suffragan [bishop] could act in extra-diocesan matters without his metropolitan, nor the metropolitan without his suffragans."[36] That was simply how the Church founded on the apostles and their successors operated.

This canon gives the appropriate context for rightly understanding various statements by St. Cyprian that seem to contradict each other. On the one hand, the great African bishop acknowledges that the Church of Rome is "the *ecclesia principalis* [foremost church] and the point of origin of the *unitas sacerdotalis* [priestly unity]." Cyprian states, moreover, that the heretics did not realize "that the Romans, whose faith was proclaimed and praised by the apostle, are men into whose company no perversion of faith can enter" (*Epist.* 59, 14). On the other hand, in the same letter and to Quasten's bewilderment, St. Cyprian "expects her [Rome] not to interfere in his own diocese 'since to each separate shepherd has been assigned one portion of the flock to direct and govern and render hereafter an account of his ministry to the Lord' (*Epist.* 59, 14)."[37] As one can see, Cyprian acknowledges Rome's principality over his African diocese while at the same time clarifying that such principality does not imply a jurisdiction all-embracing and unlimited.

St. Cyprian, we know, is jealous about the authority he has received directly from God, not from the pope. And he says so very clearly: "So long as the bond of friendship is maintained and the sacred unity of the Catholic Church is preserved, each bishop is master of his own conduct, conscious that he must one day render an account of himself to the Lord" (*Epist.* 55, 21). Quasten adds:

> In his controversy with Pope Stephen on the rebaptism of heretics he voices as the president of the African synod of September 256 his opinion as follows:

---

[35] Newman, 243–44.
[36] Newman, 253.
[37] All of Quasten's citations are taken from Johannes Quasten, *Patrology*, vol. 2: *The Ante-Nicene Literature after Irenaeus* (Westminster, MD: Christian Classics, 1983), 373–78.

The Duty of the Bishop and the Jurisdiction of the Pope

"No one among us sets himself up as a bishop of bishops,[38] or by tyranny and error forces his colleagues to compulsory obedience, seeing that every bishop in the freedom of his liberty and power possesses the right to his own mind and can no more be judged by another than he himself can judge another. We must all await the judgment of our Lord Jesus Christ, who singly and alone has power both to appoint us to the government of his Church and to judge our acts therein" (*CSEL* 3/1, 436).

Obviously, this latter statement must be seen in the light of what we have stated earlier. The bishop of Rome has a power over the other bishops, but neither an all-embracing nor a tyrannical power. The exclusion of tyranny Cyprian supports with a clear Scriptural precedent:

Even Peter, whom the Lord first chose and upon whom He built His Church, when Paul later disputed with him over circumcision, did not claim insolently any prerogative for himself nor make any arrogant assumptions nor say that he had the primacy and ought to be obeyed.[39]

That the aforementioned apostolic canon provides the key to harmonize all these texts appears with clarity in the reaction St. Cyprian had to Pope Cornelius's inquiries about the consecration of Fortunatus, which Cyprian had performed without first consulting Rome. In his reply, the African prelate recognizes his obligation to report to the Pontiff any matter of major importance:

I did not write you of it at once, dearest brother [Cornelius], for it was not a matter of enough importance or gravity to be reported to you in great haste. . . .[40] Since I supposed that you were aware of these facts and believed that you would certainly be guided by your memory and sense of discipline, I did not consider it necessary to notify you immediately and hurriedly of the heretics' antics. . . . And I did not write you of their performance because we despise all these doings

---

[38] He states it more strongly at a different place: "*hoc erant utique et ceteri apostoli quod fuit Petrus, pari consortio praediti et honoris et potestatis*" (*De unit.* 4) : "Certainly the other Apostles also were what Peter was, endued with an equal fellowship both of honor and power."

[39] *Epist.* 71, 3.

[40] Quasten adds (377): "The same reason explains exactly the same behavior when, during the vacancy following the death of Pope Fabian (250), the mere clergy of the capital city expressed their disapproval of Cyprian's going into hiding; in this case also, he yields a report of his conduct, and, over and beyond that, adopts the Roman line of action with regard to the *lapsi*; in short, he feels an obligation, not only to the ordinary, but, in his absence, to the very see."

and I was soon to send you the names of the bishops who govern the brethren soundly and correctly in the Catholic Church. It was the judgment of us all in this region that I should send these names to you.[41]

This interpretation is confirmed when St. Cyprian acknowledges the primacy of Peter and of the bishop of Rome:

> The primacy was given to Peter and in such way is taught that there is one only Church and one only Chair. That the Shepherds are many but the flock is one is taught because it is shepherded by all the apostles in perfect consensus. How could anybody who departs from the Chair of Peter on whom the Church was founded be confident about being in the Church?[42]

Saint Basil's experience

In Asia at the time of St. Basil, the Faith was in danger due to the great quantity of heresies that had made their way to the faithful, even among the bishops. At this critical juncture, the great Cappadocian Father asked Rome to help him, yet he did not receive help. He did not shrink from the defense of the Faith for that reason. In that context he complained about the Holy See.[43] In the light of these events, St. John Henry Newman states:

> And in like manner, the dissatisfaction of Saints, of St. Basil, or again of our own St. Thomas [Becket], with the contemporary policy or conduct of the Holy See . . . is no reflection either on those Saints or on the Vicar of Christ.

---

[41] *Epist.* 59, 9, cited by Quasten, 377.

[42] *De unitate Ecclesiae* 4 (my translation). "*Primatus Petro datur et una ecclesia et cathedra una monstratur. Et pastores sunt omnes, sed grex unus ostenditur qui ab apostolis omnibus unanimi consensione pascatur. Qui cathedram Petri super quem fundata ecclesia est, deserit, in ecclesia se esse confidit?*" Thus went the original edition, according to recent research, adds Quasten (377). I disagree with Quasten's interpretation when he holds that Cyprian thought that the pope was just "first among equals" and had primacy only of honor. As I have pointed out, it seems to me that Quasten did not realize the implications of the Apostolic Canon cited above.

[43] Here the reader can see a text describing the situation: "In the course of three years, Basil's tone changes about his brethren: he had cause to be dissatisfied with them, and above all with Pope Damasus, who showed little zeal for the welfare of the East. Basil's opinion of him is expressed in various letters. For instance, a fresh envoy was needed for the Roman mission; he had thoughts of engaging his brother Gregory, bishop of Nyssa. 'But,' he says, 'I see no persons who can go with him, and I feel that he is altogether inexperienced in ecclesiastical matters; and that though a candid person would both value and improve his acquaintance, yet *when a man is high and haughty*, and *sits aloft*, and is, in consequence, unable to hear such as speak truth to him from the earth, what good can come for the common weal, from his intercourse with one *who is not of the temper to give in to low flattery?*' (Ep. 215). This is not complimentary to Damasus" (Newman, *Church of the Fathers*, 83).

The Duty of the Bishop and the Jurisdiction of the Pope

Nor is his infallibility in dogmatic decisions compromised by any personal and temporary error into which he may have fallen, in his estimate, whether of a heretic such as Pelagius, or of a Doctor of the Church such as Basil. Accidents of this nature are unavoidable in the state of being which we are allotted here below.[44]

Even from these tensions that occurred in the history of the Church, God can draw lessons to enlighten and guide us. Clearly, since the Church exists for the keeping of the deposit of Faith and of the means through which we can ordinarily receive God's grace, Basil as a bishop owes more allegiance to these means and this deposit than even to Pope St. Damasus. This is the point we are going to explain now.

The priority of the Faith

Among the Fathers we find another doctrine that is rooted in Holy Scripture and has been reaffirmed by the Second Vatican Council. It is a crucial teaching for the times we live in, especially if it is connected to the texts presented in the previous section. We start with the text of the Dogmatic Constitution *Dei Verbum* (no. 10):

> The task of authentically interpreting the word of God, whether written or handed on, has been entrusted exclusively to the living teaching office of the Church, whose authority is exercised in the name of Jesus Christ. This teaching office is not above the word of God, but serves it, teaching only what has been handed on, listening to it devoutly, guarding it scrupulously and explaining it faithfully in accord with a divine commission and with the help of the Holy Spirit, and it draws from this one deposit of faith everything which it presents for belief as divinely revealed.

The Magisterium, including the papal Magisterium, is not above the Word of God but serves it. The duty of the bishops, therefore, above all else, is to preserve the received divinely-revealed Faith and to protect and keep their flock in that Faith. These duties, it is evident, are *in se* above the duty of obedience to the Bishop of Rome.

One Father who underlined this point in a very beautiful way was St. Vincent of Lérins. Consider his argument: with the exception of the Virgin Mary who is their Queen, the angels are above any merely human authority, even if it is vicarious of Christ. Why? Because if God sends an angel to reveal something, as He did to Moses, it is as if God Himself was speaking, and that is how Moses received God's angel. However,

---

[44] Advertisement to the third edition, p. x.

Unresolved Tensions in Papal-Episcopal Relations

because public revelation ended with the death of the last Apostle, St. Vincent explains St. Paul's doctrine thus:

> "But although (quoth he) we or an Angel from heaven evangelize unto you beside that which we have evangelized, be he anathema." What meaneth this that he saith, "But although we?" Why did he not rather say, "But although I?," that is to say: Although Peter, although Andrew, although John, yea, finally, although the whole company of the Apostles, evangelize unto you otherwise than we have evangelized, be he accursed. A terrible censure, in that for maintaining the possession of the first faith, he spared not himself, nor any other of the Apostles! But this is a small matter: "Although an *Angel from heaven* (quoth he) evangelize unto you, beside that which I have evangelized, be he anathema."[45]

Please note: the Apostle Peter is no exception to this rule; much less will his successor be. If a pope commands that we believe something different from what has been revealed, from what has been always and everywhere believed (as we shall see), he would be accursed and must be disobeyed.

Does this doctrine leave us in the condition of Protestants who are forced to use their "private judgment"? Not at all! Because a Catholic bishop will define what must be believed based on Holy Scripture, Tradition, and the solemn Magisterium of the Church. If a pope teaches anything against the dogmas defined at the Council of Trent, for example, nobody is obliged to believe what he proposes and, for the good of the pope's soul, one should disobey and warn him that, if he obstinately perseveres in that material heresy, he is running the risk of committing formal heresy and becoming accursed.[46]

What is the apostolic rule that states what must be received as revealed?

> This is the great canon of the *Quod semper, quod ubique, quod ab omnibus,* which saves us from the misery of having to find out the truth for ourselves from Scripture on our independent and private judgment.[47]

On this rule St. Vincent comments:

> Again, within the Catholic Church itself we are greatly to consider that we hold that which hath been believed *everywhere, always,* and *of all men*: for that

---

[45] Newman, *Church of the Fathers*, 135.
[46] In the opinion of some, a bishop may not *declare* him accursed because there is no authority over and above the pope that can judge him. Nevertheless, Pope Honorius was declared a heretic by an Ecumenical Council after his death.
[47] Newman, *Church of the Fathers*, 132.

is truly and properly *Catholic* (as the very force and nature of the word doth declare) which comprehendeth all things in general after an universal manner, and that shall we do if we follow *universality, antiquity, consent*. Universality shall we follow thus, if we profess that one faith to be true which the whole Church throughout the world acknowledgeth and confesseth. Antiquity shall we follow, if we depart not any whit from those senses which it is plain that our holy elders and fathers generally held. Consent shall we likewise follow, if in this very Antiquity itself we hold the definitions and opinions of all, *or at any rate almost all, the priests and doctors together*.[48]

This teaching was solemnly repeated in the First Vatican Council's Dogmatic Constitution *Dei Filius*:

That must be considered as the true sense of Sacred Scripture which Holy Mother Church has held and holds, whose office it is to judge concerning the true understanding and interpretation of the Sacred Scriptures; and, for that reason, no one is permitted to interpret Sacred Scripture itself contrary to this sense, or even contrary to *the unanimous agreement of the Fathers*.[49]

In order to proceed with due responsibility, the Magisterium of the Roman Pontiff for this reason may not dispense with a serious investigation of Scripture, preceding Magisterium, and the teachings of the Fathers. If, despite all these warnings from Scripture and Tradition, an ecclesiastical authority departs from the revealed deposit, that would be a means through which God would purify the elected or approved ones in the Church. This is what St. Vincent expressly teaches:

"If a prophet shall rise up in the midst of thee," and straight after, "thou shalt not hear the words of that prophet." Why so? "Because (quoth he) your Lord God doth tempt you, whether you love Him or no". . . . According to the laws of Deuteronomy we are given most clearly to understand, that if at any time any ecclesiastical teacher strayeth from the faith, that God's providence doth suffer that for our trial, whether we love Him or no in our whole heart, and in our

---

[48] Chapter 2, 3, in Newman, *Church of the Fathers*, 134; italics at the end are mine. Here, I think that we could add a beautiful and needed clarification made by St. John Henry Newman, "The Fathers are principally to be considered as *witnesses*, not as *authorities*. They are witnesses of an existing state of things, and their treatises are, as it were, *histories*—teaching us, in the first instance, matters of fact, not of opinion. Whatever they themselves might be, whether deeply or poorly taught in Christian faith and love, they speak, not their own thoughts, but the received views of their respective ages" (*Church of the Fathers*, 136).

[49] Vatican I, *Dei Filius*, ch. 2 *in fine*. My italics.

whole soul.... Which being so, he is a true and genuine Catholic, that loveth the truth of God, the Church, the body of Christ; that prefers nothing before the religion of God,... but whatsoever doctrine new and never heard of... brought in of some one man ... let him know that such doctrine doth not pertain to religion, but rather to temptation, especially being instructed with the sayings of the blessed Apostle St. Paul.... This is the cause why the authors of heresies are not straight rooted out by God, that the approved may be made manifest.[50]

There are those today who despise this subjection to the divine revelation that culminated in Jesus Christ. These dissenters are not actually Christian, having no idea about what Eternity is or about what Infinity is. They live immersed in what merely flows and are unable to distinguish necessary from contingent beings. They feed themselves more from Modernism and evolutionism than from a true philosophy. They despise what they do not understand. But the Church of Christ acts in a different way. Let us now see St. Leo the Great's doctrine:

Not only in the exercise of virtue and the observance of the commandments, but also in the path of faith, strait and difficult is the way which leads to life; and it requires great pains, and involves great risks, to walk without stumbling along the one footway of sound doctrine, amid the uncertain opinions and the plausible untruths of the unskillful, and to escape all peril of mistake when the toils of error are on every side.[51]

Why is the Church so careful about orthodoxy? St. John Henry Newman offers an admirable answer:

Surely the Church exists, in an especial way, for the sake of the faith committed to her keeping. But our practical men forget there may be remedies worse than the disease; that latent heresy may be worse than a contest of "party"; and, in their treatment of the Church, they fulfil the satirist's well-known line: "*Propter vitam vivendi perdere causas*" [to destroy, for the sake of life, the reasons for living].[52]

This, of course, does not mean that one cannot deepen the understanding of the deposit of revelation. Of course one can—as long as one does not *alter* it. St. Vincent, once more, offers us a precious teaching:

---

[50] Newman, *Church of the Fathers*, 141–42.
[51] *Serm.* 25, in Newman, 130–31.
[52] Newman, 128.

The Duty of the Bishop and the Jurisdiction of the Pope

Let posterity rejoice for coming to the understanding of that by thy means, which antiquity without that understanding had in veneration. Yet for all this, in such sort deliver the same things which thou hast learned, that albeit thou teachest *after a new manner*, yet thou never teach *new things*.[53]

The duty of the pastors/shepherds

If, by the inscrutable designs of Providence, God allowed that the man of lawlessness (cf. 2 Thess 2) be seated on the Chair of Peter, in the Holy Temple of God, the Catholic bishops would have to know that their authority comes *from Christ*, not from the pope, and that their duty before God is to fulfill their ministry for the good of the flock entrusted to them *by Him*. The Successor of Peter has a universal jurisdiction, but that jurisdiction is itself subject to the apostolic canons. The keeping of the Faith and/or the usages requires that the pope have a disciplinary authority over the other bishops. Nevertheless, the bishops have their own proper authority over their particular flocks. They may not be removed from their see without a due canonical reason related to the keeping of the Faith and/or the Church's usages. The Church is a monarchy, not a tyranny.

Salus animarum, suprema lex. A bishop may not yield his flock to a heretical sect, to an authority that teaches propositions contrary to what has been defined by the solemn Magisterium and/or to what has been unanimously taught by the Fathers as being contained in Scripture. While the bishop may not judge the pope and declare that he commits formal heresy, for he has no authority *over* him, he may and must judge whether the pope is concurring in material heresy, and the bishop must prevent his flock from being devoured by demons—which is what would happen if the people abandon the revelation received from Christ.

There could be situations in which fulfilling this duty becomes difficult. Perhaps a bishop could be forced, during the time of unleashed lawlessness, to live in a private house and abandon his episcopal palace. That is how the Apostles lived and also many of the ancient bishops. That is how the bishops in China have lived, and how the priests in France lived during the abomination of the Revolution; it is how they lived in Mexico and in many other places when persecution was raging. Remember St. Augustine's teaching:

> The ministers of Christ, who are under the pressure of persecution, are *then* at liberty to leave our posts, when no flock is left for us to serve. . . . But when the people remain, and the ministers flee, and the ministration is suspended, what

---

[53] Cited by Newman, 144, emphasis added.

Unresolved Tensions in Papal-Episcopal Relations

is that but the guilty flight of hirelings, who care not for the sheep? For then the wolf will come—not man, but the devil, who is accustomed to persuade such believers to apostasy, who are bereft of the daily ministration of the Lord's Body; and by your, not knowledge, but ignorance of duty, the weak brother will perish, for whom Christ died.[54]

Is there not, perchance, the same problem if a diocese is left in the hands of a heretic? Even if a bishop may not judge the pope, he can judge the situation and also the man who tries to replace him and usurp his authority. He may determine that that man is, indeed, a heretic who rejects (for example) *Humanae Vitae*'s doctrine, or rejects the words of Christ concerning the indissolubility of marriage, or the doctrine of the Council of Trent regarding the Eucharist or penance or justification, or does not accept that Christ is the only Mediator between God and man, and so on and so forth. A true Shepherd may not abandon his flock to robbers and adventurers. He must be prepared to suffer confiscation and live from alms.

---

[54] Letter of Saint Augustine to Honoratus, cited by Newman, 165–66.

3

Why a Good Bishop Should Not Ignore but Obey His Unjust Deposition by a Pope

José Antonio Ureta

Responding to press reports that the pope will ask for his resignation, Bishop Joseph Strickland wrote on his blog: "I have said publicly that I cannot resign as Bishop of Tyler because that would be me abandoning the flock that I was given charge of by Pope Benedict XVI. I have also said that I will respect the authority of Pope Francis if he removes me from office as Bishop of Tyler."[55] Prior in time to that statement, Dr. Peter Kwasniewski had advised Bishop Strickland to ignore the pope's possible removal decree by remaining in the diocese and exercising jurisdiction as if his pope-appointed successor were an intruder. That was not an *abrupt* reaction but a sequence of three interventions: first, in a long July interview,[56] and then in two successive articles, one published by *Crisis Magazine*[57] and the other by *OnePeterFive*,[58] which is an edited transcript of that interview.

In his *Crisis* article, Dr. Kwasniewski mentioned the case of Most Rev. Isidore Borecky, the Ukrainian Catholic Eparch of Toronto, as an example to be emulated. Bishop Borecky refused to submit his resignation when he reached the age of 75, claiming that the discipline of the Latin Rite Church did not apply to Eastern Rite ones, and, therefore, he did not recognize his successor, a Pope John Paul II appointee.

Dr. Kwasniewski presents several arguments in these articles. They are briefly summarized below and presented logically, not necessarily following the original order, partly because, in the original interview and hence in the article based on it, he had to follow the interviewer's questions. Here are his main arguments:

First published at *OnePeterFive*, October 17, 2023.

[55] Joseph E. Strickland, "A Brief Update from Bishop Strickland," BishopStrickland.com, September 20, 2023.
[56] See "Bishop Joseph Strickland Must Resist Pope Francis if Told to Step Down," *John-Henry Westen Show*, LifeSiteNews, July 12, 2023.
[57] The full text may be found in Appendix 3, under a different title than its original one.
[58] The full text may be found in Appendix 2.

Unresolved Tensions in Papal-Episcopal Relations

1. It is not the pope who makes a bishop, but Jesus Christ. In his own diocese, a bishop is not a "vicar of the pope" but a vicar of Christ, receiving his episcopacy from God at the pope's delegation.
2. The bishop's power to rule and care for the flock comes from Christ, not the pope. Therefore, bishops have prior and legitimate rights rooted in apostolic succession that papal authority must respect, regardless of its primacy. Overemphasizing the papal primacy concerning other elements of ecclesiastical life is an erroneous extrapolation and a narrow or positivistic reading of the dogmatic definition of the First Vatican Council.
3. Once someone is made bishop, he is a bishop forever. Bishops are put in place by Christ and are permanently in place unless they give just cause for the grave step of deposition. Pius XII refused to purge the French bishops accused of collaboration with the Vichy regime, declaring that such a thing had never been done before.
4. Bishops are wedded to their local church, just as Christ is the Bridegroom of the whole Church. Arbitrary removal would be tantamount to an ecclesiastical "no-fault divorce." Therefore, a bishop, like a good father, should be prepared to die rather than discontinue caring for his flock, which would be at risk of being deprived of the sacraments, sound doctrine, and moral guidance.
5. Popes are given authority for the common good of the Church. When they arbitrarily remove a good bishop, they act *ultra vires*, i.e., beyond their legal authority. Such an act would be null and void and should be ignored. The new bishop is an imposter and usurper.
6. In emergencies, doing things not allowed in a normal situation is permissible. The momentary chaos of having two concurrent bishops claiming jurisdiction over the same diocese is a lesser evil compared to abandoning the flock to the wolves.

While these six arguments contain elements of truth, the overall presentation of the relationship between the papal primacy and the ordinary power of bishops in their dioceses seems unbalanced. That is because Dr. Kwasniewski omits a fundamental point of Catholic theology, the distinction between the hierarchy of order and that of jurisdiction. This omission leads to a one-sided solution to the problem of a bishop's unjust deposition because it does not take due account of the universal and immediate

Why a Good Bishop Should Obey His Unjust Deposition by a Pope

character of the sovereign pontiff's power of jurisdiction over the whole Church in matters of government and discipline as defined in the dogmatic declaration *Pastor Aeternus* of the First Vatican Council.[59]

It is insufficient to base a solution on sections 20, 23, and 27 of the Second Vatican Council's constitution *Lumen Gentium* on the ordinary power of bishops in their dioceses as successors of the apostles and not as delegates of the pope.[60] In order to theologically justify the novelty of *collegiality* as the participation of all the bishops in the supreme government of the Church, that conciliar document failed to refer explicitly to the traditional distinction between the hierarchy of order and the hierarchy of jurisdiction. Further, it opposed the Church's traditional magisterium when declaring that the "episcopal consecration, together with the office of sanctifying, also confers the office of teaching and governing" (no. 21).

Canon 108 § 3 of the 1917 Code, still in force during the Council, showed this distinction clearly: "By divine institution, the sacred hierarchy in respect of orders consists of bishops, priests, and ministers; by reason of jurisdiction, [it consists of]

---

[59] *Pastor Aeternus*, ch. 3: "Wherefore we teach and declare that, by divine ordinance, the Roman Church possesses a pre-eminence of ordinary power over every other Church, and that this jurisdictional power of the Roman Pontiff is both episcopal and immediate. Both clergy and faithful, of whatever rite and dignity, both singly and collectively, are bound to submit to this power by the duty of hierarchical subordination and true obedience, and this not only in matters concerning faith and morals, but also in those which regard the discipline and government of the Church throughout the world."

[60] *Lumen Gentium* states: "Just as the office granted individually to Peter, the first among the apostles, is permanent and is to be transmitted to his successors, so also the apostles' office of nurturing the Church is permanent, and is to be exercised without interruption by the sacred order of bishops" (no. 20); "The individual bishops, who are placed in charge of particular churches, exercise their pastoral government over the portion of the People of God committed to their care, and not over other churches nor over the universal Church. But each of them, as a member of the episcopal college and legitimate successor of the apostles, is obliged by Christ's institution and command to be solicitous for the whole Church, and this solicitude, though it is not exercised by an act of jurisdiction, contributes greatly to the advantage of the universal Church. For it is the duty of all bishops to promote and to safeguard the unity of faith and the discipline common to the whole Church, to instruct the faithful to love for the whole mystical body of Christ, especially for its poor and sorrowing members and for those who are suffering persecution for justice's sake, and finally to promote every activity that is of interest to the whole Church, especially that the faith may take increase and the light of full truth appear to all men" (no. 23); "The pastoral office or the habitual and daily care of their sheep is entrusted to them [the bishops] completely; nor are they to be regarded as vicars of the Roman Pontiffs, for they exercise an authority that is proper to them, and are quite correctly called 'prelates,' heads of the people whom they govern. Their power, therefore, is not destroyed by the supreme and universal power, but on the contrary it is affirmed, strengthened, and vindicated by it, since the Holy Spirit unfailingly preserves the form of government established by Christ the Lord in His Church" (no. 27).

the supreme pontificate and the subordinate episcopate; by institution of the Church other grades can also be added."[61]

Why is this traditional distinction and its obliteration by the Second Vatican Council so important for our case? True, through the sacrament of Holy Orders, it is Christ who makes the episcopally consecrated person a bishop and gives him the *munera* to sanctify, teach, and govern his flock. However, it is also true that there is a difference in how these powers are received. While the bishop receives the power to sanctify directly from Christ, he receives the jurisdictional power to teach and govern directly from the pope and only indirectly from Our Lord.

In the episcopal consecration, the aptitude to receive jurisdiction is given *in radice* but accidentally. For the power to teach and govern to become effective, the pope must grant the consecrated person a diocese or some other group of the faithful to govern. Since the hierarchy of order and the hierarchy of jurisdiction are not confused, there are many bishops without a flock or jurisdiction—e.g., auxiliary bishops, bishops emeritus, bishops who are apostolic nuncios or work in the Roman Curia. Similarly, there are shepherds without episcopal consecration who have subjects and jurisdiction—e.g., apostolic delegates, vicars capitular, and superiors of religious orders and congregations.

That distinction was so clear in the past that the old Code of Canon Law specified that a cleric who was appointed bishop assumed the diocesan governance from the moment he received the apostolic letters of appointment and was given three months to receive the episcopal consecration.[62] Even more significant is the case of the supreme pontiffs who were not bishops when elected pope. They received the primacy of jurisdiction when they consented to be the pope.[63] For example, Pope Adrian V was just a simple deacon when elected and died before being ordained priest and bishop. However, he is number 186 on the list of legitimate popes. That Pope Adrian V had full and universal jurisdiction from the moment he accepted the papacy was so clear that, in the short period of his thirty-nine-day pontificate, he validly suspended the application of the bull *Ubi Periculum*, promulgated two years earlier, which had established, for the first time, the closed conclave as the method of electing the pope.

---

[61] Edward N. Peters, ed., *The 1917 Pio-Benedictine Code of Canon Law: In English Translation with Extensive Scholarly Apparatus* (San Francisco: Ignatius Press, 2001), 61.
[62] See *The 1917 Pio-Benedictine Code*, can. 333, in Peters, 134.
[63] See can. 176, in Peters, 80.

Why a Good Bishop Should Obey His Unjust Deposition by a Pope

Contrary to *Lumen Gentium*'s assertion that episcopal consecration confers the office of teaching and governing,[64] these examples make it clear that popes and bishops who exercised their office of government before receiving episcopal consecration already possessed jurisdiction. The pope's jurisdiction was full and universal; that of the bishops was limited to their dioceses.

The above may seem like a digression far removed from Dr. Kwasniewski's proposal to Bishop Strickland. In reality, it is the premise for subsequent conclusions. It lays bare the ambiguity of some formulations of the well-known traditionalist writer that inform his proposed solution, which I believe is incorrect.

These two powers (of order and jurisdiction) are distinct for several reasons. First of all, they have different origins. One is conferred by ordination and the other by the canonical mission. Second, they differ as to their proximate ends. The power of order tends toward the sanctification of individuals through the sacraments, the power of jurisdiction to the government of the community. Third, they differ as to their properties, as we can see here:

The power of order
- cannot be extinguished (because Holy Orders imprints an indelible sacramental character on the soul);
- cannot be delegated;
- is equal in all who possess it; and
- can be exercised validly, even if unlawfully, despite any prohibition (think of the power to celebrate Holy Mass or to ordain priests and consecrate bishops).

The power of jurisdiction
- can be lost;
- can be delegated;
- is different depending on who possesses it; and,
- cannot be exercised validly against Church laws.

---

[64] *Lumen Gentium*, no. 21 (emphasis ours): "For the discharging of such great duties, the apostles were enriched by Christ with a special outpouring of the Holy Spirit coming upon them, and they passed on this spiritual gift to their helpers by the imposition of hands, and it has been transmitted down to us in episcopal consecration. And the Sacred Council teaches that by episcopal consecration the fullness of the sacrament of Orders is conferred, that fullness of power, namely, which both in the Church's liturgical practice and in the language of the Fathers of the Church is called the high priesthood, the supreme power of the sacred ministry. But *episcopal consecration, together with the office of sanctifying, also confers the office of teaching and of governing*, which, however, of its very nature, can be exercised only in hierarchical communion with the head and the members of the college."

Unresolved Tensions in Papal-Episcopal Relations

With the above in mind, let us now return to Dr. Kwasniewski's articles. Their initial misdirection stems from his ambiguous assertion that "his [the bishop's] power to rule and care for the flock comes from Christ, not from the pope." As we saw, the power to sanctify is given to the bishop directly by Our Lord at his consecration. However, the power to govern a portion of the flock is given to him indirectly by God and directly by the pope with the apostolic letter of appointment.

Thus, the phrase "once someone is a bishop, he's a bishop forever" is misleading. It is true only concerning the power of order (the episcopal character is never lost—whether in heaven or in hell, a bishop will always be a bishop). Still, it is untrue concerning the power of jurisdiction because a prelate ceases to be the "Bishop of X" in the event of resignation, transfer, or deposition.

Also misleading is the sentence that immediately follows: that the bishops "are put in place by Christ and are permanently in place unless they actually do something to forfeit being in their place." The sentence fails to mention that bishops are appointed to their dioceses by the pope and receive the power to govern that portion of the flock directly from him and indirectly from Christ. That is why the pope can remove or depose them even without "a just cause for the grave step of deposition," because their removal could be justified by a higher good of the Church (for example, by replacing European-born bishops in Africa with ones who were born there, during the turbulent period of postwar decolonization).

As the adage goes, *omnis comparatio claudicat* (all metaphors limp), i.e., every comparison is somewhat flawed. The analogy between the bishop's union with his diocese and the bonds of marriage is limited since the latter are indissoluble until death separates the spouses. In contrast, the former can be terminated by resignation, transfer, or deposition. Even weaker is the comparison of an arbitrary deposition with a no-fault divorce, because in marriage every divorce is illegitimate since, except for the Pauline privilege, no human power can dissolve the bonds of a marriage that is *ratum et consummatum*.

Can the dismissed bishop appeal "from the pope to the pope," purely on principle, by introducing an administrative appeal, for example, before the Dicastery for Bishops? In any case, an arbitrarily deposed bishop can unquestionably remain spiritually united with his former flock and must be prepared to die so that his former subjects may continue to receive the sacraments, good doctrine, and sound moral guidance. To do so, he must use all the moral prestige acquired by his good shepherding. However, this does not allow him to self-reinstate the jurisdictional powers removed from him. Nor may he consider his successor a usurper, for, as seen above, the power of jurisdiction cannot be validly exercised against Church laws.

Why a Good Bishop Should Obey His Unjust Deposition by a Pope

In this sense, the examples provided by Dr. Kwasniewski, i.e., Ukrainian Eparch Isidore Borecky's refusal to accept his successor and Pius XII's statement that he would not depose the French collaborationist bishops, are not conclusive. There are many and much more expressive examples to the contrary. Consider, for example, the deposition of Cardinal József Mindszenty from the primatial archdiocese of Esztergom, Hungary, to facilitate relations between the Holy See and the Communist government of that nation. That unjust removal was followed by the appointment of Bishop László Lékai as apostolic administrator, who hastened to urge Catholics to be loyal citizens of the Communist regime (as do Chinese Patriotic Association bishops today). Despite the monstrous injustice of deposing a hero to foster a no less monstrous policy of rapprochement with the Communist regime, the cardinal-martyr never considered the appointed administrator a usurper. Nor did he carry out any jurisdictional act in his former archdiocese.

Even more significant was the case of the French bishops who had emigrated because of the French Revolution's fierce persecution. They were forced to renounce their dioceses by Pope Pius VII's brief *Tam Multa* to comply with the 1801 concordat Cardinal Consalvi had negotiated with Napoleon Bonaparte on the pope's behalf. In return, the First Consul agreed to demand the resignation of intruding "bishops" who had joined the schismatic church established by the Civil Constitution of the Clergy. A new French episcopate was thus established, chosen by Bonaparte from among *juring* and faithful *non-juring* bishops, with the pope pledging to give all of them the respective canonical recognition. Something similar happened in Communist China after its government's secret agreement with the Holy See.

The arbitrariness of *Tam Multa* was all the more obvious because, to return to France, the bishops who resigned were also obliged to swear an oath of obedience to the Constitution of the Year VIII, which officialized the Consulate. The State's domination of the Church was so extensive that Napoleon imposed on the pope respect for the territorial reconfiguration of the dioceses established by the Civil Constitution of the Clergy so that the diocesan territories matched the departments invented by the Revolution.

In the end, 47 of the 82 émigré bishops still alive in September 1801 resigned, and 35 refused to submit their resignations. Their dioceses were either suppressed or taken over by other bishops appointed by civil authorities and recognized by the pope. Nonetheless, the non-resigning bishops who remained faithful to the Holy See never claimed jurisdiction over their former dioceses, not even after Napoleon's 1814 fall and the restoration of the Bourbon dynasty.

In Church history, it is difficult to find such an arbitrary removal of so many good bishops who suffered tremendous hardships to avoid joining a schismatic church.

Unresolved Tensions in Papal-Episcopal Relations

Those who refused to resign could have argued that Pius VII was acting *ultra vires*, i.e., beyond his legal authority, that the brief *Tam Multa* should be "ignored" as "null and void," and that the new bishops should be deemed usurpers or imposters. They could have added that it was an "emergency" and the chaos of having two bishops claiming jurisdiction over the same diocese was preferable to abandoning the flock to a wolf appointed by Napoleon.

However, they did not do so, although their leader, Most Rev. Arthur Richard Dillon, Gallican archbishop of Narbonne, exiled in London, claimed that the pope "could not remove a bishop on his own authority without a canonical and regular trial."[65] Only three bishops who refused to resign continued giving orders to the clergy and faithful of their former dioceses, thus giving rise to the anti-1801 French Concordat schism known to history as the *Petite Église*.[66]

God has mysterious designs for His Church that belie the best human calculations. While the *Petite Église* experienced a rapid decline during the nineteenth century, French Catholicism, albeit led by a large number of bishops who were successors to those appointed by Napoleon, emerged rejuvenated from these troubles and saw the birth of numerous saints, new congregations, and missionary endeavors that took the Gospel to the furthest ends of the earth. We must maintain this supernatural spirit and not search for overly human solutions to the Church's current crisis—the greatest she has known in her 2,000-year history.

Pope Francis and his evil advisors and agents would be delighted if bishops who are unjustly removed from their dioceses for resisting this papacy's Church-demolishing agenda were to rebel against the papal order, going on to establish a twenty-first century anti-progressive *Petite Église*.

---

[65] Alfred Boulay de la Meurthe, *Histoire du rétablissement du culte en France (1802–1805)* (Tours: Maison Alfred Mame et Fils, 1925), 12.

[66] See "Petite Église," *Wikipedia*, accessed September 26, 2023.

4

On the Papal Deposition of Bishops

JOHN LAMONT

José Antonio Ureta's article "Why a Good Bishop Should Not Ignore but Obey His Unjust Deposition by a Pope"[67] was an attempt to refute Dr. Peter Kwasniewski's claim, repeated on more than one occasion,[68] that a pope does not have the power to simply remove a bishop at will and that a bishop should refuse to go along with an unjust attempt by the pope to remove him from office. Dr. Kwasniewski's claim was made in the context of reports that Bishop Joseph Strickland of Tyler, Texas, was to be removed from his see, despite the absence of any evidence of his having failed in the exercise of his office, or of any other good reason for removing him. Mr. Ureta argued, against Dr. Kwasniewski, that the pope has the power to legally remove any bishop from his diocese if he so chooses, and hence that a bishop should accept his removal by the pope regardless of whether or not this removal was justified.

The question is a topical one, because on November 11, 2023, Pope Francis announced that Bishop Strickland has been removed from his office as Bishop of Tyler, without giving any explanation for this action. Mr. Ureta, unlike Pope Francis, has provided a theological argument for the pope having the right to take such an action. This argument needs to be addressed in order to understand whether or not this is the case. Its importance is not limited to the power of the pope to remove bishops; it concerns the fundamental nature of papal power.

Everyone will accept that there are situations where the pope can legally remove a bishop and name another bishop to his diocese. There are therefore two questions to be answered:

Does the pope have the power to remove a diocesan bishop from his diocese *purely* as an exercise of his power of jurisdiction, without needing legal grounds that establish that the bishop is unfit to retain his office or that his removal or the suppression of his diocese is justified by the good of the Church?

First published at *Rorate Caeli*, December 18, 2023.
[67] See the preceding chapter.
[68] See Appendices 2 and 3 below.

Unresolved Tensions in Papal-Episcopal Relations

If the pope does not have this power, what conditions must be satisfied for the pope to validly remove a diocesan bishop from office?

The second question requires more detailed discussion than the first. I will not attempt to answer it. There are many factors which could make a bishop unfit for office, from illness to moral turpitude. The history and present state of canon law on the grounds for removal of bishops will be the best guide to them.[69] It is the former question that will be considered here.

Mr. Ureta argues for his position as follows:

A. The power of order and the power of jurisdiction are distinct. The power of jurisdiction is not conferred with the power of order. Clerics who are appointed to a diocese can exercise jurisdiction in it before they are consecrated as bishops. Bishops can be consecrated without being appointed to a diocese or given any other kind of jurisdiction.

> In the episcopal consecration, the aptitude to receive jurisdiction is given *in radice* but accidentally. For the power to teach and govern to become effective, the pope must grant the consecrated person a diocese or some other group of the faithful to govern. Since the hierarchy of order and the hierarchy of jurisdiction are not confused, there are many bishops without a flock or jurisdiction—e.g., auxiliary bishops, bishops emeritus, bishops who are apostolic nuncios or work in the Roman Curia. Similarly, there are shepherds without episcopal consecration who have subjects and jurisdiction—e.g., apostolic delegates, vicars capitular, and superiors of religious orders and congregations.

B. The power of order is received immediately from God in consecration. The power of jurisdiction, however, is received mediately from God and immediately from the pope. The immediate episcopal reception of the power of jurisdiction from the pope is the teaching of the Church. It follows from "the universal and immediate character of the sovereign pontiff's power of jurisdiction over the whole Church in matters of government and discipline as defined in the dogmatic declaration *Pastor Aeternus* of the First Vatican Council."

> Through the sacrament of Holy Orders, it is Christ who makes the episcopally consecrated person a bishop and gives him the *munera* to sanctify, teach, and govern his flock. However, it is also true that there is a difference in how these

---

[69] See chapter 10.

powers are received. While the bishop receives the power to sanctify directly from Christ, he receives the jurisdictional power to teach and govern directly from the pope and only indirectly from Our Lord. . . . [T]he power to sanctify is given to the bishop directly by Our Lord at his consecration. However, the power to govern a portion of the flock is given to him indirectly by God and directly by the pope with the apostolic letter of appointment. . . . Even more significant is the case of the supreme pontiffs who were not bishops when elected pope. They received the primacy of jurisdiction when they consented to be the pope. For example, Pope Adrian V was just a simple deacon when elected and died before being ordained priest and bishop. However, he is number 186 on the list of legitimate popes.

C. Since the power of jurisdiction is given by the pope to the bishops, the pope can withdraw it as he chooses, just as the entire power of an official of a Roman congregation comes from the pope, and can be withdrawn by the pope at will.

Bishops are appointed to their dioceses by the pope and receive the power to govern that portion of the flock directly from him and indirectly from Christ. That is why the pope can remove or depose them even without "a just cause for the grave step of deposition," because their removal could be justified by a higher good of the Church (for example, by replacing European-born bishops in Africa with ones who were born there, during the turbulent period of postwar decolonization).

Mr. Ureta's assertion that the removal of a bishop by the pope can be justified by a higher good of the Church is not relevant to the question at issue, because such a justification would be a reason for considering that the removal is just. We are considering whether or not a bishop should accept as valid and legally binding his removal by the pope *regardless* of the cause of his removal, on the grounds that the pope has the power to remove bishops at will.

The assertion that the power of order and the power of jurisdiction are distinct is true. However, it cannot be used as an argument against Dr. Kwasniewski without begging the question. The question is whether or not the pope's power of jurisdiction enables him to remove a bishop at will.

The thesis that bishops derive their jurisdiction indirectly from Christ and directly from the pope has long been a disputed question among Catholic theologians. The issues therefore are:

Unresolved Tensions in Papal-Episcopal Relations

- Is Mr. Ureta right in claiming that the teaching of the theological school that he supports is taught by the magisterium?
- If not, which theological school is in fact correct?

We need first to describe the competing theological positions.

I. Theological positions on the origin of episcopal jurisdiction and the nature of papal authority

The two positions that Catholic theologians have advanced on this subject are described by Valton in the *Dictionnaire de théologie catholique*:

> Bishops are established by divine law. This is a dogma of faith defined by the Council of Trent, sess. XXIII, can. 6: "Si quis dixerit in Ecclesia catholica non esse hierarchiam divina ordinatione institutam quae constat ex episcopis, presbyteris et ministris, anathema sit." But if it is beyond doubt that the power of order is conferred immediately by God upon bishops, in such a manner that the Church cannot modify it in any way, the question is not so certain when it comes to the power of jurisdiction. Is the divine origin of episcopal jurisdiction immediate or only mediate, so that, while resting upon divine law, it flows immediately from the sovereign pontiff? The question is a subject of controversy among Catholics, as can be seen in Bellarmine, *De romano pontifice*, 1. IV, c. XXII sq. Some maintain that jurisdiction is conferred immediately by Christ on bishops in the very act of episcopal consecration, although the exercise of this jurisdiction is bound until the sovereign pontiff assigns a territory and subjects to the new bishop. . . . Others think, with St. Thomas, that the jurisdiction of bishops is directly connected to that of the vicar of Christ, to whom not only a portion but the whole of ecclesiastical power has been granted.[70]

These two positions exclude conciliarist and Gallican views, which deny that the pope alone holds supreme ecclesiastical jurisdiction. Both schools accept that this is the case; but one position asserts, and the other denies, that the pope possesses not just *supreme* power of jurisdiction, but *the whole of* the power of jurisdiction. The latter view will be termed the strong view of papal jurisdiction, and the former view will be termed the moderate view of papal jurisdiction. The claim that God has granted the pope the whole of ecclesiastical power provides the justification for the claim that bishops

---

[70] E. Valton, "Évêques: questions théologiques et canoniques," *DTC* 5, col. 1702. The original French may be found in Appendix 4.

receive the power of jurisdiction directly from the pope and only mediately from God, and hence that the pope can remove a bishop from office at will.

Some authors have stated that the thesis that the pope possesses the whole of ecclesiastical power and is the direct source of episcopal jurisdiction was asserted by the First Vatican Council in its teaching that the pope possesses the plenitude of power, *plenitudo potestatis*, in the Catholic Church. This is not the case. "Plenitude of power" in this conciliar text means having all the power of jurisdiction that it is possible to have, not all the power of jurisdiction that exists. Possession of all the power of jurisdiction that it is possible to have is subject to the limits on the power of jurisdiction that are imposed by divine and natural law. The question in dispute is concerned with what these limits are.

Theologians have tried to deduce the claim that the pope has all the power of jurisdiction that exists from the teaching that he has the plenitude of power, but this is a theological inference that can be challenged, not a magisterial teaching. The above citation from Valton in the *Dictionnaire de théologie catholique*, which dates from after the First Vatican Council, acknowledges this, by treating this thesis as an open question among Catholic theologians. Domenico Palmieri, an adherent of the strong view whose arguments will be considered below, also writes after the First Vatican Council and treats this debate as an open question. There are magisterial documents that have been presented as settling this question—as will be seen below—but they are pronouncements of Pius XII, not the documents of Vatican I.

St. Thomas Aquinas holds the strong view that all power of jurisdiction whatsoever in the Church derives from papal power:

> I answer that a superior power and an inferior power can relate to each other in two different ways. In one way, the inferior power originates entirely from the superior power; and in this case, the entire power of the inferior is founded on the power of the superior; and then the power of the superior is to be obeyed *simpliciter* rather than the inferior, and is so to be obeyed in all things, just as in natural causes, the first cause acts more on an effect produced by a secondary cause than the secondary cause itself does, as is stated in the *Liber de causis*. This is the way in which the power of God is related to all created powers; it is the way in which the power of the Emperor is related to the power of the proconsul; and it is the way in which the power of the pope is related to all other spiritual powers in the Church, since every dignity in the Church is distributed and ordered by the pope, whose power is in a certain manner the foundation of the Church, as

is shown by Matthew ch. 16. And therefore we are bound in all things without distinction to obey the pope more than bishops or archbishops, or [more than] a monk is to obey an abbot. In another way, the power of a superior and an inferior are related by the both of them having originated from a higher power, which subordinates the one to the other as it chooses; and in this way the one is only superior to the other in so far as it has been subordinated to the other by a higher power, and the superior is to be obeyed rather than the inferior only in so far as it has been given authority by the higher power. The powers of bishops and archbishops, which are established by the pope, are related in this way.[71]

St. Thomas argues from Matthew 16, but he supplements this scriptural argument with an appeal to the Neoplatonic metaphysical conception of causation, where the actions of a lower agent are also the actions of the higher agents that cause the lower one. In consequence, his position is somewhat different from that of later theologians, because this Neoplatonic conception asserts that all higher agents act immediately in the lower agents whose existence and action they bring about.[72] It cannot therefore entirely correspond to the later claim that the power of jurisdiction is received immediately from the pope and mediately from God. We should note as well that he makes no mention of the power of the pope to remove bishops at will.

A classic exposition of the strong view is given by Palmieri in his *Tractatus de romano pontifice* (1891). We will take this exposition as presenting the best case for the strong view. It has the advantage of directly addressing the question of whether or not the pope can remove bishops at will.

Since this work and others like it are difficult of access and have not been translated into any modern language, it is necessary to translate excerpts from them at some length in order to give the *status quaestionis*. It is a recovery of material that has been forgotten, but that is of the first importance for the Church in her current situation.[73]

Palmieri writes:

The plenitude of power that is being discussed is not absolute, but is relative to the society that is ruled; it is plenitude of power in a polity and for a polity. To give clarity, we can say that it can be understood in two ways: only positively, or exclusively. It is understood in a positive sense only, if the supreme ruler can by his ordinary legal authority perform everything that is useful and necessary

---

[71] *In II Sent.*, Dist. 44, Q. 2, art. 3, expos. For the Latin text, see pp. 128–29 below.
[72] See *Summa contra gentiles* III, ch. 67.
[73] Appendix 4 contains the original Latin text of Palmieri.

for the entire polity and every one of its subjects, although there are subordinate powers together with him and under him that exercise authority that is not derived from him. It is understood in an exclusive sense, if the supreme ruler's authority is such that every power in the polity is either his own power, or is derived from his own power in such a way that the supreme power either formally or virtually contains every other power by which the polity is ruled. Such is the power of absolute monarchy in a political society.

It is easy to show that the plenitude of power belongs to the Roman Pontiff in the first sense. This supreme power requires the following characteristics: it requires the power given by the ordinary process of law to do everything required for the ruling of a society, whether in making laws, establishing courts, or coercively enforcing the law; and there must be nothing that can be legitimately done against its will, so that all other power in the society depends directly on it. . . . Such is the power of the Roman Pontiff in the Church. . . .

But the greatest difficulty arises with respect to another conception of the plenitude of power. This comes down to the question of whether the jurisdiction of a bishop in his diocese comes immediately from Christ, or whether it comes from Christ mediately through the Roman Pontiff, that is, immediately from the Roman Pontiff. No one denies that this power is from Christ, since all power in the Church is from Him, or that it is immediately from God in that God acts immediately in and with the action of all other causes. The question is of the immediate principle of this power—a power that is immediate in that any second cause between the first and principal cause and its effect is excluded.

There are some who suppose that the ordinary jurisdiction of bishops is received immediately from Christ. They use the arguments given above, by which we demonstrated the divine institution of the episcopate. They generally explain the immediate derivation of power from Christ by Christ's conferring this power in episcopal ordination itself, but however in first act only, and bound as to its exercise and not reduced to second act unless the Supreme Pontiff, confirming the bishop, assigns to him a territory and subjects. They believe that in this way the subordination of the bishops to the Roman Pontiff remains secure, for even if it is allowed that both pope and bishop receive their jurisdiction immediately from God, the bishop is still subject to the power of the Roman Pontiff; it is not necessary that every jurisdiction proceeding immediately from God be independent. As against this view, many others think that although Christ instituted the episcopate willing that His Church be ruled by bishops, ordinary jurisdiction is conferred by the pope on individual bishops, in such a way that, before this bestowal by the pope, in no way, even in first act, does the bishop possess jurisdiction in virtue of his ordination. The ordination of a bishop gives him only the aptitude to receive jurisdiction, in virtue of Christ's institution.

In the first hypothesis, it is asserted that the Roman Pontiff cannot licitly and validly remove or restrict the jurisdiction of a bishop without just cause: once the condition of the Roman Pontiff having assigned subjects to a bishop is satisfied, the jurisdiction received by bishops is given by God, for it is this jurisdiction of divine origin that is exercised. The Roman Pontiff may indeed regulate and modify this jurisdiction for reasons derived from just causes. He can even in certain cases declare that this jurisdiction has been lost, in virtue of his right to interpret divine law. He cannot however directly remove jurisdiction from a bishop, because this jurisdiction does not exist in its subject through him, but by divine law; and divine law takes precedence over papal authority.

In the second hypothesis, the pope cannot indeed licitly remove a bishop without cause, but he can certainly validly do this, and his act will have force on its own; a bishop in this situation cannot claim jurisdiction for himself on the pretext that there is no just cause for his removal. It is apparent from what has already been stated that this is not a question of words, as will become more clear further on: it touches on the nature of the papal primacy and the whole economy of ecclesiastical jurisdiction. The jurisdiction of the bishop in his diocese is the question that is now being considered—the question of the jurisdiction held in ecumenical councils over the whole Church will be considered later in its proper place. The question under consideration is currently a subject of discussion among Catholic theologians. . . .

III. We therefore maintain that the plenitude of power of the Roman Pontiff in the Church is such that all power by which the Church is ruled either formally or virtually is included in it, and therefore that it is the immediate source from which the jurisdiction of bishops is derived. . . .

We assert firstly that this is required by the nature of the primacy that was instituted by Christ, whose carefully framed words are to be investigated through an analysis. Certainly the Roman Pontiff holds under Christ the keys of that kingdom of heaven that is the Church: but now, in keeping with what was stated in the first thesis above, the power and function of the possessor of the keys is portrayed as being such that he can open and no one can shut, that he can close and no one can open. But if we suppose that someone has the power to open and close a house, for example, then he is provided with such a power that no one else can open or close it unless he himself opens or closes it at the same time, or gives that other person the power to open or close. If therefore it is possible to open and close without him, or without a power made by him, then someone could also close what he has opened, and open what he has closed. The proper force of this image of the keys by which he can open and none can close, and by which he can close and none can open, can therefore be seen to also signify that without his cooperation, or a power conferred by him, none can open or close. Furthermore, if this is transferred to the thing that is signified by the image, which is power over the kingdom—which is certainly the Church—it is manifest that it signifies the power of Peter to be such that no one can exercise power in the Church—a power metaphorically described as that of opening and closing—unless he [sc. Peter] cooperates with this exercise of power, or gives the faculty to exercise power.

And indeed the Roman Pontiff can bind and loose everything in this kingdom. If things are considered in themselves, an act of this power can also validly remove the jurisdiction of any bishop at all, without a determinate cause and without giving any reason. Certainly, the good of the Church, like the good of other societies, does not require that the power of the supreme authority be exercised simply at the discretion of the ruler: but the good of the Church may require that the supreme power be of such a nature that even if it is frequently exercised without a just cause, all of its acts remain valid—although the very nature of the society, the interest of the ruler, recognition of the moral law, and divine providence will prevent such exercise being of frequent occurrence. Power of this kind in the supreme authority is certainly demanded by the many things that are subject to political authority; in civil society the supreme power is exercised in this way, and the end of civil society—which is well-ordered peace between all—requires such power. Christ was therefore able to confer on the Roman Pontiff the authority to remove a bishop from office even without a just cause. But if this is the case, the words of Christ, "Whatever you bind, etc." must be interpreted as including this power. For Christ did not leave out any act from the supreme jurisdiction, but included all within it. If any limits are to be fixed for this jurisdiction, they must be determined by the end of this jurisdiction, which is the good of the Church. But this rule is to be used with caution in limiting jurisdiction, in order to avoid error. In particular, it must not be used in such a

Unresolved Tensions in Papal-Episcopal Relations

way as to include in the supreme jurisdiction only those things that are necessary and sufficient to attain this good, or that seem to be so to us; for Christ may have willed to include more than this, and Christ's words must be interpreted with the fullest possible extension. This norm is to be interpreted as excluding only those things that are incompatible with the common good of the Church, or that are incompatible with some other institution established by Christ. If now such a power of rule over the Church is not excluded from the jurisdiction of the Roman Pontiff, as it is not excluded from the supreme authority in temporal political societies, then it is not excluded from the power of the Roman Pontiff by that other institution of Christ which is the episcopate. Christ fittingly combined his will that there be bishops with willing that the jurisdiction of bishops should depend entirely on the Roman Pontiff. Therefore, the words of Christ to Peter contain a granting of this power. But the Roman Pontiff would not possess this power unless he himself conferred jurisdiction on bishops, as we observed above; so jurisdiction is conferred on bishops by the Roman Pontiff.

And certainly the jurisdiction of the Roman Pontiff is the jurisdiction of the Vicar of Christ, that is, it is the jurisdiction of Christ Himself communicated to the Roman Pontiff; it is therefore a universal jurisdiction for the entire kingdom. The institution of such vicarial power requires that whatever jurisdiction is exercised by Christ in his Church is exercised by his vicar; but to confer jurisdiction is an act of jurisdiction; therefore the jurisdiction of bishops is conferred upon them by the Roman Pontiff.

The power of the Roman Pontiff was understood in this way by Optatus. . . . [Palmieri here cites other authorities such as Ambrose, Leo, and Innocent III whom he presents as holding his position on the jurisdiction of the pope.]

Another demonstration in proof of the thesis that episcopal jurisdiction is conferred immediately by the Roman Pontiff can be deduced from an analysis of the opposite view, which contains a contradiction.

This opposing view affirms both that bishops possess jurisdiction through their consecration, and that the Roman Pontiff must assign subjects to them in order for this jurisdiction to pass into act. Therefore, before the assignation of subjects by the Roman Pontiff, no one is subject to the consecrated bishop, and there are no faithful who can be designated as being subject to the authority of the bishop and as being obliged to obey him. But this is contradictory; jurisdiction is essentially a relation that requires a certain term for the relation, namely the subjects over which it is held. It is possible for jurisdiction to exist only as

On the Papal Deposition of Bishops

a *habitus* that is not exercised, as in the case of a king expelled by force from his kingdom. But in this case, jurisdiction exists *in habitu* [i.e., as a power not exercised] because there are existing persons whom it is possible to designate as *per se* bound to obey this jurisdiction, viz., the citizens of the kingdom, although this obligation is *per accidens* suspended. If there is no one who can be said to be subjects of the king, his jurisdiction no longer exists. But a king with no subjects is in the position of a bishop who has only been consecrated, according to the hypothesis of the opposing view. No one exists or can be designated as the subjects of a bishop who has only been consecrated. The demand of the people, the nomination of a prince, or the election of a chapter cannot be said to designate subjects for such a bishop. It is certain that election or nomination does not confer jurisdiction on a bishop, or create any obligation for any of the faithful to obey him. Therefore, according to the opposing view, a bishop both has and does not have jurisdiction before the Roman Pontiff ascribes subjects to him; so the opposing view is false.

This can also be shown from a lack of sufficient reason for the opposing view. This view asserts that jurisdiction is conferred by consecration. Can jurisdiction be conferred by the Roman Pontiff before consecration? If the answer to this question is in the affirmative, it must be denied that jurisdiction was so instituted by Christ as to be received directly from God, and hence there can be no reason for saying that jurisdiction is conferred immediately by God. If the answer is in the negative, it rejects the practice of the Apostolic See and the sense of the Church, which holds that those whom the Roman Pontiff has chosen and confirmed exercise true episcopal jurisdiction even if they have not been consecrated as bishops. To avoid this consequence, it would be necessary to affirm that such persons exercise a different form of jurisdiction, or that the power or stability of their jurisdiction is different, because it has been conferred in a different way. But what is the reason for holding this statement about their jurisdiction to be true? For it is clear that such unconsecrated persons can do whatever consecrated bishops can do, when it comes to jurisdiction. As for the stability of their jurisdiction, the explanation for the fact that the stability of the jurisdiction of non-consecrated persons is not the same as the stability of the jurisdiction of bishops is that by Christ's institution, bishops are those who are to rule over churches in general. This proves indeed that by Christ's institution bishops should be set over the churches, but it does not prove that bishops obtain jurisdiction directly from Christ.

Unresolved Tensions in Papal-Episcopal Relations

Finally, we can argue as Bellarmine does from the inequality of jurisdiction. If God conferred episcopal jurisdiction by ordination, then all bishops would have equal jurisdiction, just as they all have equal power of orders. God has not determined the individual power of jurisdiction of bishops, and not all bishops have the same power of jurisdiction, either extensively or intensively; therefore, God does not confer episcopal jurisdiction by ordination.

Therefore, the plenitude of power of the Roman Pontiff is of such a nature that all the jurisdiction by which the Church is ruled in found in it as in its source.

A recent assertion of the strong view was made by Cardinal Gianfranco Ghirlanda, in a press conference on March 21, 2022 introducing the apostolic constitution *Praedicate Evangelium*:

> The question of the admission of the laity to the exercise of the power of governance in the Church involves a broader question: whether the power of governance is conferred on the bishops by canonical mission and on the Roman Pontiff by divine mission or by the sacrament of Holy Orders. If the power of governance is conferred through canonical mission, it can also be conferred on the laity in specific cases; if it is conferred by the sacrament of Orders, the laity cannot receive any office in the Church that involves the exercise of the power of governance. Therefore, it is worth offering some data to understand the novelty brought.
>
> The issue is very complex and divides authors. Here suffice it to say that it was debated repeatedly at the Second Vatican Council, but in the end the latter did not want to settle it in the sense of origin from the sacrament of Orders, having changed the only text of *Lumen Gentium* (the beginning of no. 28) that had remained formulated in this sense.[74]
>
> During the process of reforming the Code of Canon Law the issue was again discussed, and the Plenary Congregation of the Enlarged Commission, held October 20–29, 1981, was asked to delete the current canons 129 §2 and 1421 §2 on the possibility of having a lay judge in a court of three judges, based on the assertion that the Second Vatican Council had affirmed the origin of all governing power in the Church from the sacrament of Orders. The two canons remained, so the commission rejected the request on the grounds that

---

[74] [Note in Ghirlanda] Cf. *Acta Synodalia* III/I, 225; III/VIII, 96–97.

there was no evidence that the Council had affirmed such a thing.[75] Since the reason brought for the suppression was doctrinal in nature, the fact that the two canons remained assumes doctrinal significance.

John Paul II in no. 43 of *Pastores Gregis* of October 16, 2003, referring to can. 381 §1 CC 1983 and can. 178 CCEO (footnote no. 166), explicitly stated that the bishop "is invested, by virtue of the office he has received, with an objective juridical power, destined to express itself in potestative acts by means of which he implements the ministry of governance (*munus pastorale*) received in the Sacrament."[76]

The fact, then, that Pope Francis's motu proprio *Mitis Iudex Dominus Iesus* of August 15, 2015,[77] in Article 1673 §3, admits that out of a college of three judges two may be laity, while providing that the president must be a cleric, comes to reinforce the provision of canon 1421 §2, because it cannot be questioned that it may be the laity, who, exercising the power of judicial government received with the canonical mission, determine the nullity or otherwise of the marriage in question.

Along these lines are Principles and Criteria, no. 5, and Article 15 of the Apostolic Constitution *Praedicate Evangelium*. They come to settle the question of the ability of the laity to receive offices involving the exercise of the power of governance in the Church, provided they do not require the reception of Holy Orders, and indirectly affirm that the power of governance in the Church does not come from the sacrament of Holy Orders, but from the canonical mission, otherwise what is provided for in the Apostolic Constitution itself would not be possible.[78]

The moderate view on papal power is best represented by Francisco de Vitoria O.P. in his *Relectiones*.[79] These are lectures given by Vitoria at the University of Salamanca

---

[75] [Note in Ghirlanda] Cf. Pontificium Consilium de Legum Textibus Interpretandis, *Congregatio Plenaria diebus 20–29 octobris 1981 habita*, Vatican City, 1991, 35–38.

[76] [Note in Ghirlanda] AAS 96 (2004) 825–927. Also along the same lines are nos. 8 and 9 of the same Exhortation and nos. 12, 64 and 159 of Dir. *Apostolorum Successores* of the Congregation for Bishops of February 22, 2004, in *Enchiridion Vaticanum* 22/1567–2159. It should be noted that proponents of the origin, from the sacrament of Orders, of the power of governance do so on the basis of the identification between *munus* and *potestas*, due to the incorrect interpretation of the Dogm. Const. *Lumen Gentium* 21b.

[77] [Note in Ghirlanda] Cf. AAS 107 (2015) 958–70.

[78] "Conferenza Stampa di presentazione della Costituzione Apostolica 'Praedicate Evangelium' sulla Curia Romana e il suo servizio alla Chiesa nel mondo. Intervento del Prof. Gianfranco Ghirlandis, S.I.," March 21, 2022; https://press.vatican.va/content/salastampa/it/bollettino/pubblico/2022/03/21/0192/00417.html#ghirlanda.

[79] Vitoria's original Latin text may be found in Appendix 4. Gabriel Vazquez S.J. also puts the case for the moderate view; see his *In primam secundae Sancti Thomae* (Lyons, 1631), II, 31.

Unresolved Tensions in Papal-Episcopal Relations

in 1532 and 1533 and published posthumously in 1604. The lecture format explains the personal references in the text. Vitoria was an eminent Dominican theologian, the founder of the School of Salamanca (Salmanticenses). He is best known today for having argued that the inhabitants of the New World had a right to their property and formed legitimate states, that the Spanish Crown had no right to wage a war of conquest on them or seize their lands and property, and that the pope had no right to award sovereignty over them to the Spanish and Portuguese—a position that provoked the rage of the Emperor, Charles V. His works were ordered to be placed on the Index by Sixtus V, who objected to his views on the papacy, but this pope died before the order could be promulgated, and it was withdrawn by his successor at the request of Philip II of Spain.[80]

From the *Relectio I de potestate ecclesiae* (1532):

> The power of the Church is therefore twofold: the power of orders, and the power of jurisdiction. The power of orders is ordered to the real Body of Christ, that is, to the Eucharist: the power of jurisdiction is ordered to the mystical Body of Christ, that is, to the governance of the Christian people ordered to the end of supernatural happiness. By the power of orders is understood the power not only to consecrate the Eucharist, but also to properly dispose and render men worthy for the Eucharist: that is, to ordain priests and confer other orders, to administer the sacraments to all, to remit sins, and to do everything that in any way pertains to the consecration of the Eucharist. Therefore, the power of orders is said to be a power to consecrate in many ways. The power of jurisdiction pertains to the government of the Christian people outside the consecration and ministry of the sacraments; that is, to make and abrogate laws, to excommunicate, to pronounce justice outside the sacrament of penitence, and to do all other things of this sort.
>
> All the spiritual and ecclesiastical power that now exists in the Church stems from divine positive law, either mediately or immediately. . . .

Relectio II de potestate ecclesiae (1533):

> It now remains for us to determine in whom this power resides, and to trace it back to its original source. Our first conclusion is that all the power of the Church, both of orders and of jurisdiction, existed in the apostle Peter. This is indicated by the text of the Gospel of Matthew 16: "I give to thee the keys of the kingdom of heaven, and upon this rock I shall build my church." And by

---

[80] Vicente Beltrán de Heredia, "Vitoria (François de)," *DTC* 15/2, col. 3131.

the Gospel of John: "Feed my sheep." Our second conclusion is that the power of orders and of jurisdiction existed in all the apostles. This can be seen from the fact that it was said to all the apostles together, "Do this in memory of me, etc.: Whomsoever's sins you shall remit, and Whatsoever you loose." Luke 22, Luke 18, John 20.

There is however a first doubt that arises concerning this question. Did all the apostles have power immediately from Christ, or did only Peter receive it immediately from Christ, and the others from Peter? . . . In the case of the power of jurisdiction, the better part of Catholic authors, and the most authoritative among them, assert that only Peter received this power directly from Christ, and that the others received it from Peter.

In proof of this, the authority of great men is first offered; as Anacletus, Cyprian, Augustine, Leo, and Alexander. I refrain from reciting the words of these men, for it is apparent that their meaning is not what the defenders of this thesis wish it to be. Those who wish to see this can consult Cardinal Torquemada, *De Ecclesia*, book 2, ch. 54. The assertions of these saints were directed simply at this, to assert that all authority after Peter took its origin in Peter, and that Peter himself was the ruler both of the other apostles and of the entire Church of Christ. Be it far from us to deny this claim, which we hold it intolerable to contradict. But if these testimonies do not prove what they want, they appeal to argument to vindicate it. The first argument they offer is that since Christ did not personally assign subjects to the other apostles, therefore he did not assign jurisdiction to them, since there can be no jurisdiction without subjects. They base the antecedent of this argument on the following reasoning. Either Christ assigned all men as subjects to the apostles, or he assigned only some men as subjects. We cannot choose to affirm the former, because it is not mentioned in the Gospels, and it seems that Christ did not give all men as subjects to the apostles. For there were many pastors, and there would hence be several equal rulers having the plenitude of power in the Church, which is a defective form of rule in any kingdom. It is pernicious for there to be many princes, as Aristotle states in *Metaphysics* 12. And "every kingdom that is divided among itself shall be made desolate." Moreover, there would not be one flock and one pastor for Christ's sheep if there were many shepherds with equal powers; and it cannot be understood how Peter would be the prince and head over the other apostles, if all of them had received the same power as Peter from Christ.

Unresolved Tensions in Papal-Episcopal Relations

It is because the Gospels truly support the contrary view that I draw the conclusion that all the power that the apostles possessed was received by them immediately from Christ. This is proved firstly by the fact that in Matthew 18, "Whatever you loose upon earth," etc., is said to all the apostles; and likewise in Luke 22, where "Do this in memory of me" is addressed to all of them; in John 20, "Whomsoever's sins you remit," in the last chapter of Matthew, "Go throughout all the world and preach the Gospel to all," John 20, "As the Father sends me, so I send you." It is written, "Christ made them all apostles," as is plain from Matthew 10, Mark 3, Luke 6, 1 Corinthians 2, Ephesians 4. But the powers of both orders and jurisdiction belong to apostles: therefore both of these powers were given to the apostles by Christ. It should be considered that three things pertain to the dignity of an apostle. The first is the power to govern the faithful; the second is the office of teaching; and the third is the power of miracles. This is shown first by Luke 9, where it is written; "Calling together the twelve apostles, Jesus gave them power over all demons, and to cure diseases, and sent them to preach the kingdom of God and to heal the sick." Matthew in his last chapter writes, "The Lord said to them, Go forth into all the world, teach and baptize all nations, and teach them to follow everything that I have commanded you." The first epistle to the Corinthians chap. 12 states: "[God] has sent some into the Church as apostles." The gloss on this text states: "all were ordainers and judges." Thus, if Christ made them apostles, they could not have been without the powers of orders and jurisdiction; therefore, they received both of these powers from Christ. Moreover, it is apparent that none of the other apostles received less power from Christ than the apostle Paul: but all the power that Paul possessed, he received from Christ. Paul himself stated in Galatians 1 that he did not receive his power from man or through man. He put this in a different way in Galatians 2, where he said that he had received nothing from the other apostles, and specifically that he had received nothing from Peter. For Paul said that "those who seemed to be something added nothing to me, for he who worked through Peter in the apostolate to the circumcised worked through me in the apostolate to the Gentiles." Therefore, it seems to me certain that it must be declared and believed that all the apostles received both powers from Christ.

But there remains a doubt as to whether all the apostles received the same power as Peter; and both answers to this question have their adherents. But because the hasty supporters of the majority view on this question do not

On the Papal Deposition of Bishops

provide the reasons upon which both sides base their conclusions, I assert this conclusion: all the apostles had the same power as Peter. I understand this in the sense that every apostle had ecclesiastical power covering the whole world, for all the acts that Peter had power to do; I do not speak of those acts that pertain only to the Supreme Pontiff, such as the assembling of a general council. The first part of this claim is proved by the text of Matthew already cited, "Go throughout all the world," etc. And these statements were made without exception: "Whatsoever you loose," etc., "Those whose sins you remit," etc., Matthew 18 and John 20, "As the Father sent me," etc. But Christ was sent to the whole world; therefore, the apostles were also sent to the whole world. The second part, to the effect that the apostles had the power to do all that Peter could do, can be seen to be proved by the fact that possession of the authority of government is essential to being an apostle. There is no reason for holding that this authority was limited, since there are no grounds for saying that it was limited to certain acts and not to others; on the contrary, it is established by the acts of the apostles themselves, who founded churches and named bishops all over the world, and laid down laws through their own power. Nor is it apparent what Peter could do that the other apostles could not do, save those acts that only the Supreme Pontiff can do. Moreover, St. Paul in Galatians chapters 1 and 2 sufficiently defends the claim that he has equal power with Peter. This is clearly the view of St. Cyprian in his Epistle to the Novatians on the unity of the Church, where in question 14 he states: "I tell you this: the rest of the apostles and Peter were given the same fellowship, honour, and power." The gloss that states that this is to be understood as referring to the power of orders and not to the power of jurisdiction is to be rejected, as can be seen by reading this letter of the saint.

And lest anyone should suspect that I wish to derogate in any way from the dignity, prerogatives, or primacy of Peter, which I not only confess with the Catholic Church but have defended before men, I will state some theses. [Vitoria then gives a number of Scriptural arguments for the primacy of Peter.] . . . Although it is true to state that the apostles were equal in power to Peter in the sense given above, nonetheless Peter's power was greater. Firstly, it was an ordinary power, whereas the power of the apostles was an extraordinary one. Secondly—which follows from this—the power of Peter remained in the Church, whereas the power of the [other] apostles did not. Thirdly, the power of the others was neither over Peter nor over one another, but Peter's

Unresolved Tensions in Papal-Episcopal Relations

power extended over the other apostles. Fourthly, the power of the others was subordinate to the power of Peter; the authority of Peter prevailed over the authority of the others. . . .

Aside from the holy apostles, no one else in the Church received ecclesiastical power from Christ . . . and thus we have the first origin of ecclesiastical power; for the twelve apostles were the first and only persons to receive this power from Christ, our Lord and Redeemer.

It now remains to treat of how this ecclesiastical power continued in the Church and reaches us; with this, the whole business concerning the subject of ecclesiastical power that I have undertaken will be complete.

The first proposition on this topic is that ecclesiastical power existed not just in the apostles, but also in others. This can be seen from the Scriptures: Paul made Titus and Timothy bishops. . . .

The second proposition is that after the death of Christ's apostles, all the power of orders and jurisdiction that existed in the apostles continued to exist in the Church. This is proved by the fact that the grades of power in the Church were instituted by Christ not only for the time of the apostles, but for all the times in which the Church will exist. . . .

The third proposition is that all the power of orders in the Church is derived from and depends immediately upon the bishops. . . .

The fourth proposition is that after the death of the apostle Peter, someone succeeds Peter with the same authority and power of jurisdiction over all the world. . . . Just as Adam had certain personal gifts that he could not transmit to his posterity, such as the plenitude of knowledge, and certain common gifts that pertained to the state of innocence, such as grace and immortality, so Peter had certain personal gifts that do not exist in his successors (and are not necessary for them), such as the grace of miracles and the gift of tongues. There are certain gifts however that he received so as to be transmitted to his successors, such as the power of the keys, which he received not for himself but for the Church. The order established in the Church in the beginning by Christ, whereby there is one head and one ruler over all, was the best one for the administration of the Church. . . .

It remains for us to address the question of the successors of the other apostles. Concerning them this first proposition is asserted: no one succeeds the other apostles with the authority and power of jurisdiction that they had, that is to say, with the plenitude of power in all the world that these apostles had, as was shown above. For we read of no one who acted as the bishop of the universal Church except the Roman Pontiff; those close to the apostles were said to be bishops of Jerusalem, of Antioch, or of some other city. Secondly, it is asserted that because this universal power in the other apostles was an extraordinary and personal power, as has been stated, and one that they could not pass on to their successors—whereas the power of Peter was an ordinary one that remains in perpetuity—no one receives such a power from the Church, who is incapable of granting this power, even when lacking her head. Nor do we read of anyone being appointed by the Supreme Pontiff, that is, from Peter or Clement, to substitute for any of the apostles with a power of that extent. Thirdly, there would be the greatest occasion for schism and dissension among the successors of the apostles—who are not confirmed in grace, as the apostles were—if they did not have distinct provinces of their own.

Second proposition. Any of the apostles aside from Peter could leave a successor, not a universal one, but in any province that he wished, who would be the true bishop of that province. I know that this proposition will not please all the doctors, both theologians and canonists, and that it does not please the Cardinals Torquemada and Cajetan themselves. For all of them were once seized by the conviction that all power of jurisdiction so depends on the Roman Pontiff that no one can possess the most minimal spiritual power save by the command or law of that Pontiff: no one, that is, after the apostles, who by a unique privilege had spiritual power granted to them by Christ, which no one else can receive save from Peter. But I will manifestly prove this proposition: any of the apostles could in his lifetime create a bishop in any province that he wished, and this power would not be lost with the death of the apostle; therefore, bishops can leave successors. It should first be noted that Paul made Titus and Timothy bishops, and all the other apostles had the right to do the same; and in this sense, the proposition cannot be denied by anyone. But I assert the proposition to be true in the sense that successors to Peter could be nominated: that is, a successor who in truth would have no power until after the death of the apostle; thus, I say, John in Asia could nominate Ignatius, so that he would be bishop after him in that province. The proposition can be proved thus. As was abundantly proved above, all the apostles had the same power as Peter, so that they could establish laws to the effect that the apostles while living should choose their successors; therefore, the apostle could by that law himself first choose his successor. Certainly there does not seem to

Unresolved Tensions in Papal-Episcopal Relations

be any doubt about the antecedent, that all the other apostles were given equal authority with Peter. And if Peter could establish such laws in a province, why could Paul not do so as well? On the contrary, it is certain that he did not need other apostles to act, awaiting Peter's command for all the things that had to be done in the provinces. And so it seems to me that the proposition is not only probable, but beyond a doubt.

Third proposition. Not only the Apostles could leave successors, but any of their successors could similarly do so. This is manifestly proved by the second proposition. For by the law passed by John, or by Paul, to the effect that a living bishop can nominate a successor, Titus could nominate his own successor. But I further add something that is seemingly more difficult, but that I nonetheless consider to be true: even if no law on this subject was instituted by Paul, Titus and Timothy could have named their own successors, even without consulting the successors of Peter; and the same is true for all the other bishops. This is proved by the fact that a bishop is the pastor and ruler of his province by divine law. Therefore, unless impeded by a higher power, he can do all things that are expedient for the welfare of his province. But at that time it could have been of the greatest importance that a bishop nominate his successor during his lifetime; therefore a bishop could do this, and could indeed legislate that it be done in perpetuity. How could it be that a bishop could legislate about the election of an abbot, or a parish priest, or about any other matter, but not about the election of a bishop? This is confirmed by the fact that it would not only be possible and proper, but necessary at all times. How could a dead bishop in the farthest reaches of India await a mandate from Peter to meet the need of a new bishop? And thus the discussion of the power of jurisdiction is complete. As for the power of orders, if the episcopate is said to be an order or a power distinct from the presbyterate and from jurisdiction, as almost all consider it to be, it is necessary to combine with the choice of the bishop some form of consecration, for the institution of the pope as for the institution of a bishop. But this can be done by any living bishop consecrating his successor; or, if the bishop is dead, by another bishop of the same province, who can consecrate the successor who has already been chosen and nominated.

Last proposition. Any bishop, even without consulting the see of Peter, can establish a law stating that priests elect the bishop, or that bishops are instituted by some other form. This follows from the other points already made; the bishop can make appropriate laws for his province on this subject, as on others. This is the reason why the authority and dignity of a bishop can be derived successively from one bishop to the next until it reaches us, and through the bishop all other inferior power.

But notwithstanding these things (lest anyone think that I wish to detract from the Roman See and its dignity), I state this conclusion: the successors of Peter can at their discretion create bishops in new provinces, abolish existing laws on the succession of bishops, establish new laws on this subject, divide provinces, and do all things pertaining to these matters by their own judgment and power. Everything that has been said on this matter should be understood as obtaining unless it is established otherwise by the See of Peter. This proposition is clearly proved by the fact that it was said to Peter, "Feed my sheep," with no limitations or exceptions. Therefore all direction pertains to Peter without any exception, and in consequence even the creation of bishops falls under his power. For if any of the other apostles could and did do this—and it is clear that they did—so much more are Peter and his successors able to do likewise. From this the corollary clearly follows that one cannot now become a bishop except according to the forms laid down by the Supreme Pontiff, and that if anyone attempts to do otherwise, nothing will result; such an attempt will be null and void. I state this however about the authority of jurisdiction, for what pertains to consecration is different. Secondly, it follows that all ecclesiastical power, whether of orders or of jurisdiction, depends mediately or immediately on the see of Peter. This is apparent from the fact that all bishops depend on the pope, and all priests and other inferior orders and powers depend on the bishops.[81]

II. Evaluation of the theological debate

As we have seen, there are two related questions being considered: the question of the nature and origin of episcopal jurisdiction, and the question of the right of the pope to remove bishops at will. The latter question is not entirely dependent on the former, but it cannot be settled independently of it. The former is the more fundamental question. We can assume that the pope has at least the power and supremacy granted to him by the moderate view, since to deny that he has at least this power is to reject the Catholic faith. The debate thus turns upon the strength of the arguments for the strong view.

St. Thomas is the earlier and greater of the advocates of the strong view. Like Palmieri and other advocates of this position, he appeals to the text of Matthew 16 in support of

---

[81] Francisco de Vitoria O.P., *Relectiones*, in *Arbor magna iurisdictionis ecclesiasticae* (Venice, 1640).

Unresolved Tensions in Papal-Episcopal Relations

this view. This appeal in fact uses the strong view to interpret the biblical text, and then cites the text as proof of the strong view, thus reasoning in a circle. The text, reasonably interpreted, does not decide between the strong and moderate views.

St. Thomas does more than appeal to this tendentious exegesis; he also argues from his Neoplatonic conception of causation. This conception applies to the metaphysical category of efficient causation in the created world. Those who accept it are bound to agree that it describes every instance of such causation. But although God exercises efficient causation in causing the power of jurisdiction to exist in the Church, that does not mean that the power of jurisdiction that he causes is itself an instance of efficient causation. This power has connections to efficient causation and resembles it in some analogous ways, but it is not in fact a power of efficient causation or an exercise of such a power. So St. Thomas's argument from causation fails.

Amicus Thomas, sed magis amica veritas. St. Thomas's position on papal authority is not compatible with his own theory of grace and the sacraments.

Ecclesiastical jurisdiction confers divine authority, not natural authority. It cannot arise from any natural basis of authority. If it is a proper and ordinary jurisdiction, it is a supernatural *gratia gratis data* that cannot originate in any created cause. Hence, it can only be conferred by God alone.[82] It can be produced by the action of a created cause only when the created cause is an instrumental cause used by God as the principal cause and agent.[83] The assertion of later theologians that episcopal jurisdiction is derived immediately from the pope and only mediately from God is thus incompatible with the fact that episcopal jurisdiction is a supernatural rather than a natural power. If the conferring of episcopal jurisdiction is only mediately from God, then it cannot be caused by God as the principal agent.

St. Thomas's own view does not face this problem, because he does not describe episcopal jurisdiction as being only mediately from God; indeed the Neoplatonic conception that he uses to argue for the strong view of papal power excludes this possibility, stating as it does that "the first cause acts more on an effect produced by a secondary cause than the secondary cause itself does."

However, St. Thomas's position is ruled out by the nature of a sacrament. A created cause that is a sign, and is used by God to directly produce supernatural grace, is a sacrament.[84] The conferring of the power of jurisdiction upon a bishop is a gift of a supernatural grace that is done through a sign. It must therefore be done through a

---

[82] See *Summa theologiae* I-II, Q. 112, art. 1.
[83] See ibid., ad 2.
[84] See *Summa theologiae* III, Q. 60, art. 2.

sacrament. Both the consecration of bishops and the assignation of subjects to a bishop by the pope are signs; they are speech acts with intelligible meanings that effect what they signify. But only the consecration of a bishop is a sacrament. The assignation of territory and subjects to a bishop by the pope is not a sacrament. The source of the jurisdiction of bishops must therefore originate in the sacrament of their consecration. St. Thomas's Neoplatonic conception of causation explains how authority received by a bishop in consecration is received directly by Christ.

St. Thomas's claim that the power of bishops is related to the power of the pope in the same way as the power of proconsuls is related to the power of the Emperor effectively reduces the bishops to vicars of the pope. This claim is no longer accepted by Catholic theologians in the light of the teaching of the Council of Trent, as Valton states:

> We must indeed recognize that although the bishops are dependent upon the supreme pontiff, who holds the universal primacy, they are not simply his vicars; rather, their power is an ordinary one, flowing from the very office—*ratione muneris*—which has been confided to them, that is to say from the pastoral responsibility through which the Holy Spirit has made them bishops with the mission of governing the Church of God. For the bishops are the successors of the apostles, as the Council of Trent has taught, loc. cit. ch. 4; *in locum apostolorum successerunt*.[85]

Dom Baucher, in his article in the *Dictionnaire de théologie catholique* on jurisdiction, states:

> The bishops belong by divine right to the hierarchy of the Church; they govern the part of Christ's flock that is confided to them with a proper and ordinary power of jurisdiction, and, although this power can be more or less restrained by the superior authority of the pope, it is nonetheless a complete power, extending to every aspect of ecclesiastical government in both the external and internal forum. The council of Trent affirms this doctrine in the most categorical fashion: "the holy Synod declares that, besides the other ecclesiastical degrees, bishops, who have succeeded to the place of the apostles, principally belong to this hierarchical order; that they are placed, as the same apostle [Paul] says, by the Holy Ghost, to rule the Church of God" (Session 23, ch. 4). We can see that the Council appeals principally to the words addressed by St. Paul to the

---

[85] Valton, "Évêques: questions théologiques et canoniques," *DTC* 5, col. 1703.

persons governing the church at Ephesus, whatever the actual titles of these persons may have been.[86]

The scriptural reference here is to Ephesians 4:11–12, "his [sc. Christ's] gifts were that some should be apostles, some prophets, some evangelists, some pastors and teachers, to equip the saints for the work of ministry, for building up the body of Christ." Bishop Zinelli, the relator for the conciliar document of the First Vatican Council *Pastor Aeternus*, explained the term "ordinary" as meaning a power that belongs to its possessor in virtue of the possessor's office, and is not delegated to its possessor by another person who holds it in virtue of his own office.[87]

Palmieri offers several arguments for the strong view, in addition to the scriptural appeal to Matthew 16. He asserts that absolute monarchy is the best form of government, because it is the one the best promotes the common good. But God will give the Church the best form of government; therefore, he has made the Church an absolute monarchy with the pope at its head.

Such a priori reasoning about what God must have done presumes too much on the reasoner's supposed knowledge of what God ought to do. The claim that absolute monarchy is the perfect form of civil government is open to objections too obvious to require detailing here; and in any case the inference from the best form of civil government to the best form of government of the Church is fallacious.

The character of this fallacy deserves examination in this case. Civil states all cover a part of the world and of the human race. Pure monarchical government can be argued to be the best form of government for such states (remember that Aristotle, who is always quoted in favour of monarchical government, thought that a proper state was the size of a smallish Greek polis). The Catholic Church however is not meant to extend to part of the world or part of the human race, but to the whole of it. A pure monarchical form of government would thus be unsuited to it. A mixture of monarchy and aristocracy, with a supreme ruler and subordinate rulers possessing real power under him, would be suited to its universal nature; and this is what the moderate view holds to be the case.

Palmieri's argument from the fact that persons can possess the power of episcopal jurisdiction prior to consecration as a bishop is also fallacious. This jurisdiction can be explained as papal jurisdiction supplied to its possessor, which is replaced by properly episcopal jurisdiction when its possessor is consecrated. His argument must assume that this is not the case, and that the jurisdiction possessed does not change at time

---

[86] "Jurisdiction," *DTC* 8/2, col. 1992.
[87] Mansi 52:1105.

of episcopal consecration, in order to prove its conclusion. But this assumption is false. The jurisdiction held by a person who has been appointed to a diocese but not consecrated a bishop cannot be the same as the jurisdiction possessed by a person who is the bishop of a diocese. The latter jurisdiction is episcopal; it is essentially connected to the bishop's membership of the episcopal order. The former is not, since the person is not a bishop. It can only be supplied by papal jurisdiction. The only way for jurisdiction possessed before and after episcopal consecration to be the same is for bishops to possess their jurisdiction as vicars of the pope, which is ruled out by Catholic teaching.

Palmieri begs the question when he claims that the strong view of papal jurisdiction should enjoy the benefit of the doubt, and be accepted as true unless very good reasons can be given to the contrary. He also disregards the fact that there are strong prima facie objections to his thesis. As we saw above, the Council of Trent states that bishops "are placed, as the same apostle [Paul] says, by the Holy Ghost, to rule the Church of God." They thus rule as bishop by divine authority. How is this compatible with their jurisdiction being derived from the pope, and with the pope being able to remove this jurisdiction at will? A proper and ordinary divine authority must be derived from God, and can only be taken away by Him: no merely human authority can remove it. But a pope deposing a bishop at will, independently of the divine law, is not acting with divine authority. Palmieri states:

> It is false that according to our position the bishops are the vicars of the pope. For bishops do not exist in the Church in right of papal authority, but in right of the authority of Christ, and the pope cannot abolish the episcopal dignity and authority: furthermore, the power and tribunal of the pope and of bishops are two different things, because Christ willed that besides the chair of Peter there should also be an episcopal chair. Nor are the bishops delegates of the pope, because they possess an ordinary jurisdiction through the power of the office that Christ has instituted. The bishops rule their flock as their own, for by Christ's institution they must be pastors of a portion of the sheep, over which they exercise the power of binding and loosing. And although the Roman Pontiff may remove jurisdiction from any and all, he is nonetheless bound to ensure that other bishops exist, in order that there may always be bishops in the Church; for he may not abolish episcopal authority itself.[88]

---

[88] Domenico Palmieri, *Tractatus de romano pontifice* (Prato, 1891), art. 1, thesis XIV, p. 457.

Unresolved Tensions in Papal-Episcopal Relations

But this evades the issue. The point is not that the episcopate as a whole exists by divine right, and cannot be abolished by the pope, but that according to the Catholic Church individual bishops in their dioceses rule by divine right derived from their order and their office.

Palmieri's argument that the moderate view entails a contradiction about jurisdiction is fallacious. He asserts that there can be no jurisdiction without subjects over which this jurisdiction can be exercised. The answer of the moderate view to this objection is that jurisdiction exists in a consecrated bishop in first act, that is, as a power to exercise jurisdiction once subjects for it are designated. Potential subjects for jurisdiction always do exist at the time of the consecration of a bishop, because of the existence of Christian faithful over whom such jurisdiction can be exercised. Palmieri's example of jurisdiction existing in first act, as a power which requires further conditions for its activation, is an actually existing jurisdiction over specified subjects whose exercise is impeded (a king exiled by force). In order to derive his contradiction, Palmieri assumes that this is the only form of jurisdiction that can exist in first act. But this assumption is false.

The historical origins of Palmieri's thesis are worth noting. The conception of absolute monarchy to which he appeals is the conception of the authority of the Emperor in Roman law. The corpus of Roman law was lost during the Dark Ages, and then recovered early in the Middle Ages. Thereafter, Roman law and its conception of the authority of the ruler had an enormous influence on the formation of the conception of civil authority in European states and on the conception of papal authority developed by medieval canonists. It is this tradition of thought concerning authority to which Palmieri is appealing in his argument for a papal absolute monarchy; he is not just advancing his own outlandish and extreme authoritarianism. The strength and erstwhile general acceptance of this tradition of thought explains much of the support for the strong view of papal authority among Catholic theologians.

It remains to address Cardinal Ghirlanda's argument in favour of the strong view. It is not a serious one, but it should be considered because of Cardinal Ghirlanda's influential position at the moment. The argument has no logical connection to its conclusion. As we have seen, the question that has been debated by theologians is not whether the sacrament of orders in itself or canonical mission confers jurisdiction, but whether it is ordination to the episcopate or assignment of jurisdiction to a bishop by the pope that confers episcopal jurisdiction. No Catholic author has ever maintained that ordination to the priesthood and/or the diaconate confers any form of the power of jurisdiction. Dom Baucher observes:

On the Papal Deposition of Bishops

No one belongs to the divinely instituted hierarchy of jurisdiction in the Church except for bishops. The only persons who belong to this hierarchy are those who exercise governance in the Church with proper and ordinary jurisdiction, and only bishops satisfy this condition.[89]

It is simply a *non sequitur* to argue that because the sacrament of orders—which includes consecration to the episcopate, the priesthood, and the diaconate—does not as such confer jurisdiction, the jurisdiction of bishops is derived from their canonical mission from the pope. The ordination of bishops is related to jurisdiction, whereas the ordination of priests and deacons is not. It makes the person ordained a member of the group that has the role of ruling the Church. That is why there is a separate rite for the ordination of bishops.

The grant of the power of jurisdiction to laymen is irrelevant to the strong view of papal power. The power of jurisdiction in the Church in the external forum includes the legislative power, the judicial power, and the executive and coercive power. The bishop of a diocese possesses *ex officio* all three of these powers over his flock, excepting acts of juridical power reserved by the legislation of the universal Church to the Apostolic See. Such jurisdiction cannot be possessed by a layman, because no one except a bishop can have jurisdiction of this kind. Any jurisdiction possessed by a layman must be received from an authority that does possess ordinary and proper jurisdiction. This is indeed the case with jurisdiction possessed by ordained persons such as parish priests and religious superiors, not only with that possessed by laymen. To assume that jurisdiction of this kind can only be received from the pope, and not from any other bishop, is to beg the question at issue.

Although it is true that the sacrament of orders as such does not confer jurisdiction, it should be pointed out that Cardinal Ghirlanda's position on the independence of the power of governance from the sacrament of orders is open to question. Theologians have maintained that the clerical status is a necessary condition for receiving any power of jurisdiction in the Church.[90] This was asserted by the 1917 Code of Canon Law; however, that Code did not restrict the clerical status to those in major orders, but defined clerics as those who had been tonsured, a necessary step before the reception of both minor and major orders (can. 108). It did restrict the grant of a power of jurisdiction that involved a cure of souls to those who had been ordained as priests (can. 154). In doing so it followed the decrees of the Council of

---

[89] Baucher, "Juridiction," *DTC* 8/2, col. 1994.
[90] See Baucher, col. 1991.

Unresolved Tensions in Papal-Episcopal Relations

Lyon in 1245 and the Council of Trent.[91] This position was supported by the Second Vatican Council:

> Though they differ from one another in essence and not only in degree, the common priesthood of the faithful and the ministerial or hierarchical priesthood are nonetheless interrelated: each of them in its own special way is a participation in the one priesthood of Christ. The ministerial priest, by the sacred power he enjoys, teaches and rules the priestly people [*populum sacerdotalem efformat ac regit*]; acting in the person of Christ, he makes present the Eucharistic sacrifice, and offers it to God in the name of all the people. But the faithful, in virtue of their royal priesthood, join in the offering of the Eucharist. They likewise exercise that priesthood in receiving the sacraments, in prayer and thanksgiving, in the witness of a holy life, and by self-denial and active charity.[92]

The logic of this position is clear. The power of orders is directed at the sanctification of the Church and her members. It provides grace to its recipients to achieve this end, a grace that is not given to those who do not receive the sacrament of ordination. The power of jurisdiction in the Church is directed at the same end as the power of orders; the supernatural end of sanctifying the members of the Church and bringing them to heaven. In consequence, there is no sense in giving the power of order to one group of men, and the power of jurisdiction to an at least partially different group of men. Nor is there sense in giving the sanctifying task of rule over the Church to persons who have not received the power to sanctify others through the grace of ordination.

This position also corresponds to the importance attached to the liturgy by the Second Vatican Council, which asserted that "the liturgy is the high point towards which the activity of the Church is directed."[93] Since the liturgy is the most important part of the activity of the Church, it makes sense that the hierarchy of juridical authority within the Church correspond to the hierarchy that exists in liturgical function. This correspondence was apparent in the older canonical legislation that restricted all power of jurisdiction to clerics. As we have seen, "cleric" in this sense was not limited to those who had received sacramental ordination; it covered all those members of the

---

[91] "Le pape Innocent IV, au concile général de Lyon, en 1245, établit que tout clerc appelé à gouverner une Église devait, dans l'année même, recevoir l'ordre de la prêtrise. S'il ne le faisait pas, il était de droit et sans autre monition privé de sa charge. *Sext. Décret.*, I. I, tit. vi, c. 14. Le concile de Trente est encore plus précis sur ce point: *Neminem etiam deinceps ad dignitatem, canonicatum, aut portionem recipiant, nisi qui eo ordine sacro sit initiatus quam illa dignitas, praebenda aut portio requirit.* Sess. xxiv, de Reform., c. xii" (ibid.).

[92] *Lumen Gentium*, no. 10.

[93] *Sacrosanctum Concilium*, no. 10.

On the Papal Deposition of Bishops

Church who had some liturgical function and office. Jurisdiction was thus limited to those with a liturgical function, and jurisdiction involving a cure of souls was limited to those with a liturgical office that required priestly ordination.

Cardinal Ghirlanda claims that the Second Vatican Council did not link the rule of the people of God with the ministerial priesthood, on the grounds that the drafters of the 1983 Code of Canon Law denied that it did, and amended the canons to permit laymen to exercise judicial power by sitting on a canonical court. However, canons of the Code of Canon Law and their drafters do not enjoy total exemption from error, and the text of *Lumen Gentium* says what it says. The 1983 Code of Canon Law is in fact not clear on this subject. It states:

> Can. 129 §1. Those who have received sacred orders are qualified, according to the norm of the prescripts of the law, for the power of governance, which exists in the Church by divine institution and is also called the power of jurisdiction.[94]
>
> §2. Lay members of the Christian faithful can cooperate in the exercise of this same power according to the norm of law.

Can. 129 §1 only makes sense as asserting that the power of jurisdiction is restricted to those in sacred orders. It can hardly mean that the power of jurisdiction is *possible* for those in sacred orders; it would be absurd to state this in a canon. But this raises the difficulty of how laymen can cooperate in the exercise of this power, as stated in 129 §2. The only solution to this difficulty is to interpret the canon in the light of the previous canonical tradition, and limit the cooperation of laymen to exercises of jurisdiction that do not include the cure of souls. This would mean that the participation of laymen in ecclesiastical tribunals is illicit, if they are granted a share in the juridical power of such tribunals. But there is nothing impossible about the participation of laymen in ecclesiastical tribunals being illicit. Such participation cannot be justified as licit by the existing canon, since that canon need not be interpreted as permitting it. Nor does the actual fact of laymen being given a juridical role in ecclesiastical tribunals justify such participation, since this can be considered as an abuse, and there is no reason for thinking that abusive and illicit practices cannot exist in ecclesiastical tribunals.

The arguments that theologians have offered for the strong view of papal jurisdiction are thus unpersuasive. The merits of Vitoria's arguments for the moderate view should be apparent to the reader. His historical sense is particularly worthy of note; he discerned that the patristic texts commonly cited in favour of the strong view did not mean what

---

[94] "Potestatis regiminis, quae quidem ex divina institutione est in Ecclesia et etiam potestas iurisdictionis vocatur, ad normam praescriptorum iuris, habiles sunt qui ordine sacro sunt insigniti."

the adherents of the strong view claimed that they did. It is a fact that no one in the first millennium of the Church ever thought of this view, or would have taken it seriously if they had thought of it; and that it would have been completely impractical—as Vitoria points out—to have put it into practice during this period.

Msgr. Joseph Clifford Fenton objects to Vitoria's arguments on the grounds that "Victoria, outstanding theologian though he was, seems to have misconstrued the question at issue, and to have imagined that in some way the traditional teaching involved the implication that all bishops had been placed in their sees by appointment from Rome."[95] As we have seen, this characterisation of Vitoria is mistaken. He argues against the strong view on the grounds of the positive right of apostles and bishops to leave successors in their sees, in virtue of the power of their respective offices.

It is melancholy to reflect that Vitoria's undoubtedly superior arguments were made 358 years before those of Palmieri. The fact is that during and after Vitoria's time, the pope was engaged in a struggle with Catholic monarchs over control of the Church. The conception of the pope as an absolute monarch was considered to be the best weapon for the papacy in this struggle, and was naturally felt to be true in itself by the popes. In consequence, theologians and religious orders who sided with the pope and looked to the papacy for support and reward backed the idea of the pope as absolute monarch. This idea also conformed to the dominant understanding of authority during this period, which saw the growth of the power and prestige of absolute monarchy. Theologians who did not take the side of the papacy in this dispute generally looked to Catholic monarchs for support and reward, and supported Gallicanism, Febronianism, or similar positions that denied the authority of the pope over the Church. The topic of the nature of papal authority and the papal office became a battleground for these two opposing camps. The moderate view of papal authority retained the status of a permitted theological opinion because of its intrinsic probability and the eminence of its principal upholders, but it remained a minority view. As with his position on the rights of the Indians, the truth of Vitoria's claims did not prevail against political realities.

III. Magisterial teaching on papal and episcopal jurisdiction

Mr. Ureta claims that the strong view of papal jurisdiction is taught by the magisterium of the Church. He is followed in this by a number of Catholic authors, and it seems that the strong view is taken for granted by many orthodox Catholics as being Catholic teaching. This is not in fact the case, but the position of the magisterium on this subject

---

[95] See Joseph Clifford Fenton, "Episcopal Jurisdiction and the Roman See," *American Ecclesiastical Review*, vol. 120, no. 4 (April 1949): 337–42.

is not expressed in a simple manner. A careful analysis of a number of magisterial texts is required in order to identify what this position is.

An important text on papal and episcopal jurisdiction is found in Leo XIII's encyclical *Satis Cognitum*:

> 14. But if the authority of Peter and his successors is plenary and supreme, it is not to be regarded as the sole authority. For He who made Peter the foundation of the Church also "chose twelve, whom He called apostles" (Lk 6:13); and just as it is necessary that the authority of Peter should be perpetuated in the Roman Pontiff, so, by the fact that the bishops succeed the Apostles, they inherit their ordinary power, and thus the episcopal order necessarily belongs to the essential constitution of the Church. Although they do not receive plenary, or universal, or supreme authority, they are not to be looked upon as vicars of the Roman Pontiffs, because they exercise a power really their own, and are most truly called the *ordinary* pastors of the peoples over whom they rule.
>
> But since the successor of Peter is one, and those of the Apostles are many, it is necessary to examine the relations which exist between him and them according to the divine constitution of the Church. Above all things the need of union between the bishops and the successors of Peter is clear and undeniable. This bond once broken, Christians would be separated and scattered, and would in no wise form one body and one flock. "The safety of the Church depends on the dignity of the chief priest, to whom if an extraordinary and supreme power is not given, there are as many schisms to be expected in the Church as there are priests" (S. Jerome, *Dialog. contra Luciferianos*, no. 9). It is necessary, therefore, to bear this in mind, viz., that nothing was conferred on the apostles apart from Peter, but that several things were conferred upon Peter apart from the Apostles. St. John Chrysostom in explaining the words of Christ asks: "Why, passing over the others, does He speak to Peter about these things?" And he replies unhesitatingly and at once, "Because he was pre-eminent among the Apostles, the mouthpiece of the Disciples, and the head of the college" (Hom. 88 *in Joan.*, no. 1). He alone was designated as the foundation of the Church. To him He gave the power of binding and loosing; to him alone was given the power of feeding. On the other hand, whatever authority and office the Apostles received, they received in conjunction with Peter. "If the divine benignity willed anything to be in common between him and the other princes, whatever He did not deny to the others He gave only through him. So that whereas Peter

Unresolved Tensions in Papal-Episcopal Relations

alone received many things, He conferred nothing on any of the rest without Peter participating in it" (S. Leo, Sermon 4, ch. 2).

15. From this it must be clearly understood that bishops are deprived of the right and power of ruling, if they deliberately secede from Peter and his successors; because, by this secession, they are separated from the foundation on which the whole edifice must rest. They are therefore outside the *edifice* itself; and for this very reason they are separated from the *fold*, whose leader is the Chief Pastor; they are exiled from the *Kingdom*, the keys of which were given by Christ to Peter alone.

This description of the jurisdiction of the pope and the bishops on the face of it expresses the moderate view. It cannot be taken as a decisive resolution of the theological debate between the strong and the moderate views, however, because it does not mention this debate or contain a statement that definitively rules out the strong view. It does lend weight to the moderate view, as being the theological position that best conforms to Leo XIII's teaching.

Those Catholic theologians who assert that the strong view is taught by the magisterium of the Church base their claim upon the teaching of Pope Pius XII in his encyclical *Mystici Corporis*. Van Noort asserts:

> Prior to *Mystici Corporis*, two opinions were held by Catholics: 1. Some theologians held that God directly confers episcopal jurisdiction in each individual instance, either by the very consecration of the bishop, or in some other way. . . . 2. The other, and always the majority opinion, maintained that bishops received their jurisdiction not directly, but indirectly from God.[96]

Finally, in his epoch-making encyclical, *Mystici Corporis*, Pius XII states explicitly and without any qualification that the bishops receive their jurisdiction directly from the pope:

> As far as each one's diocese is concerned, they [the bishops] each and all as true Shepherds feed the flocks entrusted to them and rule them in the name of Christ. Yet in exercising this office they are not altogether independent, but are duly subordinate to the authority of the Roman Pontiff: and although their jurisdiction is inherent in their office, yet they receive it directly from the same Supreme Pontiff.[97]

---

[96] G. van Noort, *Dogmatic Theology*, vol. II: *Christ's Church*, trans. and rev. John J. Castelot and William R. Murphy (Westminster, MD: Newman Press, 1957; repr. Waterloo, ON: Arouca Press, n.d.), 325.

[97] "Quamobrem sacrorum Antistites non solum eminentiora universalis Ecclesiae membra habendi sunt, ut qui singulari prorsus nexu iunguntur cum divino totius Corporis Capite, atque adeo iure vocantur «partes membrorum

On the Papal Deposition of Bishops

Following this explicit, even though brief, declaration by Pius XII the first opinion is, we feel, no longer tenable. We would agree with Cardinal Ottaviani's statement that the second opinion "should now . . . be rated as absolutely certain because of the words of the Supreme Pontiff, Pius XII."[98]

The text of *Mystici Corporis* that van Noort cites runs thus, in full:

> 41. They, therefore, walk in the path of dangerous error who believe that they can accept Christ as the Head of the Church, while not adhering loyally to His Vicar on earth. They have taken away the visible head, broken the visible bonds of unity and left the Mystical Body of the Redeemer so obscured and so maimed, that those who are seeking the haven of eternal salvation can neither see it nor find it.
>
> 42. What we have thus far said of the Universal Church must be understood also of the individual Christian communities, whether Oriental or Latin, which go to make up the one Catholic Church. For they, too, are ruled by Jesus Christ through the voice of their respective bishops. Consequently, bishops must be considered as the more illustrious members of the Universal Church, for they are united by a very special bond to the divine Head of the whole Body and so are rightly called "principal parts of the members of the Lord"; moreover, as far as his own diocese is concerned, each one as a true shepherd feeds the flock entrusted to him and rules it in the name of Christ. Yet in exercising this office they are not altogether independent, but are subordinate to the lawful authority of the Roman Pontiff, although enjoying the ordinary power of jurisdiction which they receive directly from the same Supreme Pontiff. Therefore, Bishops should be revered by the faithful as divinely appointed successors of the apostles, and to them, even more than to the highest civil authorities should be applied the words: "Touch not my anointed one!" For Bishops have been anointed with the chrism of the Holy Spirit.

Pius XII made a similar statement in his encyclical *Ad Sinarum Gentem* (1954), addressed to the Catholic bishops and people of China:

Domini primae» (S. Greg. Magn. *Moral.* 14, 35, 43); sed, ad propriam cuiusque Dioecesim quod spectat, utpote veri Pastores assignatos sibi greges singuli singulos Christi nomine pascunt ac regunt (cfr. Conc. Vat. *Const. de Eccl.* cap. 3); id tamen dum faciunt, non plane sui iuris sunt, sed sub debita Romani Pontificis auctoritate positi, quamvis ordinaria iurisdictionis potestate fruantur, immediate sibi ab eodem Pontifice Summo impertita."

[98] van Noort, *Dogmatic Theology*, 2:325–26, citing Alfredo Ottaviani, *Institutiones juris publici ecclesiastici* (Rome, 1947), I, 413.

Unresolved Tensions in Papal-Episcopal Relations

11. In fact, even then, as you well know, it will be entirely necessary for your Christian community, if it wishes to be part of the society divinely founded by our Redeemer, to be completely subject to the Supreme Pontiff, Vicar of Jesus Christ on earth, and be strictly united with him in regard to religious faith and morals. With these words—and it is well to note them—is embraced the whole life and work of the Church, and also its constitution, its government, its discipline. All of these things depend certainly on the will of Jesus Christ, Founder of the Church.

12. By virtue of God's will, the faithful are divided into two classes: the clergy and the laity. By virtue of the same will is established the twofold sacred hierarchy, namely, of orders and jurisdiction. Besides—as has also been divinely established—the power of orders (through which the ecclesiastical hierarchy is composed of bishops, priests, and ministers) comes from receiving the Sacrament of Holy Orders. But the power of jurisdiction, which is conferred upon the Supreme Pontiff directly by divine right, flows to the Bishops by the same right, but only through the Successor of St. Peter, to whom not only the simple faithful, but even all the Bishops must be constantly subject, and to whom they must be bound by obedience and with the bond of unity.

13. Finally by the same Divine Will, the people or the civil authority must not invade the rights and the constitution of the ecclesiastical hierarchy (cf. Council of Trent, Sess. XXIII, De Ordine, canons 2–7; Vatican Council, Sess. IV, canons 108–9).

Pius XII repeated this assertion in his encyclical *Ad Apostolorum Principis* (1958), addressed to the Catholic bishops and people of China:

38. For it has been clearly and expressly laid down in the canons that it pertains to the one Apostolic See to judge whether a person is fit for the dignity and burden of the episcopacy, and that complete freedom in the nomination of bishops is the right of the Roman Pontiff. But if, as happens at times, some persons or groups are permitted to participate in the selection of an episcopal candidate, this is lawful only if the Apostolic See has allowed it in express terms and in each particular case for clearly defined persons or groups, the conditions and circumstances being very plainly determined.

39. Granted this exception, it follows that bishops who have been neither named nor confirmed by the Apostolic See, but who, on the contrary, have been elected and consecrated in defiance of its express orders, enjoy no powers of

On the Papal Deposition of Bishops

teaching or of jurisdiction since jurisdiction passes to bishops only through the Roman Pontiff, as We admonished in the Encyclical Letter *Mystici Corporis* in the following words: "As far as his own diocese is concerned, each [bishop] feeds the flock entrusted to him as a true shepherd and rules it in the name of Christ. Yet in exercising this office they are not altogether independent but are subordinate to the lawful authority of the Roman Pontiff, although enjoying the ordinary power of jurisdiction which they receive directly from the same Supreme Pontiff."

40. And when We later addressed to you the letter *Ad Sinarum Gentem*, We again referred to this teaching in these words: "The power of jurisdiction which is conferred directly by divine right on the Supreme Pontiff comes to bishops by that same right, but only through the successor of Peter, to whom not only the faithful but also all bishops are bound to be constantly subject and to adhere both by the reverence of obedience and by the bond of unity."

41. Acts requiring the power of Holy Orders which are performed by ecclesiastics of this kind, though they are valid as long as the consecration conferred on them was valid, are yet gravely illicit, that is, criminal and sacrilegious.

These papal assertions cannot be said to settle the question. The issue is a debate between different schools of Catholic theology that lasted for centuries. Both sides of this debate were strongly argued for at an ecumenical council, the Council of Trent,[99] and no agreement was arrived at. It is a question of the first importance that concerns the fundamental structure of the Church. In order to end a dispute of this kind by a magisterial intervention, such an intervention must clearly describe the question, express the intention of settling it, specify the position being taught, and make it clear that the teaching is binding on all Catholics.

Of the texts cited above, only the encyclical *Mystici Corporis* could satisfy these criteria, because it is the only document that is addressed to the entire Church. But it does not in fact satisfy them. Such a question cannot be settled by a subordinate phrase of a sentence in a papal encyclical—a phrase, moreover, that does not explain the

---

[99] This was pointed out by Benedict XIV in his *De synodo diocesana* (Venice: Typographia Bassanensi, Sumptibus Remondinianis, 1767), lib. 1, c. 4, II: "quaestio eodem est inter Tridentinos Patres summa contentione jamdiu exagitata, nec definita, de qua Cardinalis Pallavicinius in *Historia Concilii Tridentini* lib. 18, c. 14 et lib. 21, c. 11 et 13 an Episcopi illam accipiant immediate a Christo, aut potius a summo Pontifice." See also Karl Joseph von Hefele et al., *Histoire des conciles d'après les documents originaux* (Paris: Letouzey et Ane, 1907ff.), IX, 747ff. and 776ff.; Sforza Pallavicini, *Histoire du concile de Trente* (Montrouge: Migne, 1844), Lib. XVIII, chs. 14ff.; Lib. XXI, chs. 11 and 13, II, 1347ff.; III, 363ff.

Unresolved Tensions in Papal-Episcopal Relations

character of the direct jurisdiction it refers to, make mention of the theological debate in question, or express the intention to bind Catholics to reject one of the competing theories and accept the other. There is no mention of the Scriptural texts that are given by theologians to support this position. There is indeed no clear indication in the encyclical of a will to teach that bishops receive their ordinary power of jurisdiction directly from the pope. The goal of the passage in which this statement occurs is to teach the necessity of loyally adhering to the Supreme Pontiff and submitting to his authority. The statement that bishops receive their ordinary power of jurisdiction directly from the pope is given as a reason for this loyalty and submission; that is not the same as presenting this claim about episcopal power of jurisdiction as a teaching to be held by Catholics. This reason need not be accepted in order to accept the necessity of loyalty and submission to the pope. Such loyalty and submission is required by both of the theological positions that we have been considering.

The encyclicals to the Chinese bishops and people are by their nature incompetent to pronounce a definite and final teaching on the subject of episcopal jurisdiction, because they are not addressed to the whole Church. The point about the goal of the passage in *Mystici Corporis* that mentions this issue applies to these encyclicals as well. They are intended to recall the duty of obedience and subjection to the Supreme Pontiff, and to state that bishops who have been elected and consecrated in defiance of the express orders of the Apostolic See enjoy no powers of teaching or of jurisdiction. Their claims about episcopal jurisdiction are given as reasons for this statement, not as an independent teaching.

The passages from the encyclicals of Pius XII that are cited above cannot be seen as a proper and responsible exercise of the papal teaching office. One may speculate that these passages were included in the texts of these encyclicals by drafters at the Holy Office (of which Cardinal Ottaviani was the head at the time) in order to further the cause of a theological opinion that they accepted, without having to face the opposition that would arise if this opinion were presented in a direct and above-board fashion as a position that was being definitively taught by the pope.

The dogmatic constitution *Lumen Gentium* takes a different position on the nature of episcopal jurisdiction. It states:

> 21. And the Sacred Council teaches that by episcopal consecration the fullness of the sacrament of Orders is conferred that fullness of power, namely, which both in the Church's liturgical practice and in the language of the Fathers of the Church is called the high priesthood, the supreme power of the sacred

ministry. But episcopal consecration, together with the office of sanctifying, also confers the office of teaching and of governing, which, however, of its very nature, can be exercised only in hierarchical communion with the head and the members of the college....

22.... But the college or body of bishops has no authority unless it is understood together with the Roman Pontiff, the successor of Peter as its head. The pope's power of primacy over all, both pastors and faithful, remains whole and intact. In virtue of his office, that is as Vicar of Christ and pastor of the whole Church, the Roman Pontiff has full, supreme, and universal power over the Church....

24.... The canonical mission of bishops can come about by legitimate customs that have not been revoked by the supreme and universal authority of the Church, or by laws made or recognized by that authority, or directly through the successor of Peter himself; and if the latter refuses or denies apostolic communion, such bishops cannot assume any office....

27. Bishops, as vicars and ambassadors of Christ, govern the particular churches entrusted to them by their counsel, exhortations, example, and even by their authority and sacred power.... This power, which they personally exercise in Christ's name, is proper, ordinary, and immediate, although its exercise is ultimately regulated by the supreme authority of the Church, and can be circumscribed by certain limits, for the advantage of the Church or of the faithful.... The pastoral office or the habitual and daily care of their sheep is entrusted to them completely; nor are they to be regarded as vicars of the Roman Pontiffs, for they exercise an authority that is proper to them, and are quite correctly called "prelates," heads of the people whom they govern.

Nota explicativa praevia (Preliminary note of explanation):

2. A person becomes a member of the College by virtue of episcopal consecration and by hierarchical communion with the head of the College and with its members. Cf. no. 22, § 1 *in fine*. In his consecration a person is given an ontological participation in the sacred functions [*munera*]; this is absolutely clear from Tradition, liturgical tradition included. The word "functions" [*munera*] is used deliberately instead of the word "powers" [*potestates*], because the latter word could be understood as a power fully ready to act. But for this power to be fully ready to act, there must be a further canonical or juridical determination

through the hierarchical authority. This determination of power can consist in the granting of a particular office or in the allotment of subjects, and it is done according to the norms approved by the supreme authority. An additional norm of this sort is required by the very nature of the case, because it involves functions [*munera*] which must be exercised by many subjects cooperating in a hierarchical manner in accordance with Christ's will. It is evident that this "communion" was applied in the Church's life according to the circumstances of the time, before it was codified as law.

For this reason it is clearly stated that hierarchical communion with the head and members of the Church is required. Communion is a notion which is held in high honor in the ancient Church (and also today, especially in the East). However, it is not understood as some kind of vague disposition, but as an organic reality which requires a juridical form and is animated by charity. Hence the Commission, almost unanimously, decided that this wording should be used: "in hierarchical communion." Cf. Modus 40 and the statements on canonical mission (no. 24). The documents of recent Pontiffs regarding the jurisdiction of bishops must be interpreted in terms of this necessary determination of powers.

These passages from *Lumen Gentium* assert that bishops receive their jurisdiction through their ordination. They present an understanding of papal power and episcopal jurisdiction that agrees with the moderate view, and reject an essential component of the strong view; and they assert that the encyclicals of Pius XII are to be understood as being in harmony with their position.

For this reason, Mr. Ureta rejects the teachings of *Lumen Gentium* on this subject. He asserts:

> It is insufficient to base a solution on sections 20, 23, and 27 of the Second Vatican Council's constitution *Lumen Gentium* on the ordinary power of bishops in their dioceses as successors of the apostles and not as delegates of the pope. In order to theologically justify the novelty of *collegiality* as the participation of all the bishops in the supreme government of the Church, that conciliar document failed to refer explicitly to the traditional distinction between the hierarchy of order and the hierarchy of jurisdiction. Further, it opposed the Church's traditional magisterium when declaring that the "episcopal consecration, together with the office of sanctifying, also confers the office of teaching and governing" (no. 21).

On the Papal Deposition of Bishops

This position is untenable. *Lumen Gentium* mentions the distinction between order and jurisdiction, as the passages cited above indicate. It is a dogmatic constitution of an ecumenical council, which constitution explicitly sets out to give Catholic teaching on the nature of the Church. The documents of the Second Vatican Council are of different kinds, and many of these kinds of document—decrees, declarations, etc.—do not have a great degree of authority. The case of a dogmatic constitution is different. Such constitutions are a recognized form of conciliar teaching; the documents *Dei Filius* and *Pastor Aeternus* of the First Vatican Council are dogmatic constitutions. They express by their titles the intention of teaching Catholic dogma in an authoritative fashion. A dogmatic constitution has a much higher degree of authority than the encyclicals of Pius XII cited above, which are the only magisterial statements that support Mr. Ureta's position.

It is not denied that some passages of the documents of Vatican II could be or are contrary to Catholic teaching. However, this has to be proven for any passage of these documents; and the presumption is that the documents express Catholic truth, since they were produced by a valid ecumenical council. In the case of the conciliar teaching on episcopal jurisdiction, it can be shown that the position of *Lumen Gentium* does *not* contradict Catholic teaching. The main reason for this is that the assertion that episcopal consecration confers the office of teaching and governing is a recognized position in Catholic theology, as we have seen above. It is supported by the teaching of Leo XIII, and it is not ruled out as inadmissible by the statements of Pius XII on episcopal jurisdiction. It cannot be claimed to be a view that was introduced into the document by modernists wishing to advance their cause. It is stated in the *Nota praevia*, a text that was added to the dogmatic constitution in order to remove the objections of conservative bishops at the council who objected that the original text of the constitution could be interpreted as supporting conciliarism or otherwise denying the papal primacy. The statements of *Lumen Gentium* on episcopal jurisdiction are therefore authoritative and final, and must, as far as they go, be accepted.

Mr. Ureta appeals to the precedent of Pius VII's brief *Tam Multa* to support his position. This precedent is important for our subject. Mr. Ureta describes this historical episode as follows:

> Even more significant was the case of the French bishops who had emigrated because of the French Revolution's fierce persecution. They were forced to renounce their dioceses by Pope Pius VII's brief *Tam Multa* to comply with the 1801 concordat Cardinal Consalvi had negotiated with Napoleon Bonaparte on

Unresolved Tensions in Papal-Episcopal Relations

the pope's behalf. In return, the First Consul agreed to demand the resignation of intruding "bishops" who had joined the schismatic church established by the Civil Constitution of the Clergy. A new French episcopate was thus established, chosen by Bonaparte from among *juring* and faithful *non-juring* bishops, with the pope pledging to give all of them the respective canonical recognition. . . .

In the end, 47 of the 82 émigré bishops still alive in September 1801 resigned, and 35 refused to submit their resignations. Their dioceses were either suppressed or taken over by other bishops appointed by civil authorities and recognized by the pope. Nonetheless, the non-resigning bishops who remained faithful to the Holy See never claimed jurisdiction over their former dioceses, not even after Napoleon's 1814 fall and the restoration of the Bourbon dynasty.

In Church history, it is difficult to find such an arbitrary removal of so many good bishops who suffered tremendous hardships to avoid joining a schismatic church. Those who refused to resign could have argued that Pius VII was acting *ultra vires*, i.e., beyond his legal authority, that the brief *Tam Multa* should be "ignored" as "null and void," and that the new bishops should be deemed usurpers or imposters. They could have added that it was an "emergency" and the chaos of having two bishops claiming jurisdiction over the same diocese was preferable to abandoning the flock to a wolf appointed by Napoleon.

However, they did not do so, although their leader, Most Rev. Arthur Richard Dillon, Gallican archbishop of Narbonne, exiled in London, claimed that the pope "could not remove a bishop on his own authority without a canonical and regular trial." Only three bishops who refused to resign continued giving orders to the clergy and faithful of their former dioceses, thus giving rise to the anti-1801 French Concordat schism known to history as the *Petite Église*.

This account does not give a correct picture of events. In the brief *Tam Multa* of August 15, 1801, Pius VII requested the bishops of all the dioceses then located in France to resign their sees within ten days for the good of the Church, in order to permit an agreement with Bonaparte (then the First Consul) that would regularize the situation of the Catholic Church in France. The request did not leave them a free choice about their decision, but it did not inform them that they had been removed from their sees. All the bishops who resided in France agreed to this request, but 36 bishops who had fled the country refused it. In response to this refusal Pius VII issued on November 29, 1801 the bull *Qui Christi Domini*. This bull suppressed all the existing dioceses of France and withdrew all jurisdiction from the bishops who had not submitted their resignation.

In response to this action, thirteen expatriate bishops residing in London published a document explaining their refusal to resign their office. This document asserted the Gallican principle that the pope and the bishops acting in moral unanimity are the only possessor of supreme authority in the Church, and argued from this principle that the pope did not have the power to remove them or demand their resignations. When new bishops began to be appointed to their sees, many of the bishops who had refused to resign declared that they delegated their powers to the new appointees, and that the faithful should obey them, without conceding that their successors held office legitimately. A considerable number of Catholics followed the bishops and priests who refused to accept the concordat with Napoleon and the actions of Pius VII. As these bishops and priests died out, the number of this group—the "Petite Église"—dwindled, and its last members submitted to the Church in 1911.

The following points about this episode are important for our question:

- Pope Pius VII did not demand the resignation of the bishops, or suppress their dioceses and remove them from office, purely on the basis of his authority as pope. He gave a justification for doing so that could be presented as having legal force; the step was described as necessary for the restoration of the Church in France, and thus was required by the good of the Church and the French nation.
- The majority of the bishops chose to resign their sees in response to his initial request. This action did not concede that the pope had power to require them to resign or to remove them from office.
- The bishops who refused to resign protested against his action as an abuse of power. Most of them did not attempt to continue to exercise their jurisdiction over their dioceses, but this was a necessity imposed on them by being in exile. The bishops of Blois and La Rochelle did however attempt to govern their dioceses from outside the country, until Bonaparte had them arrested by the King of Spain.
- The position of these recusant bishops was not, be it noted, a simple denial of the pope's power to remove them from office; they also advanced a false, Gallican position on the character of supreme power in the Church, and used this position to justify their action. The question at issue between these bishops and the Holy See was thus not only a dispute over the pope's right to remove bishops. There were, accordingly, other grounds for holding these bishops to be schismatic and for treating them as such.

Unresolved Tensions in Papal-Episcopal Relations

❖ The action of Pius VII was criticized at the time by eminent ecclesiastics as an abuse of power, and has never been accepted as above all objection.

The actions of Pius VII in *Tam Multa* and *Qui Christi Domini* thus cannot be used to sustain the thesis that the pope has the right to remove diocesan bishops at will.

The sequel to this episode is extremely important for our question. Archbishop Deschamps of Malines presented a postulatum to the First Vatican Council in 1870 in connection with the "Petite Église." He requested a formal condemnation of this movement as schismatic. He proposed an amendment to the Council's chapter on the Roman primacy that would assert the pope's power to suppress dioceses, and supported this amendment by reference to Pius VII's actions in 1801.[100] The Council Fathers refused to accept this amendment.[101] This claim about papal power therefore cannot be described as having been taught by the First Vatican Council. The Council chose not to include this claim in its description of papal primacy when asked to do so.

Mr. Ureta asserts that "while the *Petite Église* experienced a rapid decline during the nineteenth century, French Catholicism, albeit led by a large number of bishops who were successors to those appointed by Napoleon, emerged rejuvenated from these troubles and saw the birth of numerous saints, new congregations, and missionary endeavors that took the Gospel to the furthest ends of the earth." This gives too rosy a view. The French Church lost the struggle with its anticlerical and anti-Christian enemies during the nineteenth and twentieth centuries. France became more and more secularized in the twentieth and twenty-first centuries, with the practicing Catholics in that country now being a tiny minority. The French Church is in ruins and faces extinction. The actions of Pius VII in *Tam Multa* and *Qui Christi Domini* greatly weakened the Church in France, and hence contributed to this result. By suppressing the ancient Catholic dioceses of France, Pius VII deprived French Catholics of their spiritual homes and histories. By removing many of their bishops, often the ones who had shown the most fidelity to the Church in the French Revolution, he deprived them of their spiritual fathers. A list of the achievements of the French Church after the French Revolution does not explain why the Catholic Church in France failed to conquer the challenge of the Revolution.

---

[100] The amendment reads: "aut sustinent R. Pontificem non posse, vi huius iurisdictionis, ad bonum religionis uti mediis extraordinariis (quale ineunte hoc saeculo XIX. ad religionis cultum in Galliis resturandum adhibuit P. M. Pius VII., plures Dioeceses extinguendo et novas erigendo), ac ideo huiusmodi ordinationibus obtemperare nolentes, Sanctae Sedi et constitutis ab Ea legitimis Episcopis obedientiam detrectantes, a vera Christi Ecclesia seiuncti, in schismate versantur." February 25, 1870. *Acta et decreta sacrosancti oecumenici concilii Vaticani*, vol. 7 (Freiburg, 1892), 855. See E. Mangenot, "Anticoncordataires," *DTC* 1/1, col. 1377.

[101] *Acta et decreta sacrosancti oecumenici concilii Vaticani*, 7:368.

On the Papal Deposition of Bishops

This was the goal that the Church needed to achieve, and it was far from impossible after revolutionary ideas had revealed their destructive and criminal face. *Tam Multa* and *Qui Christi Domini* are a major part of the explanation for this failure. Bonaparte showed a sinister cunning in getting Pius VII to agree to his proposals. By offering the pope an unprecedented extension of his power over the Church, he recruited Pius VII as an agent of revolutionary destruction.

This review of magisterial teaching gives valuable insight into the progressives of Vatican II and their heirs. A main progressive theme was the irrelevance, abstractness, futility, etc. of traditional scholastic and neoscholastic theology. However, the traditional theological debate between the strong and moderate views of papal authority is, as we have seen, of immediate interest for the Church and raises fundamental and important questions. When we need to decide these questions, the only thing to do is to go back to this traditional debate by digging up texts written only in Latin in the nineteenth century or earlier. Progressive theology is useless here.

The support of progressives for Pope Francis and his actions in removing bishops reveals their hypocrisy. The supposed ecumenical goals of progressives should lead them to insist on a clear rejection of the strong view and its conception of the pope as an absolute monarch. The strong view on the nature of papal primacy is unacceptable to the Orthodox, although they are generally ready to concede some sort of primacy to the pope. It is outrageous and abhorrent to Protestants. Rejecting it is thus a necessary step for any kind of ecumenical progress. There is however no effort to do this on the part of progressives. That is because ecumenism is really of interest to them as a tool for destroying Catholic belief, not as a path towards Christian reconciliation. Thus, when a pope acts in their interests, as is the case with Pope Francis, they present the strong view of papal power as the gospel truth: when he opposes their cause, as sometimes happened with John Paul II and Benedict XVI, they proclaim the right to resist and disobey the pope.

IV. Resolution of the question

Both the balance of argument and the teaching of the Church indicate that the strong view of papal jurisdiction should be rejected. This view is rejected by the dogmatic constitution *Lumen Gentium* in clear terms—an unusual step for the Second Vatican Council. It is not historically or theologically credible.

The claim that the pope has the right to remove bishops at will is justified by its adherents on the basis of the strong view. Since the strong view is false, this claim lacks any grounds for acceptance. As noted above, it cannot be reconciled with the fact that bishops have by divine right a proper and ordinary jurisdiction over their diocese. A jurisdiction of this kind by its very nature can be lost only for a just reason and through the process of law. The claim must therefore be rejected.

There is more that can be said about this claim. Palmieri thus characterises the moderate view:

> It is asserted that the Roman Pontiff cannot licitly and validly remove or restrict the jurisdiction of a bishop without just cause: once the condition of the Roman Pontiff having assigned subjects to a bishop is satisfied, the jurisdiction received by bishops is given by God, for it is this jurisdiction of divine origin that is exercised. The Roman Pontiff may indeed regulate and modify this jurisdiction for reasons derived from just causes. He can even in certain cases declare that this jurisdiction has been lost, in virtue of his right to interpret divine law. He cannot however directly remove jurisdiction from a bishop, because this jurisdiction does not exist in its subject through him, but by divine law; and divine law takes precedence over papal authority.

The question that should be raised here is: what could the pope *lose* by this being true? What benefit to the Church could arise from his *not* having to have a just cause in order to remove a bishop? The idea that there could be some such benefit is absurd. The pope would not benefit from the power to depose bishops at will regardless of the justice of their deposition. This is a despotic power. Despotism is a weak form of government, judging by the standard of the purposes to which government is directed. It makes the ruler of a despotic polity strong, or makes him feel strong, but it ensures that the polity over which he rules is unjust, inefficient, and malfunctioning—and thus weak. Undoubtedly, the opposite is the case; there are great benefits to the Church from his having to have some just cause for removing a bishop. These benefits go further than ruling out arbitrary and unjust removal of bishops by the pope. They go to the foundations of the structure of the Church, to the fact that the Church is a polity ruled and structured by law rather than by arbitrary power. The rule of law in the Church is identical with the rule of God in the Church, and hence departure from the rule of law is departure from the rule of God. The fact that the rule of law could have been rejected by so many Catholic thinkers for such a long time in favour of the strong view of papal authority indicates a serious and troubling pathology in the Catholic understanding of authority.[102]

---

[102] For a detailed analysis of this pathology, see my essay "The Catholic Church and the Rule of Law" in Kwasniewski, ed., *Ultramontanism and Tradition*, 78–106, as well as numerous other essays in that anthology.

On the Papal Deposition of Bishops

Dr. Kwasniewski was therefore correct in saying that Bishop Strickland was not bound to resign his diocese simply because Pope Francis removed him. Our analysis of papal and episcopal jurisdiction permits us to draw further conclusions about this situation. In attempting to remove Bishop Strickland without good reason, Pope Francis was breaking the divine law. He was not just breaking the moral law established by God; he was also breaking the public divine law established by Christ to govern the Church. Those who break this public divine law are criminals; Pope Francis is therefore a criminal. This will not be a surprise to those who have studied Pope Francis's career.[103]

There are other bishops whom Pope Francis has removed in violation of the divine law. The criminal character of these removals is obvious. There is another interesting feature of the divine law as applied to his actions that has not been so well explored as the unjust removal of bishops and that merits consideration. The moderate view asserts that the pope can remove bishops only when this is required by divine law, and that he may not do so otherwise. Is it also the case that the pope *must* remove bishops when the divine law calls for them to be removed, and that he is breaking the divine law and thus committing a crime if he does not do so? The moderate view seems to imply this, but the question has not been much explored by theologians. There are many criminal bishops whom Pope Francis has protected and left in place after it became apparent that they had to be removed for the good of the faithful and of the Church. By so doing, Pope Francis has provided a fruitful area of research for future theologians.

---

[103] See Kwasniewski, ed., *Ultramontanism and Tradition*, 386–440.

5

It Is Churchmen Who Need Reform, Not the Church: In Defense of Papal Prerogatives

José Antonio Ureta

On December 18, 2023, the same day that the Dicastery for the Doctrine of the Faith released *Fiducia Supplicans*, Dr. John Lamont published a study "On the Papal Deposition of Bishops" at *Rorate Coeli*.[104] It was an attempt to refute my article titled "Why a Good Bishop Should Not Ignore but Obey His Unjust Deposition by a Pope,"[105] about Bishop Joseph Strickland's removal from the Tyler, Texas diocese. The Christmas and New Year festivities and the follow-up to the debate surrounding Cardinal Fernández's bombshell document explain the relative lateness of this rejoinder.

The core of the controversy is whether the pope has the power to dismiss from his diocese a bishop who has committed no severe misconduct and absent some proportionate reason that makes it necessary. The issue is not whether an arbitrary removal is licit—it is not—but whether it is valid. The dismissed bishop can ask the pope to reconsider his decision only if it is first valid. He cannot appeal to any lower authority (*prima sedes a nemine iudicatur*, the first see is judged by no one). Here, we do not consider the case where revocation would occur for a reason of faith, i.e., where the justification of the sanction is the fidelity of the bishop to a dogma openly denied by the pope. In this case, the bishop has full right to remain in his see. Otherwise, the dismissed bishop must cede his post to the administrator or Vatican-appointed successor, as did Bishop Strickland and other bishops whom Pope Francis unjustly removed. The same was done by Cardinal József Mindszenty, whom Pope Paul VI unjustly removed from Hungary's primatial see of Esztergom. If the removal were null or invalid (which would be difficult to establish because the pope dictates the law; who could judge that except the pope himself or a successor?), the deposed bishop would have every right to remain in possession and consider his pope-appointed replacement as an intruder.[106]

First published in two parts at *Rorate Caeli* on February 14 and March 4, 2024.

[104] See the preceding chapter. Italics used in quotations represent emphases added by Dr. Lamont or myself.
[105] See chapter 3.
[106] In his article "Bishop Strickland's Removal Was Against Canon Law" (see chapter 10), Fr. Gerald Murray analyzes the canonical irregularities incurred in the procedures to remove these bishops, which would make

It Is Churchmen Who Need Reform, Not the Church

In turn, the validity or invalidity of this arbitrary removal depends on the immediate origin of episcopal power. Since the Middle Ages, theology and canon law have distinguished between two powers in the episcopal office: the fullness of the power of order, aimed at the sanctification of the faithful, and the power of jurisdiction, aimed at teaching and governing the flock. All theologians admit that the fullness of the power of order is received directly from God at the episcopal consecration. However, there is disagreement as to the immediate origin of a bishop's power of jurisdiction. The Jesuit theologian Domenico Palmieri (1829–1909), quoted at length in Dr. Lamont's work in an excellent translation which we thank him for, briefly describes the two positions and their respective consequences for the matter in dispute:

> No one denies that this power [of jurisdiction] is from Christ, since all power in the Church is from Him, or that it is immediately from God in that God acts immediately in and with the action of all other causes....
>
> There are some who suppose that the ordinary jurisdiction of bishops is received immediately from Christ.... Many others think that although Christ instituted the episcopate willing that His Church be ruled by bishops, ordinary jurisdiction is conferred by the pope on individual bishops....
>
> In the first hypothesis, it is asserted that the Roman pontiff cannot licitly and validly remove or restrict the jurisdiction of a bishop without just cause: once the condition of the Roman pontiff having assigned subjects to a bishop is satisfied, the jurisdiction received by bishops is given by God, for it is this jurisdiction of divine origin that is exercised. The Roman pontiff may indeed regulate and modify this jurisdiction for reasons derived from just causes. He can even in certain cases declare that this jurisdiction has been lost, in virtue of his right to interpret divine law. He cannot however directly remove jurisdiction from a bishop, because this jurisdiction does not exist in its subject through him, but by divine law; and divine law takes precedence over papal authority.
>
> In the second hypothesis, the pope cannot indeed licitly remove a bishop without cause, but he can certainly validly do this, and his act will have force on its own; a bishop in this situation cannot claim jurisdiction for himself on the pretext that there is no just cause for his removal.

---

them invalid. While his analysis is conclusive and worthy of endorsement, it addresses the issue from an exclusively canonical perspective rather than the theological one in which the current controversy with Dr. Lamont is being held.

Unresolved Tensions in Papal-Episcopal Relations

The discussion about the immediate origin of the power of jurisdiction arose in the twelfth century, shortly after the distinction between the power of order and the power of jurisdiction was made in Western theology and canon law. Following in the footsteps of Saint Thomas Aquinas, the majority current, which included authors of great authority such as Saints Bonaventure and Robert Bellarmine, asserted that the power of episcopal jurisdiction came from the canonical mission granted or corroborated by the pope. Since the Second Vatican Council, the once minority position has prevailed, according to which episcopal consecration, "together with the office of sanctifying, also confers the office of teaching and governing" (*Lumen Gentium*, no. 21). Otherwise, the "collegiality" novelty that all bishops also possess supreme and permanent power over the universal Church headed by the pope and in communion with him would lose its foundation. Therefore, the conciliar innovators had to premise the thesis that one becomes a member of the episcopal college, the juridical subject of this supreme power, by virtue of consecration.

In his study, Dr. Lamont decidedly sides with the post-conciliar current, now in the majority. Dr. Lamont does not put forward arguments used by neo-modernist theologians, defenders of collegiality and pioneers of synodality, who consider the distinction between the power of order and the power of jurisdiction outdated and technical, and insist on the indivisible unity of the three *munera* (sanctifying, teaching, and governing). He does accept this distinction in a bishop's powers but tries to base the direct divine origin of the power of jurisdiction on the few authors who belong to the minority current before Vatican II. However, his analysis contains several errors, which I will point out in this article.

In the first part, I will limit myself to showing the following inconsistencies that weaken Dr. Lamont's argument from an external point of view: mistranslation of an important text; a misrepresentation of the thought of the two leading authors he quoted; an underrating of Pius XII's teaching; an overvaluing of Vatican II's magisterial authority; and an insufficient explanation of an insurmountable historical-canonical obstacle. In the second part, I will turn to more fundamental philosophical and theological issues.

I

A fatal mistranslation

The first section of Dr. Lamont's study is titled "Theological Positions on the Origin of Episcopal Jurisdiction and the Nature of Papal Authority." He begins with a quotation from the *Dictionnaire de théologie catholique*, which he translates as follows: "Some maintain that jurisdiction is conferred immediately by Christ on bishops in the very act of episcopal consecration. . . . Others think, with St. Thomas, that the jurisdiction of bishops is directly connected to that of the vicar of Christ, to whom not only a portion but *the whole of* ecclesiastical power has been granted."

Then he adds that "the claim that God has granted the pope *the whole of* ecclesiastical power provides the justification for the claim that bishops receive the power of jurisdiction directly from the pope and only mediately from God, and hence that the pope can remove a bishop from office at will." Yet again he uses the expression *"the whole of* ecclesiastical power" and, in another instance, "the pope has *all the power of* jurisdiction." Dr. Lamont labels this position "the strong view of papal jurisdiction" since it holds that the pope possesses "not just *supreme* power of jurisdiction, but *the whole of* the power of jurisdiction" and the opposite position, which denies it, "the moderate view of papal jurisdiction."

It turns out that the translation of the *Dictionnaire* serving as the basis for characterizing the current he calls the "strong view" is incorrect. The French original says that the pope has been entrusted with "la *plenitude* du pouvoir ecclésiastique," literally, "the *fullness* of ecclesiastical power," not "the *whole* of ecclesiastical power." The first meaning (fullness) is all the more precise because the phrase refers to chapter 3 of the dogmatic constitution *Pastor Aeternus*, which, referring to the pope's primacy, quotes the Council of Florence's statement that "to him [the pope], in blessed Peter, *full power* has been given by our Lord Jesus Christ to feed, rule and govern the universal Church" (*plena potestas pascendi, regendi et gubernandi*).[107] Further on, the constitution refers to the "*supreme power* which the Roman Pontiff has in governing the whole Church."[108]

Now, saying that the pope enjoys full and supreme power ("full power was given to him . . . to feed, rule, and govern") is very different from affirming that he received "the whole of ecclesiastical power," meaning that he is the only one who holds power in the Church and that all other powers would be a delegation of his. Dr. Lamont recognizes the difference between the two concepts, as he attacks the windmill he created with his mistranslation by stating (this time with a correct translation): "'*Plenitude* of power' in this conciliar text [*Pastor Aeternus*] means having all the power of jurisdiction that it is possible to have, not all the power of jurisdiction that exists."

---

[107] Heinrich Denzinger, *The Sources of Catholic Dogma*, trans. Roy J. Deferrari (Fitzwilliam, NH: Loreto Publications, n.d.), 230; Denz.-Rahner, 694.
[108] *Pastor Aeternus*, ch. 3, nos. 1, 6.

Unresolved Tensions in Papal-Episcopal Relations

Misrepresentation of Palmieri and Vitoria

It so happens that this restricted interpretation of *plena potestas* is exactly the position of the theologian Domenico Palmieri, whose *Tractatus de romano pontifice*. Dr. Lamont quotes at length but mistakenly calls the "best case for the strong view" (i.e., "the whole of ecclesiastical power"). It is enough to quote his own words to prove that Palmieri upholds the narrow interpretation that Dr. Lamont subscribes to and calls the "moderate view of papal jurisdiction":

> The [pope's] plenitude of power that is being discussed is not absolute, but is relative to the society that is ruled; it is plenitude of power in a polity and for a polity. To give clarity, we can say that it can be understood in two ways: only positively, or exclusively. It is understood in a positive sense only, if the supreme ruler can by his ordinary legal authority perform everything that is useful and necessary for the entire polity and every one of its subjects, *although there are subordinate powers together with him and under him that exercise authority that is not derived from him*. It is understood in an exclusive sense, if the supreme ruler's authority is such that every power in the polity is either his own power, or is derived from his own power in such a way that the supreme power either formally or virtually contains every other power by which the polity is ruled. Such is the power of absolute monarchy in a political society. *It is easy to show that the plenitude of power belongs to the Roman Pontiff in the first sense.*

What Dr. Lamont calls the "strong view," Domenico Palmieri calls the "exclusive sense," which he rejects; and what Dr. Lamont calls the "moderate view," Palmieri calls the "positive sense," the restricted sense he defends. Therefore, it is absolutely inappropriate to classify it as the "best case for the strong view."

Unfortunately, this misrepresentation of the position of those who deny that the power of jurisdiction is granted to bishops at consecration—as if they thought that bishops are mere delegates of the pope, who supposedly would hold "the whole of ecclesiastical power"—runs through and disqualifies Dr. Lamont's entire study.

Lamont misrepresents not only the position of Domenico Palmieri, however, but also that of Francisco de Vitoria, the author he introduces as the supposed champion of the thesis of the sacramental origin of the power of episcopal jurisdiction. In his eyes, Vitoria's *Relectiones* are the ones that best represent the "moderate view on papal jurisdiction."

In the long text quoted, the great theologian and founder of the Salamanca School begins by proving, with the support of passages from Scripture, that the Twelve received

It Is Churchmen Who Need Reform, Not the Church

the apostolic mission and consequent power directly from Jesus Christ and that "every apostle had ecclesiastical power covering the whole world, for all the acts that Peter had power to do," except those that belong exclusively to the supreme pontiff, such as convening a general council. Vitoria then goes on to maintain that "any of the apostles aside from Peter could leave a successor, not a universal one, but in any province that he wished, who would be the true bishop of that province"—as Saint Paul did with Titus and Timothy. Furthermore, "not only the apostles could leave successors, but any of their successors could similarly do so" because "at that time it could have been of the greatest importance that a bishop nominate his successor during his lifetime," since "it would not only be possible and proper but necessary at all times. How could a dead bishop in the farthest reaches of India await a mandate from Peter to meet the need of a new bishop?" Vitoria goes even further by stating that "any bishop, even without consulting the see of Peter, can establish a law stating that priests elect the bishop, or that bishops are instituted by some other form." He concludes: "This is the reason why the authority and dignity of a bishop can be derived successively from one bishop to the next until it reaches us, and through the bishop all other inferior power." This power would not contradict the pope's *plenitudo potestatis* because "the successors of Peter can at their discretion create bishops in new provinces, abolish existing laws on the succession of bishops, establish new laws on this subject, divide provinces, and do all things pertaining to these matters by their own judgment and power."

Our purpose here is not to analyze Vitoria's proposal that a bishop's election and the transmission of jurisdiction be done by his predecessor or a method established by him without the intervention of the Holy See. We want to emphasize that at no point does Vitoria say that the power of jurisdiction is granted directly by Christ in the act of episcopal consecration, which is the real issue under discussion. On the contrary, he categorically states that "Peter's power was greater" than that received by the other apostles because "firstly, it was an ordinary power, whereas the power of the apostles was an extraordinary one"; "secondly—which follows from this—the power of Peter remained in the Church, whereas the power of the apostles did not." And then he concludes: "Aside from the holy apostles, *no one else in the Church received ecclesiastical power from Christ* . . . and thus we have the first origin of ecclesiastical power; for *the twelve apostles were the first and only persons to receive this power from Christ, our Lord and Redeemer.*"

Furthermore, at the end of the passage from *Relectio II*, quoted by Dr. Lamont, Vitoria says, "It was said to Peter, 'Feed my sheep,' with no limitations or exceptions. Therefore all direction pertains to Peter without any exception, and in consequence even the creation of bishops falls under his power." He continues:

Unresolved Tensions in Papal-Episcopal Relations

> From this the corollary clearly follows that one cannot now become a bishop except according to the forms laid down by the supreme pontiff, and that *if anyone attempts to do otherwise, nothing will result; such an attempt will be null and void.* I state this however about the authority of jurisdiction, for what pertains to consecration is different. Secondly, it follows that all ecclesiastical power, whether of orders or of jurisdiction, depends mediately or *immediately* on the see of Peter.

In this paragraph, Vitoria clearly distinguishes between the power of order (granted directly by Christ), whose transmission without a license from the pope renders it illicit but not invalid, and the power of jurisdiction, whose transmission without a canonical mission granted or recognized by the pope renders it null and legally invalid.

If the issue under discussion were whether the apostles received jurisdiction directly from Christ or through Saint Peter, Vitoria's long quotation would serve its purpose. But that is not what Dr. Lamont is questioning in my article, which is not even remotely about that. He wants to prove that any bishop at his consecration receives the power of jurisdiction immediately from Christ. The quotation from Vitoria is totally inappropriate and even counterproductive for this purpose, because the Salamanca theologian explicitly says that no one after the apostles received jurisdiction directly from Christ.

Underrating of Pius XII's teaching

As mentioned, the thesis of the immediate reception of jurisdiction from the pope's hands enjoyed the support of the vast majority of the best theological authors and treatises before Vatican II. What is more, it was explicitly put into practice in the 1917 Code of Canon Law and was taught in three documents by Pius XII: the encyclical on the Church, *Mystici Corporis Christi* (1943), and the encyclicals *Ad Sinarum Gentem* (1954) and *Ad Apostolorum Principis* (1958) addressed to the Chinese Catholic bishops and people. In my article, I stated that the Second Vatican Council "opposed the Church's traditional magisterium when declaring that the 'episcopal consecration, together with the office of sanctifying, also confers the office of teaching and governing' (no. 21)." Dr. Lamont asks: "Is Mr. Ureta right in claiming that the teaching of the theological school that he supports is taught by the magisterium?" He develops the theme in section III of his study, titled "Magisterial Teaching on Papal and Episcopal Jurisdiction," which begins by recognizing that "the position of the magisterium on this subject is not expressed in a simple manner. A careful analysis of a number of magisterial texts is required in order to identify what this position is."

It Is Churchmen Who Need Reform, Not the Church

The first text Dr. Lamont analyzes is Leo XIII's encyclical *Satis Cognitum*, which affirms what no one denies, namely that "if the authority of Peter and his successors is plenary and supreme, it is not to be regarded as the sole authority," since "by the fact that the bishops succeed the apostles, they inherit their ordinary power, and thus the episcopal order necessarily belongs to the essential constitution of the Church." However, the pope adds, it is necessary to bear in mind "that nothing was conferred on the apostles apart from Peter, but that several things were conferred upon Peter apart from the apostles," so that "whatever authority and office the apostles received, they received in conjunction with Peter." Quoting his predecessor and namesake Saint Leo the Great, Pope Leo XIII even seems to contradict Francisco de Vitoria's thesis: "If the divine benignity willed anything to be in common between him [Peter] and the other princes, whatever He did not deny to the others *He gave only through him*. So that whereas Peter alone received many things, *He conferred nothing on any of the rest without Peter participating in it* (S. Leo, Sermon 4, ch. 2)."

Let us remember that the debate is not whether the apostles received power directly from Our Lord or through Saint Peter. In any case, even Vitoria, who supports the former, explicitly states that this would have been the Twelve's exclusive and non-transferable privilege. However, if Saint Leo the Great and Leo XIII maintain that even the apostles received power through the mediation of Peter, *a fortiori* they would be inclined to maintain that bishops receive jurisdiction indirectly from God but directly from the pontifical mandate, although they do not specifically address the issue.

Despite this, and without any textual support but based solely on his misrepresentation of Palmieri's position, Dr. Lamont draws the opposite conclusion. At first, he limits himself to saying that Leo XIII's description of the jurisdiction of the pope and the bishops on the face of it "expresses the moderate view." This is true if, by "moderate view," one means what the whole world agrees on, namely that the pope does not have "the whole of ecclesiastical power." But it is incorrect to ascribe to Leo XIII the opinion that bishops receive jurisdiction directly from Christ, as Dr. Lamont does later on, stating: "The assertion that episcopal consecration confers the office of teaching and governing is a recognized position in Catholic theology. . . . It is supported by the teaching of Leo XIII." The quoted papal text does not support this statement. Even the last sentence of the encyclical quoted by Dr. Lamont would incline one to deduce the opposite, for, speaking of bishops who deliberately secede from Peter and his successors, Leo XIII says: "they are exiled from the *Kingdom, the keys of which were given by Christ to Peter alone*." As is well known, all theologians teach that the keys represent the power of jurisdiction.

Unresolved Tensions in Papal-Episcopal Relations

In addition to misinterpreting the encyclical *Satis Cognitum*, Dr. Lamont attempts to diminish the magisterial value of Pius XII's encyclical *Mystici Corporis*, which states unequivocally that although the bishops' jurisdiction is inherent in their office, "they receive [it] directly from the same supreme pontiff," a statement he repeated in the encyclicals *Ad Sinarum Gentem* and *Ad Apostolorum Principis*, nine and fifteen years later respectively. Cardinal Alfredo Ottaviani went so far as to say that these statements by Pius XII meant that the traditional majority opinion that bishops receive jurisdiction from God not directly but indirectly "should now . . . be rated as absolutely certain." Dr. Lamont is right to question this statement by the last great holder of the Holy Office, explaining that "in order to end a dispute of this kind by a magisterial intervention, such an intervention must clearly describe the question, express the intention of settling it, specify the position being taught, and make it clear that the teaching is binding on all Catholics."

Even assuming that this is not the case, however, we would be in the situation described by Pius XII in *Humani Generis*:

> Nor must it be thought that what is expounded in encyclical letters does not of itself demand consent, since in writing such letters the popes do not exercise the supreme power of their teaching authority. For these matters are taught with the ordinary teaching authority, of which it is true to say: "He who heareth you, heareth me" (Luke 10:16); and generally what is expounded and inculcated in encyclical letters already for other reasons appertains to Catholic doctrine. But if the supreme pontiffs in their official documents purposely pass judgment on a matter up to that time under dispute, it is obvious that that matter, according to the mind and will of the pontiffs, cannot be any longer considered a question open to discussion among theologians.[109]

However, from Cardinal Ottaviani's supposedly exaggerated remark—*dato non concesso*—Dr. Lamont draws a conclusion that could be misleading. He states that "the passages from the encyclicals of Pius XII that are cited above cannot be seen as a proper and responsible exercise of the papal teaching office." This could be understood by people less versed in theology to mean that the ordinary papal magisterium does not constitute a proper and responsible exercise of the papal teaching office, which would consist of the promulgation of dogmas of faith. I do not believe Dr. Lamont thinks that, but it is one of the possible meanings of his phrase. Unfortunately, a reader could be led to interpret it that way because he implies right afterwards that this would not even have been Pius XII's opinion as a private doctor: "One may speculate that these

---

[109] Pius XII, Encyclical *Humani Generis*, no. 20.

passages were included in the texts of these encyclicals by drafters at the Holy Office (of which Cardinal Ottaviani was the head at the time) in order to further the cause of a theological opinion that they accepted." Regrettably, in attributing this passage from *Mystici Corporis* to Cardinal Ottaviani or his staff, Dr. Lamont failed to check dates and made a historical error. The encyclical was published in 1943, but Cardinal Ottaviani was appointed secretary of the Congregation of the Holy Office—of which the pope was the prefect—only in 1959, sixteen years later. It is hard to imagine that Ottaviani would have had enough influence in 1943 to insert a theological opinion different from Pope Pacelli's in one of his most important encyclicals.

Overvaluation of Vatican II's magisterial authority

In defending his position, Dr. Lamont not only downplays the magisterial value of *Mystici Corporis*, but magnifies the magisterial value of Vatican II's dogmatic constitution *Lumen Gentium* by taking advantage of the adjective "dogmatic" in its title to deduce that its teachings are definitive:

> The documents of the Second Vatican Council are of different kinds, and many of these kinds of document—decrees, declarations, etc.—do not have a great degree of authority. The case of a dogmatic constitution is different. Such constitutions are a recognized form of conciliar teaching; the documents *Dei Filius* and *Pastor Aeternus* of the First Vatican Council are dogmatic constitutions. *They express by their titles the intention of teaching Catholic dogma in an authoritative fashion.* A dogmatic constitution has a much higher degree of authority than the encyclicals of Pius XII cited above, which are the only magisterial statements that support Mr. Ureta's position.

This parallel between Vatican I and Vatican II constitutions is absolutely improper because it is based on an entirely secondary aspect, such as a title. A document's title is not enough to express "the intention of teaching Catholic dogma in an authoritative fashion," as Dr. Lamont correctly stated when denying the binding character of the passages quoted from Pius XII's encyclicals. As already mentioned, to be definitive, "such an intervention must clearly describe the question, express the intention of settling it, specify the position being taught, and make it clear that the teaching is binding on all Catholics." None of the Vatican II documents—including *Lumen Gentium*—expresses the intention of definitively settling a theological question, making it binding on all Catholics.

While no one doubts that the latest Council enjoyed supreme magisterial authority, everyone recognizes—except for supporters of the hermeneutic of rupture—that the

Unresolved Tensions in Papal-Episcopal Relations

Council Fathers renounced exercising their infallible authority in order to give it the pastoral character that John XXIII suggested in his inaugural speech. This is particularly true of *Lumen Gentium*, to which Paul VI ordered the addition of an appendix, namely, the following statement issued at the 123rd General Congregation:

> A question has arisen regarding the precise theological note which should be attached to the doctrine that is set forth in the Schema de Ecclesia and is being put to a vote.
>
> The Theological Commission has given the following response regarding the Modi that have to do with Chapter III of the de Ecclesia Schema: "As is self-evident, the Council's text must always be interpreted in accordance with the general rules that are known to all."
>
> On this occasion the Theological Commission makes reference to its Declaration of March 6, 1964, the text of which we transcribe here:
>
> "Taking conciliar custom into consideration and also the pastoral purpose of the present Council, the sacred Council defines as binding on the Church only those things in matters of faith and morals which it shall openly declare to be binding. The rest of the things which the sacred Council sets forth, inasmuch as they are the teaching of the Church's supreme magisterium, ought to be accepted and embraced by each and every one of Christ's faithful according to the mind of the sacred Council. The mind of the Council becomes known either from the matter treated or from its manner of speaking, in accordance with the norms of theological interpretation."[110]

The manner of speaking of the First Vatican Council's constitutions *Dei Filius* and *Pastor Aeternus* clearly expresses the will to define and concludes with anathemas for those who deny its teachings. For example, the chapter on the primacy of the pope begins by saying "We *teach and declare* that . . . ." It continues by saying "*We promulgate anew the definition of the ecumenical Council of Florence*, which *must be believed* by all faithful Christians." And it concludes by saying, "Therefore, we condemn and reject the opinions of those who hold that . . . ." And, further, "So then, should anyone, which God forbid, have the temerity to reject this definition of ours; let him be *anathema*."[111] Absolutely none of this can be found in *Lumen Gentium*'s manner of speaking or in any other document of Vatican II. Furthermore, at the close of Vatican II, Paul VI explicitly

---

[110] *Lumen Gentium*, Appendix.

[111] *Pastor Aeternus*, ch. 1, no. 1; ch. 3, no. 1; ch. 4, no 1, end.

declared that in the Council, "the teaching authority of the Church ... [did] not [wish] to issue extraordinary dogmatic pronouncements."[112]

Why, then, was *Lumen Gentium* titled "dogmatic" constitution? A malicious observer would say it was to mislead the unwary. We prefer to follow the assessment of Arnaldo Xavier da Silveira in addressing this objection: "The adjective 'dogmatic' only means that the subject matter is related to dogma. Just as everything that can be read in a manual of Dogmatic Theology is not dogma."[113]

For all of the above reasons, Dr. Lamont errs when he affirms: "The statements of *Lumen Gentium* on episcopal jurisdiction are therefore authoritative and final, and must, as far as they go, be accepted." On the contrary, it is precisely their character as an ordinary, non-dogmatic magisterium that allows scholars to question with great freedom the theological novelties of these documents, which, in their natural sense, seem to break with the traditional teaching of the Church. They include, among others, religious freedom, the salvific character of heretical or schismatic sects, and "collegiality," which breaks with the dogma of papal primacy by affirming the existence of two permanent supreme powers in the Church and which departs from the teaching of Pius XII and the past's majority current of theologians by affirming that the power of jurisdiction is received directly from God at the episcopal consecration.

It is surprising that a traditionalist author like Dr. Lamont states, in defense of this *Lumen Gentium* novelty: "It cannot be claimed to be a view that was introduced into the document by modernists wishing to advance their cause." He seems unaware that chapter 3 of *Lumen Gentium* provoked the greatest reaction from the Coetus Internationalis Patris and even prompted a letter to Paul VI signed by twenty-five cardinals and thirteen superiors of religious orders. In it, they denounced precisely the pressure from the progressive wing to have the novelty of "collegiality" and the sacramentality of the power of jurisdiction accepted. The letter, sent by Cardinal Arcadio Larraona on behalf of the others who concurred with it, states:

> The *new* doctrine has become neither more certain, nor objectively more probable than before as a result of the disturbing campaign of pressure groups who have deplorably politicized the council and disconcerted some episcopates.... Nor has it become more certain as a result of the actions of many audacious experts who, unfaithful to their true ministry, made biased propaganda instead of objectively

---

[112] Paul VI, Closing Speech at Second Vatican Council, December 7, 1965.
[113] Arnaldo Vidigal Xavier da Silveira, *Can Documents of the Magisterium of the Church Contain Errors?* (Spring Grove, PA: The American Society for the Defense of Tradition, Family, and Property, 2015), 28.

Unresolved Tensions in Papal-Episcopal Relations

enlightening the bishops by acquainting them with the *status quaestionis*. And, finally, it has not become probable through wide coverage of the press, which, with its characteristic methods—methods utilized by the progressives—has created an atmosphere which makes calm discussion difficult, fettering and hampering true liberty by making those who do not show approval appear ridiculous and unpopular. In such an atmosphere scientific reasoning can no longer exert its legitimate influence in any practical way and does not even get a hearing.[114]

Indeed, it can be claimed that the less probable view on the origin of episcopal jurisdiction was introduced into *Lumen Gentium* by modernists wishing to advance their cause.

An insufficient explanation for an insurmountable historical-canonical objection

Cardinal Enrico Dante, the famous prefect of Pontifical Ceremonies under Pius XII and John XXIII, was one of the signatories of that letter by twenty-five cardinals. During the debates of the Council's Third Session, discussing collegiality, he wrote Pope Paul VI a long letter raising one of the greatest historical-canonical obstacles to the thesis of the immediately divine origin of the power of episcopal jurisdiction.

The difficulty: for many centuries, the Church considered to be fully valid acts of jurisdiction taken before episcopal consecration by clerics appointed diocesan bishops and by popes who were simple deacons when elected. This was based on the consensus that the new pope had already been granted by Christ the power of jurisdiction at the acceptance of his election and the new bishop at his acceptance of the power of jurisdiction granted by the papal appointment. The 1917 Code of Canon Law even established a three-month period for a new bishop to be consecrated. If jurisdiction were received at the consecration, all previous acts of bishops would have been null and void, and, *a fortiori*, so would the bulls promulgated by popes before their episcopal consecration and enthronement.

In his letter to Paul VI, Cardinal Dante complained about the shallow answer the conciliar commission studying this matter gave his objection: "*Textus, ordinis generalis, ad casum tam particularem attendere non potest*" [the proposed text, of a general order, cannot attend to such a particular case]. And he insisted:

> A long catalog can be made both of popes who were elected without being bishops, and of the acts of government implemented in the period between

[114] Roberto de Mattei, *The Second Vatican Council: An Unwritten Story*, ed. Michael J. Miller, trans. Patrick T. Brannan, Michael J. Miller, and Kenneth D. Whitehead (Fitzwilliam, NH: Loreto Publications, 2010), 350.

the election and the consecration: . . . Was the Church wrong in believing that those men were supreme pontiffs already prior to their consecration and that their decisions were valid? . . . (The Commission) believes that it is enough to appeal to the fact that they had the will *"accipiendi consecrationem seu votum consecrationis"* [to accept the consecration or a desire for consecration]. Does this mean that the desire to receive a sacrament, which confers power, is sufficient to have such power? The answer given by the Commission is as absurd as saying that a seminarian who has the desire and will to be ordained a priest can already validly celebrate the Holy Mass by virtue of his *"votum ordinationis"* [desire to be ordained]. . . . (They say) that it will be up to theologians to try to explain how historical facts can be reconciled with the doctrine of the Schema. But the problem lies precisely here: Can these facts be reconciled with this doctrine?[115]

In a 2013 article for *Civiltà Cattolica*, Gianfranco Ghirlanda—then professor emeritus of Canon Law at the Pontifical Gregorian University, and created a Cardinal in the latest consistory—said that this traditional doctrine is clearly expressed in canons 109 and 219 of the 1917 Code of Canon Law, confirmed by Pius XII with the apostolic constitution *Vacantis Apostolicae Sedis* (1945), with the motu proprio *Cleri Sanctitati* (1957), and with his speech at the Second International Congress for the Apostolate of the Laity (1957). The cardinal added: "On this issue, there have been magisterial and authoritative interventions by at least six Roman pontiffs between the eleventh and twentieth centuries, which indicate the acceptance of the election to the supreme pontificate as the moment of reception by the elected of the supreme and full power over the universal Church, even if, in view of the subsequent episcopal consecration, the chosen one was not yet bishop."[116]

Vatican II innovators were so cognizant of this obstacle that, when drafting the new Code of Canon Law, they explicitly stipulated that the new bishop has the right to govern his diocese only after episcopal consecration unless it is a case of a transfer of see. In the case of the papal election of a non-bishop, the post-conciliar decrees stipulate that he be consecrated immediately after accepting the election and before receiving the act of submission from the cardinals and appearing on the balcony of St. Peter's

---

[115] Albert Kallio, "Collegialità nel Vaticano II: una nuova dottrina?" *Chiesa e post concilio*, June 23, 2018, https://chiesaepostconcilio.blogspot.com/2018/06/collegialita-nel-vaticano-ii-una-nuova.html.

[116] Gianfranco Ghirlanda, "Cessazione dall'ufficio di Romano Pontefice," *Civiltà Cattolica*, Quaderno 3905, 2013, vol. 1, pp. 445–62, n15, www.laciviltacattolica.it/articolo/cessazione-dallufficio-di-romano-pontefice/.

Unresolved Tensions in Papal-Episcopal Relations

Basilica—quite differently from Saint Gregory the Great, who ruled for almost a year as a deacon, and Stephen II and Adrian V, who died without consecration!

Fr. Umberto Betti, a conciliar expert and later rector of the Lateran University and cardinal, offered this hesitant explanation for the historical and canonical precedent contrary to the new doctrine: "It is not possible to give an answer that is absolutely satisfying. On the doctrinal level, the solution would consist, perhaps, in saying that God supplies [the power] Himself, by an anticipated effect of the episcopal consecration to which they are ordered by an intrinsic necessity from the moment of their election."[117]

Dr. Lamont has no such hesitations and confidently suggests an alternative: "This jurisdiction can be explained as papal jurisdiction supplied to its possessor, which is replaced by properly episcopal jurisdiction when its possessor is consecrated." But in this hypothesis, the transitory jurisdiction would not be properly *episcopal*. It would not be *ordinary* but pontifically delegated, like that of any apostolic delegate or apostolic administrator.. We would then have to conclude that many of the successive prelates who have governed some of the most important dioceses in Europe should be removed from the annals because they would not have been real bishops. For example, many bishops in the dioceses of the Holy Roman Empire's Prince-Bishoprics remained simple tonsured clerics until the end of their lives and obtained from the Holy See the appointment of a "chor bishop" (a kind of auxiliary bishop) to carry out on their behalf all activities required by the episcopal *munus sanctificandi* they did not possess.

In any case, this explanation, for which Dr. Lamont presented no support in theology or in Church practice, is insufficient to resolve the penetrating objection Cardinal Dante formulated to Paul VI during the discussion of the schema on collegiality.

In the next part of this chapter, I will address important underlying issues, such as the philosophical and theological arguments presented by Dr. Lamont in favor of the sacramentality of the power of jurisdiction's origin.

II

In the first part of this article, I showed external errors in Dr. John Lamont's argument against my essay on Bishop Joseph Strickland's removal. The fundamental error of Dr. Lamont's study was apparent: attributing to the traditional position—according to which the bishops receive the power of jurisdiction directly from the pope and indirectly from God—the assumption that the Vicar of Christ possesses not only the

---

[117] Kallio, "Collegialità," n30.

fullness of power but *all* power that exists within the Church, such that the bishops are merely his delegates. This is simply not true. Dr. Lamont himself quotes a passage from Palmieri that proves the inconsistency of this interpretation:

> It is false that according to our position the bishops are the vicars of the pope. For bishops do not exist in the Church in right of papal authority, but in right of the authority of Christ, and the pope cannot abolish the episcopal dignity and authority; furthermore, the power and tribunal of the pope and of bishops are two different things, because Christ willed that besides the chair of Peter there should also be an episcopal chair. Nor are the bishops delegates of the pope, because they possess an ordinary jurisdiction through the power of the office that Christ has instituted. The bishops rule their flock as their own, for by Christ's institution they must be pastors of a portion of the sheep, over which they exercise the power of binding and loosing. And although the Roman pontiff may remove jurisdiction from any and all, he is nonetheless bound to ensure that other bishops exist, in order that there may always be bishops in the Church; for he may not abolish episcopal authority itself.[118]

According to Dr. Lamont, Palmieri "evades the issue," which is that "individual bishops in their dioceses rule by divine right derived from their order and their office." But his comment is incorrect because Palmieri explicitly states that the bishops "possess an ordinary jurisdiction through the power of the office that Christ has instituted."

The same can be said of Dr. Lamont's criticism of St. Thomas Aquinas. He claims there is a supposed contradiction in the Angelic Doctor's teaching. This is what I will address next, analyzing Dr. Lamont's study no longer from an external point of view but going to the core of his argument.

Misinterpretation of St. Thomas Aquinas's doctrine on causality

Dr. Lamont recognizes that "St. Thomas is the earlier and greater of the advocates of the strong view." This statement is true if by "strong view" is meant that bishops receive the power of jurisdiction directly from the pope but govern with and under him a portion of the flock by an ordinary power of their own. But this affirmation is false if, by "strong view," one understands that every power in the Church is either the pope's power or is derived from his own power in such a way that the pope's power either formally or

---

[118] Palmieri, *Tractatus de romano pontifice*, art. 1, thesis XIV, 457, quoted by Lamont.

Unresolved Tensions in Papal-Episcopal Relations

virtually contains every other power by which the Church is ruled. Dr. Lamont erroneously attributes this second position to St. Thomas based on a misinterpretation of his metaphysics, which he identifies with Neoplatonism. He affirms:

> St. Thomas Aquinas holds the strong view that all power of jurisdiction whatsoever in the Church derives from papal power:
>
> "I answer that a superior power and an inferior power can relate to each other in two different ways. In one way, the inferior power originates entirely from the superior power; and in this case, the entire power of the inferior is founded on the power of the superior; and then the power of the superior is to be obeyed *simpliciter* rather than the inferior, and is so to be obeyed in all things, just as in natural causes, the first cause acts more on an effect produced by a secondary cause than the secondary cause itself does, as is stated in the *Liber de causis*. This is the way in which the power of God is related to all created powers; it is the way in which the power of the Emperor is related to the power of the proconsul; and it is the way in which the power of the pope is related to all other spiritual powers in the Church, since every dignity in the Church is distributed and ordered by the pope, whose power is in a certain manner the foundation of the Church, as is shown by Matthew ch. 16. And therefore we are bound in all things without distinction to obey the pope more than bishops or archbishops, or [more than] a monk is to obey an abbot. In another way, the power of a superior and an inferior are related by both of them having originated from a higher power, which subordinates the one to the other as it chooses; and in this way the one is only superior to the other in so far as it has been subordinated to the other by a higher power, and the superior is to be obeyed rather than the inferior only in so far as it has been given authority by the higher power. The powers of bishops and archbishops, which are established by the pope, are related in this way" (*In II Sent.*, d. 44 q. 2 a. 3 expos.).
>
> St. Thomas argues from Matthew 16, but he supplements this scriptural argument with an appeal to the Neoplatonic metaphysical conception of causation, where the actions of a lower agent are also the actions of the higher agents that cause the lower one. In consequence, his position is somewhat different from that of later theologians, because this Neoplatonic conception asserts that all higher agents act immediately in the lower agents whose existence and action they bring about (*Summa contra gentiles*, bk. 3, ch. 67). It cannot therefore entirely correspond to the later claim that the power of jurisdiction is received

immediately from the pope and mediately from God. We should note as well that he makes no mention of the power of the pope to remove bishops at will.

Further on, Dr. Lamont reiterates:

> St. Thomas does more than appeal to this tendentious exegeses [of Matt. 16]; he also argues from his Neoplatonic conception of causation. This conception applies to the metaphysical category of efficient causation in the created world. Those who accept it are bound to agree that it describes every instance of such causation. . . .
>
> St. Thomas's claim that the power of bishops is related to the power of the pope in the same way as the power of proconsuls is related to the power of the Emperor effectively reduces the bishops to vicars of the pope.

These passages from Dr. Lamont's study deserve various observations.

1. It is historically and intellectually unfounded to describe the Thomistic concept of causality as an expression of Neoplatonism

Until the beginning of the twentieth century, historians of medieval thought assured us that Aquinas was essentially Aristotelian. This assessment gradually changed. One of the first directors of the *Revue thomiste*, H.-A. Montagne, indicated in a programmatic statement that to delve deeper into Thomistic doctrine, it was necessary to "determine what he owes to the Stagirite, what he also owes to Plato and the other great thinkers of antiquity."[119] Two years later, he published a study by Charles Huit on this topic in that journal.[120] The movement gained greater momentum on the eve of the Second World War, notably after the publication of the study *The Metaphysical Notion of Participation* by Fr. Cornelio Fabro (1939). But to conclude that Aristotelianism in St. Thomas is an ancillary element of his Platonism, or that his concept of causality is purely Neoplatonic, is to mischaracterize his truly original thinking.

The *Dictionnaire de philosophie et de théologie thomistes*, by Dominicans Philippe-Marie Margelidon, director of the *Revue thomiste*, and Yves Floucat, member of the Pontifical Academy of St. Thomas Aquinas, contains two entries about the matter. Seen together, they provide a well-balanced view of their respective contributions. Let us see their most relevant passages:

---

[119] H.-A. Montagne, "Notre programme," *Revue thomiste*, vol. 17 (1909): 5–37, at 15.
[120] Charles Huit, "Les éléments platoniques de la doctrine de Saint Thomas," *Revue thomiste*, vol. 19 (1911): 724–66.

Unresolved Tensions in Papal-Episcopal Relations

St. Thomas's Aristotelianism

It is fair to say that the metaphysics of St. Thomas and the primary philosophy of Aristotle are in a relationship of continuity, kinship, filiation, and essential fidelity of spirit from the former to the latter. The Stagirite and Aquinas are committed to the primacy of individual substance as *ens per se* and principle of activity. The analogy of attribution finds its first authentic expression in Aristotle. . . . On the other hand, it was St. Thomas who brought to light how, beyond substantiality, the *ens per se* is called *habens esse*; it was he who brought out the formal aspect of the *actus essendi*. If the idea of creation is absent in Aristotle, as are the concepts of Providence and [divine] efficient cause, it is nonetheless true that the five ways [to prove the existence of God] find in him a framework, sometimes even their formulation (God conceived as the First Unmoved Mover). . . .

St. Thomas's relationship with Aristotle is certainly more than material, but despite their undeniable similarities, the consciously assumed heritage, and the profound intellectual debt between the former and the latter, we are dealing with something quite different. The metaphysics of St. Thomas is not Aristotelian: substance is created; it implies a metaphysics of participation and causality that crosses Platonism and biblical creationism in a superior, original synthesis.[121]

St. Thomas's Neoplatonism

Historians of medieval thought stopped long ago saying that St. Thomas was essentially a medieval Aristotelian, i.e., a sort of mixed bag (heteroclite, at worst) between Aristotle (via Averroes and Avicenna) and Augustinian philosophy inspired by (a Christianized) Neoplatonism. However, it is undeniable that if Saint Thomas has constructed an original synthesis that is not a heap of juxtaposed pieces, we can, without accusing him of plagiarism, recognize what he owes to Neoplatonism, or rather to Neoplatonic metaphysics fully assumed and integrated into the architecture of his thought. . . .

The Aristotelian site of his metaphysics is greatly enriched by the Neoplatonic contribution, even to the typically Aristotelian question of substance. Aristotle's interpretation is colored by Neoplatonic influence in various parts; God as motivating cause has become efficient cause thanks to Avicenna, who reads Aristotle in a Platonic climate. The interpretation of *De causis* was decisive for his own

---

[121] Philippe-Marie Margelidon, O.P. and Yves Floucat, O.P., *Dictionnaire de philosophie et de théologie thomistes*, 3rd ed. rev. (Paris: Parole et Silence, 2023), 56–57.

metaphysics of causes according to the principle: "Every primary cause infuses its effect more powerfully than does a universal second cause" (*Book of Causes*, prop. 1) because it is the source of its causality not only as regards its existence but also concerning its exercise and effect.... Moreover, Saint Thomas retains this capital but reinterpreted idea: "The first of created things is being (*esse*)" (*Book of Causes*, prop. 4).... The real composition of finite being (*ens*) and being (*esse*) is not found in Aristotle, but the thesis of being (*esse*) as the principle of finite being is found among medievals under Neoplatonic influence. *Esse* as *actus essendi* ["act of being"] is specific to St. Thomas, beyond all Aristotelianism and Platonism. St. Thomas's Aristotelianism is permeated by Neoplatonism; for example, the notion of participation, which is central to his account of the relationship of existing being to the universal first cause as its efficient and exemplary cause. It would be wrong, however, to speak too much of Thomism as a Neoplatonic Aristotelianism. Here again, St. Thomas is not an amalgam or a simple juxtaposition or interweaving of heterogeneous philosophies. He soars higher than eclecticism. The theology, and the metaphysics it implies, are *sui generis* and should be considered in their own right.[122]

The quotation is long, but necessary in order to understand in what sense the concept of causality in St. Thomas—and, therefore, its practical application to the kind of relationship that exists between the power of the pope and other spiritual powers in the Church—does not correspond to its interpretation in Dr. Lamont's study. If the Thomistic concept of causality were truly Neoplatonic, Dr. Lamont would be right because it would follow that second causes do not have an actual existence and, therefore, the bishops' power of jurisdiction, derived from that of the pope, has no substance of its own as an ordinary power possessed in virtue of the office. But this is not true, as we will see.

2. The Thomistic concept of causality differs radically from the Neoplatonic one

As is known, for Neoplatonic philosophers, notably Plotinus and Proclus, the One is the supreme principle, the cause of the existence of all things in the universe, which emanate from it not through a creation *ex nihilo* (as we profess in the Creed), but by the superabundance of its own being which, without undergoing any change, deploys itself in a descending and diversified hierarchy of secondary manifestations with no substance of their own, like rays emanating from the sun. According to Plotinus, "The

---

[122] Margelidon and Floucat, *Dictionnaire*, 373–74.

Unresolved Tensions in Papal-Episcopal Relations

One is all things and no one of them; the source of all things is not all things; all things are its possession—running back, so to speak, to it—or, more correctly, not yet so, they will be."[123] In other words, "the *isness* of the One is nothing but its appearance in all things";[124] for his part, each being is a mere manifestation or *image* of the One. But an image is not another being added to what is represented.

For Saint Thomas, on the contrary, beings created in their *esse simpliciter* (i.e., limited by an essence; in man, for example, it is *esse homo*) by the Creator, are autonomous and subsistent creatures. He states: "to be made and to be created properly belong to whatever being belongs; which, indeed, belongs properly to subsisting things."[125] André de Muralt, a Swiss specialist on ancient and medieval philosophy, describes the consequence of this real subsistence of creatures: "They participate as such in their cause, and particularly in their divine cause. They do not have their participative similitude to the divine as their quidditative being; their subsistence is not owed to being a modified One, nor to being 'God without anything'; they are *substances subsisting by themselves through creation*. That is why the Second Person of the Holy Trinity can unite with one of them in a true Incarnation, which does not merely give Him the appearance of human reality."[126]

The ontological difference between the pseudo-being—a mere image for Neoplatonists—and St. Thomas's subsistent substantial being bears on the concepts of causality and participation. When Neoplatonists affirm that all things engender just as the One engenders, this means for them that the lower efficient causes are merely successive and univocally similar emanations of the One. For St. Thomas, on the other hand, each second efficient cause is different since it operates through its own autonomous activity and causality, albeit participating in divine causality according to a non-univocal similarity. Thus, he rejects the idea that a creature, in its own action, exercises only a simple instrumental causality while depending entirely on the principal cause.

> If he sometimes uses the word *instrument*, it is only to mark the creature's radical dependence on the Creator, not to deny it its own autonomy in being and acting, that autonomy which participation in creation implies, establishes, causes, and manifests. . . . [The notion of participation according to Aquinas]

---

[123] Plotinus, *The Six Enneads*, trans. Stephen MacKenna and B.S. Page (Grand Rapids, MI: Christian Classics Ethereal Library), V.2.1, 360.
[124] Joshua Packwood, "Everything Is Flat: The Transcendence of the One in Neoplatonic Ontology," Doctoral Thesis, University of Arkansas, 2013, p. 143.
[125] *Summa theologiae* I, Q. 45, art. 4.
[126] André de Muralt, *Néoplatonisme et aristotélisme dans la métaphysique médiévale: Analogie, causalité, participation* (Paris: J. Vrin, 1995), 108.

makes it possible to understand that the second cause is totally dependent on divine causality insofar as it is created, and that . . . the creature participates in divine causality by exercising its various operations autonomously according to the "dignity" of its own being and causality.[127]

Therefore, that notion assumes and reconciles "the fact of every created substance's self-subsistence and the necessity of its total dependence on its Creator. Conversely, Neoplatonism emphasizes the necessity of dependence so radically that it sees the creature's participation or image-being as its very quiddity, at the risk of denying its character as an autonomous created subsistence."[128]

3. The true meaning of St. Thomas's paragraph, quoted and misinterpreted by Lamont

St. Thomas's phrase should be understood in this sense of reconciling the second cause's autonomous created subsistence with its total dependence on God: "The first cause acts more on an effect produced by a secondary cause than the secondary cause itself does, as is stated in the *Liber de causis*" (quoted by Dr. Lamont). This phrase does not mean that secondary causes lose their character of autonomous, created subsistence—one that is, moreover, free, in the case of spiritual substances endowed with an intellect and will. The obvious proof of that interpretation is that the foregoing quotation is taken from St. Thomas's commentary on the forty-fourth and last distinction of Book II of the *Sentences*, where Peter Lombard first discusses the question of whether the power to sin (*potentia peccandi*) in man comes from God or from ourselves and the devil. He answers that it comes from God. If the Angelic Doctor's phrase were to be understood in a strictly Neoplatonic sense, in which the second cause is a mere instrument without autonomy, one would have to conclude that God Himself sins through his creature, which would be blasphemy.

By interpreting this phrase from St. Thomas in a strictly Neoplatonic sense, Dr. Lamont concludes that "although God exercises efficient causation in causing the power of jurisdiction to exist in the Church, that does not mean that the power of jurisdiction that He causes is itself an instance of efficient causation." In other words, according to Dr. Lamont, the plenitude of the power of jurisdiction the pope receives from God is not a sufficient cause to transmit part of his power to his subordinates, contrary to what St. Thomas teaches in the text quoted in his study: "It is the way in which the power of the pope is related to all other spiritual powers in the Church, since every dignity in

---

[127] de Muralt, *Néoplatonisme*, 145–46.
[128] de Muralt, 146.

Unresolved Tensions in Papal-Episcopal Relations

the Church is distributed and ordered by the pope, whose power is in a certain manner the foundation of the Church."

A few pages before that, Dr. Lamont had stated that

> his [St. Thomas's] position is somewhat different from that of later theologians, because this Neoplatonic conception asserts that all higher agents act immediately in the lower agents whose existence and action they bring about (cf. *Summa contra gentiles*, bk. 3, ch. 67). It cannot therefore entirely correspond to the later claim that the power of jurisdiction is received immediately from the pope and mediately from God.

Indeed, in a Neoplatonic interpretation of the text, the pope's action as a second agent would be ineffective and, imperatively, a bishop would receive his jurisdiction directly from God. However, as we have seen, according to Thomistic doctrine, the pope operates with his own autonomous causality while participating in divine causality, and, therefore, he can indeed be the immediate source of the power of jurisdiction of the bishop to whom he entrusts part of the Lord's flock. For his part, the bishop designated by the pope, while participating in the fullness of papal power, also operates with his own and autonomous action—his ordinary power—and is not reduced to the condition of a mere vicar of the pope, as Dr. Lamont erroneously deduces.

Misinterpretation of the supernatural character of jurisdiction

Also due to a misunderstanding of St. Thomas Aquinas's true thought on causality, Dr. Lamont states in his study:

> *Amicus Thomas, sed magis amica veritas.* St. Thomas's position on papal authority is not compatible with his own theory of grace and the sacraments.
>
> Ecclesiastical jurisdiction confers divine authority, not natural authority. It cannot arise from any natural basis of authority. If it is a proper and ordinary jurisdiction, it is a supernatural *gratia gratis data* that cannot originate in any created cause. Hence, it can only be conferred by God alone (cf. I-II, Q. 112, art. 1). It can be produced by the action of a created cause only when the created cause is an instrumental cause used by God as the principal cause and agent (I-II, Q. 112, art. 1, ad 2). The assertion of later theologians that episcopal jurisdiction is derived immediately from the pope and only mediately from God is thus incompatible with the fact that episcopal jurisdiction is a supernatural rather than a natural power. If the conferring of episcopal jurisdiction is only mediately from God, then it cannot be caused by God as the principal agent.

It Is Churchmen Who Need Reform, Not the Church

Again, this passage contains inaccuracies that call for clarification.

1. Difference between the power of order and the power of jurisdiction in terms of their nature and mode of transmission

As I explained in my article on the legal validity of an unjust deposition of a bishop by the pope, the Second Vatican Council's constitution *Lumen Gentium* omitted any reference to the traditional distinction between the powers of order and jurisdiction. In its place, it adopted the three *munera* theory to designate what one receives with episcopal consecration. These functions or offices (lat. *munus, -eris*; plural *munera*) are the sanctifying (*munus sanctificandi*), teaching (*munus docendi*), and governing (*munus regendi*) of the faithful.

The *munera* theory was fabricated by John Calvin, starting in 1545, and was adopted by Lutherans in the middle of the eighteenth century. Some German-speaking Catholic theologians, obviously influenced by Protestant theology, started using it in the early twentieth century. In the second half of the nineteenth century, two lay German canonists, Ferdinand Walter and George Phillips, presented the triple *munera* for the first time, and also defended it against the traditional division of two powers: order and jurisdiction.[129]

As I wrote in earlier articles, the Council Fathers resorted to the triple *munera* argument and those powers' simultaneous transmission to bishops during their episcopal consecration to give a theological foundation to the novel notion of collegiality. It is through consecration that a bishop becomes part of the episcopal college, which is supposed to be a permanent holder, *cum Petro* and *sub Petro*, of the fullness of supreme power. Based on this conception of three inseparable *munera* received simultaneously, neo-modernist theologians logically attribute sacramental character not only to the *munus sanctificandi* but also to the *munera docendi et regendi*. However, it is problematic and illogical to attribute such a character to these two offices when one admits the traditional distinction between the power of order and that of jurisdiction and recognizes that governing and teaching are integral elements of the latter. But that is precisely what Dr. Lamont has done in his study, as one can see in the passage quoted above, where he states that the power of jurisdiction is a *gratia gratis data* that God alone can confer.

To demonstrate that this view is erroneous, it suffices to quote a few excerpts from Cardinal Journet's renowned treatise, *The Church of the Word Incarnate*. After stating that both powers differ in their purpose—the power of order, which bestows grace and

---

[129] See Josef Fuchs, S.J., "Origines d'une trilogie ecclésiologique à l'époque rationaliste de la théologie," in *Revue de sciences philosophiques et théologiques*, no. 53 (1969): 185–211, at 197, 199, 210.

Unresolved Tensions in Papal-Episcopal Relations

atones for sin, opens heaven directly, while the power of jurisdiction points the way to heaven, enabling the pope and the hierarchy to determine and preach the object of Faith, to regulate the legitimate use of the power of order, and to control all things in the Church Militant—Cardinal Journet shows their respective characters:

> 1. The two powers differ in nature. The power of order is a participation of the *priesthood* of Christ. The sacramental characters, says St. Thomas, "are nothing else than certain participations of Christ's priesthood, flowing from Christ Himself." The power of jurisdiction is a participation of Christ's *kingship*: Christ being Head of the Church in a sovereign manner and in virtue of His own proper authority, the others being heads in a dependent manner and as delegated by Christ.
>
> The end of Christ's priesthood is to pour into souls the very virtue of the Redemption. The created intermediaries are unable to produce so divine an effect save as simple instruments. The sacramental power is therefore a *purely instrumental* ministerial power. Hence it is infallible, not of course on account of its own proper virtue, but because it transmits the virtue of a Principal Agent. But the end of Christ's kingship is the outward proclamation of the full divine revelation, so that the created intermediaries can here play a freer part. The power of jurisdiction is still ministerial; but it can be said to act more in the manner of a *secondary cause*; and it will not be infallible save in so far as it is divinely aided.
>
> The power of order, which exists to bring the redemptive virtue to souls, is a *physical* spiritual participation of the spiritual power of Christ the Priest. . . . Like every sacramental character, the power of order is a physical spiritual power and hence indelible. It can persist, and can even be transmitted, in schism and heresy. The power of jurisdiction, which exists for the external preaching of Christian truth, speculative and practical, is a *moral* authority, mission, and power. . . . It is lost as soon as the subject leaves the Church. Apostolic authority, but not the power of order, was lost to Judas. No regular jurisdiction can of itself continue under conditions of heresy and schism.
>
> 2. The two powers differ in the mode of their transmission. The sacramental power, being physical, will be normally conferred by way of consecration, *per consecrationem* (consecration received from Baptism, Confirmation, Holy Orders). The power of jurisdiction, being moral, will be normally conferred by way of designation, of commission, of mandate, *ex simplici injunctione*.[130]

---

[130] Charles Journet, *The Apostolic Hierarchy*, vol. 1 of *The Church of the Word Incarnate*, trans. A.H.C. Downes (London: Sheed & Ward, 1955), 23–24.

2. The difference in the mode of transmission stems from the disparity in causality

While Dr. Lamont attributes a single cause to both powers, Cardinal Journet explains that they come from different causes:

> I. Jesus is Priest as none other is priest. There is only one redemptive sacrifice: His own. There is but one fountain of grace: His transpierced heart. As far as the sacerdotal and redemptive power is concerned, the power that obtains and dispenses grace, there is not in all the Church any other head, any other ruler, any other source, any other cause, save only Him.
>
> When the time of His visible presence among us was ended, He abandoned no part of this role. Nor did He wish to deprive us of His sanctifying contact. He availed Himself of mortal priests through whom He might carry out the acts of the Christian cultus, like an artisan using tools that need constant renewal. But it was He alone, and none other, who, through them, was to bring about the presence among us of the sacrificial intercession of the cross; He alone who, through them, was to baptize and absolve. His sacerdotal and sanctifying action was to pass through them independently of their moral worthiness or unworthiness, and to do so infallibly, for—and this is true above all on the supernatural plane—an instrument does not act by its own proper virtue, but by the virtue of him who uses it. The ministers of the sacraments, their sacerdotal power, and the sacraments themselves, are in fact no more than purely external instruments, mere transmitters of impulsions coming from Christ Himself, which, in souls made ready for them, blossom into graces.
>
> The priesthood of Christ is thus participated in the Church only in a purely instrumental manner.
>
> 2. It is not quite the same with His kingship. We have just said that Jesus is Priest as none other is priest. We must also say that Jesus is King as none other is king. He rules angels and men. . . .
>
> Jesus is the fountain-head of a universal kingship, and He never ceases to exercise it from heaven where He sits at the right hand of the Father. And yet, so that men might not be deprived of the help His living voice had brought them, He has in His mercy left them a visible power, continuing to speak with authority in His name—the power of jurisdiction. . . .
>
> To force open the door of the soul and then to pour grace into it, is possible to none but God; and creatures therefore can here avail only as instruments in His hand, and for ends beyond their scope. But to propose to minds a speculative

Unresolved Tensions in Papal-Episcopal Relations

or practical message from without, even were this message of divine origin, is a work which seems more connatural to men, and one in which they can have a greater share in the initiative. The interior influx of grace, remarks St. Thomas, cannot be transmitted save by instruments, and, in this matter, Christ alone can be Head of the Church. . . . On the contrary, the "exterior government of the Church," the "authority" over the Church, the "pastoral power" over the Church, the dignity of being a "foundation" of the Church—all that can be communicated to others. They too can be called heads of the Church, though not as Christ is called Head. For Christ is Head and Foundation of the Church in a unique way, in His quality as Principle, or, to put it another way, universally and by His own proper virtue; whereas they are heads and foundations in a dependent and secondary manner—that is, not universally but only of the Church immersed in history, or only for some few years like the pope, or for some small area like the bishops; and this not by their own virtue but in their quality as ambassadors of Christ. . . .

Consequently, the depositaries of the jurisdiction act as *second causes* rather than as mere transmitters. They have certain initiatives and certain responsibilities.[131]

And what about the *gratia gratis data* Dr. Lamont refers to? It is not something inherent to the power of jurisdiction and permanent, but is granted as an external help whenever required:

> The drawback of giving men such a privilege is that in proportion to the importance of their office their natural fallibility will threaten to invade the government of the Church. Hence, so that the Church may be directed by them and not misled, so that it may continue to be the salt of the earth, and not be reabsorbed into the world, it needs the help of a particular providence, a prophetic gift, Christ's assistance: "Go therefore, teach ye all nations . . . teaching them to observe all things whatsoever I have commanded you. And *behold I am with you all days, even to the consummation of the world*" (Matt. 28:19–20).[132]

3. Neither the pope's power of universal jurisdiction (which derives from Christ directly) nor the bishops' limited one (received through the pope's mediation) needs a sacrament for its transmission

---

[131] Charles Journet, *The Apostolic Hierarchy*, 124–26.
[132] Journet, 126.

It Is Churchmen Who Need Reform, Not the Church

Dr. Lamont states:

> St. Thomas's position is ruled out by the nature of a sacrament. A created cause that is a sign, and is used by God to directly produce supernatural grace, is a sacrament (3a q. 60 a. 2). The conferring of the power of jurisdiction upon a bishop is a gift of a supernatural grace that is done through a sign. It must therefore be done through a sacrament. Both the consecration of bishops and the assignation of subjects to a bishop by the pope are signs; they are speech acts with intelligible meanings that effect what they signify. But only the consecration of a bishop is a sacrament. The assignation of territory and subjects to a bishop by the pope is not a sacrament. The source of the jurisdiction of bishops must therefore originate in the sacrament of their consecration. St. Thomas's Neoplatonic conception of causation explains how authority received by a bishop in consecration is received directly by Christ.

We have seen how the last sentence is erroneous because St. Thomas's concept of causality is not Neoplatonic but Thomistic. However, what precedes it is also wrong, because Jesus Christ willed to make the apostles and their successors participate in His external government of the Church as second causes rather than as mere transmitters. And just as He established a difference in powers between Peter and the rest of the Twelve, He also established a difference in the manner of reception between the pope and the bishops, but in neither case does this reception take place through a sacrament. That is what Cardinal Journet says:

> Christ, as we have said, bestowed on the apostles immediately, besides certain exceptional and temporary powers of which they were the *sole* depositaries, the regular and permanent powers of which they were the *first* depositaries. However, although it was conferred on them immediately by Christ, the regular jurisdiction proper to each of the apostles, which they would hand on to their successors, did not belong to all of them in the same degree or by the same right. Not in the same degree, for in Peter it was sovereign and universal while in the others it was subordinated and particular. Not by the same right, for in Peter it dwelt as in a fountainhead, in the others as something derived. It was by a special favour, as we have seen, that Christ Himself bestowed on the apostles a jurisdictional power which, normally, was to reach them through Peter as intermediary.
>
> The consequence of this doctrine is that as time went on the jurisdictional power would devolve differently on the pope and on the other bishops. On the

Unresolved Tensions in Papal-Episcopal Relations

pope it is bestowed immediately by Christ as soon as he is validly elected. To the bishops it is given mediately, through the pope: the Saviour, says Cajetan, sends down His power first on the head of the Church, and thence to the rest of the body. When a pope is created the electors merely designate the person, and it is Christ who then confers on him immediately his dignity and power. But when the sovereign pontiff, either of himself or through others, invests bishops, the proper jurisdiction they receive does not come to them directly from God, it comes directly from the sovereign pontiff to whom Christ gives it in a plenary manner, and from whom it comes down to the bishops: somewhat after the manner of the life-pulse that begins in the heart and is transmitted thence to the other organs. And that is why the sovereign pontiff must not be conceived as merely *designating* bishops who then receive directly from Christ their proper and ordinary authority; but as himself *conferring* the episcopal authority, having first received it from Christ in an eminent form.[133]

In light of the above, this statement of Dr. Lamont is erroneous: "A proper and ordinary divine authority must be derived from God, and can be taken away only by Him: no merely human authority can remove it. But a pope deposing a bishop at will, independently of the divine law, is not acting with divine authority."

Conversely, Domenico Palmieri is right when he teaches that

the pope cannot indeed licitly remove a bishop without cause, but he can certainly validly do this, and his act will have force on its own; a bishop in this situation cannot claim jurisdiction for himself on the pretext that there is no just cause for his removal. It is apparent from what has already been stated that this is not a question of words, as will become more clear further on: it touches on the nature of the papal primacy and the whole economy of ecclesiastical jurisdiction.

A final and friendly consideration

As I finish defending the postulates of my original article, I am reminded of a recent conversation in a Paris café with a respected and erudite traditionalist priest. When I mentioned the growing exasperation of many faithful Catholics at the heresies and scandalous pastoral attitudes of Pope Francis and top Church authorities and the consequent fragmentation of opinions in the *pusillus grex*, giving rise to various theories that lead to mismatched attitudes, my learned companion said: "We must avoid the

---

[133] Journet, 403–4.

mistake of doing theology—and especially ecclesiology—starting from the anomalous reality the Church is experiencing today, because this inductive method can lead to drawing wrong conclusions."

I immediately thought of my experiences with Latin American liberation theologians in the 1970s. They sought to rework the Church's social doctrine based on situations of extreme poverty in some sectors of the population but ended up aligning themselves with Marxist thought. The big mistake of progressive German bishops and laity seeking to reinvent Church teaching on the sacrament of Holy Orders and ministries and to change Church discipline on priestly celibacy based on biased conclusions about reports of sexual abuse among the clergy also came to mind.

I fear that some friends and colleagues in the trenches defending Tradition make a similar mistake. Seeing the Vatican's current abuses of power, the lack of courage of a majority of cardinals and bishops, and the willful blindness of some conservatives who hide their heads in the sand, they deduce that one needs to reform the papacy by shrinking papal power or at least reducing it to the modalities seen in the first millennium. An even greater mistake is to try to justify such proposals based on claims and theories developed by neo-modernist theologians from before and after the Second Vatican Council.

It is not the divine and beautifully hierarchical structure established by Jesus Christ for the part of His Mystical Body militating here on Earth that needs reform. Instead, reform—one entirely based on traditional Church teaching—is needed by sinful churchmen and all of us laity, who are so badly influenced by the revolutionary and evil spirit of today's world.

6

In Defense of the Moderate Position on Papal Jurisdiction: A Reply to José Ureta

John Lamont

My article "On the Papal Deposition of Bishops"[134] was occasioned by Mr. José A. Ureta's "Why a Good Bishop Should Not Ignore but Obey his Unjust Deposition by the Pope,"[135] which advanced an historically standard view among Catholic theologians to the effect that because all bishops receive their jurisdiction immediately from the pope, they can be removed from their diocese at the will of the pope, regardless of the justice of this removal. His argument was a topical one, because it was applied by him to Bishop Joseph Strickland of Tyler, Texas, who was first asked to resign from his diocese by Pope Francis and then, having refused to do so, was removed from the diocese without a just cause. I had argued that this theological position was wrong in itself and was no longer an option for Catholic theologians, because of its rejection by the Second Vatican Council. Mr. Ureta endeavored to refute me in two responses.[136]

Because of the importance of the subject, an answer to Mr. Ureta seems to be called for. At the same time, many of the arguments he advances in his response are in fact addressed in my original article; when this is the case, the reader is best advised to compare this article and Mr. Ureta's response and decide for himself. This answer will limit itself to new questions that arise from Mr. Ureta's response, while referring the reader to the original article to complete the exposition of the position being argued for here. The reader may find some of the necessary but detailed rebuttals of Mr. Ureta's claims to be less than enthralling, but it is hoped that some substantial contribution to this important issue will be achieved.

There is an initial point to be made about Mr. Ureta's position. He states, "The core of the controversy is whether the pope has the power to dismiss from his diocese

---

First published at *Rorate Caeli* on March 14, 2024. The first paragraph has been slightly rewritten for its inclusion in this anthology.

[134] See chapter 4.
[135] See chapter 3.
[136] Combined here as chapter 5.

a bishop who has committed no severe misconduct and absent some proportionate reason that makes it necessary. The issue is not whether an arbitrary removal is licit—it is not—but whether it is valid." In distinguishing between a valid act of dismissal and a licit act of dismissal, Mr. Ureta follows Palmieri, the Jesuit theologian whom I cited as a representative of the strong view of papal jurisdiction that I oppose.

The distinction between a valid act and a licit act makes sense when applied to exercises of the power of order. For example, a sacrament such as the Eucharist can be celebrated validly but not licitly. The distinction does not however apply to exercises of the power of jurisdiction. The power of jurisdiction just *is* a power to give legally binding orders or permissions. Its object is the law and what is governed by the law. The distinction between valid acts and licit acts thus has no application when it comes to exercise of the power of jurisdiction. If the exercise of such a power is valid, then it is licit.

One might reply that a papal act of jurisdiction is valid but illicit when it contradicts existing canon law. But either the pope has the authority to override existing canon law in his actions, or he does not. In the former case, his overriding of canon law is licit, because it is an exercise of legitimate authority. In the latter case, it is not licit and hence has no force. In neither case is it valid but not licit. This is not however a final objection to Mr. Ureta's position, because the strong view of papal jurisdiction can be stated and defended without having recourse to this distinction between valid and licit acts of jurisdiction.

Palmieri and Vitoria as advocates of the strong and moderate views of papal jurisdiction

There is a certain unclarity in Mr. Ureta's exposition of the position that he defends. He asserts that I have misrepresented the thought of Domenico Palmieri S.J., whom I discuss as giving a complete and accurate presentation of the strong view of papal jurisdiction. He states:

> It is enough to quote his [viz., Palmieri's] own words to prove that Palmieri upholds the narrow interpretation that Dr. Lamont subscribes to and calls the "moderate view of papal jurisdiction":
>
>> The [pope's] plenitude of power that is being discussed is not absolute, but is relative to the society that is ruled; it is plenitude of power in a polity and for a polity. To give clarity, we can say that it can be understood in two ways: only positively, or exclusively. It is understood in a positive sense only, if the supreme ruler can by his ordinary legal

authority perform everything that is useful and necessary for the entire polity and every one of its subjects, *although there are subordinate powers together with him and under him that exercise authority that is not derived from him*. It is understood in an exclusive sense, if the supreme ruler's authority is such that every power in the polity is either his own power, or is derived from his own power in such a way that the supreme power either formally or virtually contains every other power by which the polity is ruled. Such is the power of absolute monarchy in a political society. *It is easy to show that the plenitude of power belongs to the Roman Pontiff in the first sense.*

What Dr. Lamont calls the "strong view," Domenico Palmieri calls the "exclusive sense," which he rejects; and what Dr. Lamont calls the "moderate view," Palmieri calls the "positive sense," the restricted sense he defends. Therefore, it is absolutely inappropriate to classify it as a "best case for the strong view."

But when Palmieri says that "it is easy to show that the plenitude of power belongs to the Roman Pontiff in the first sense," what he means is that it is easy to show that the plenitude of power belongs to the Roman Pontiff in *at least* the first sense; that is, that the Roman Pontiff can easily be seen to have *at least* the amount of power that is attributed to him in the first sense. What is more difficult, according to Palmieri's account, is to determine if the Roman Pontiff has not only the amount of power attributed to him in the first, restricted sense, but also the amount of power attributed to him in the exclusive sense. Palmieri holds and argues that the Roman Pontiff *does* have the power attributed to him in the exclusive sense, the power of absolute monarchy in a political society. This appears from the text of Palmieri's that follows on from the citation from Palmieri given by Mr. Ureta above, a text that for ease of reference is reproduced here:

> It is easy to show that the plenitude of power belongs to the Roman Pontiff in the first sense. This supreme power requires the following characteristics: it requires the power given by the ordinary process of law to do everything required for the ruling of a society, whether in making laws, establishing courts, or coercively enforcing the law; and there must be nothing that can be legitimately done against its will, so that all other power in the society depends directly on it. . . . Such is the power of the Roman Pontiff in the Church. . . .
>
> But the greatest difficulty arises with respect to another conception of the plenitude of power. This comes down to the question of whether the

In Defense of the Moderate Position on Papal Jurisdiction

jurisdiction of a bishop in his diocese comes immediately from Christ, or whether it comes from Christ mediately through the Roman Pontiff, that is, immediately from the Roman Pontiff. No one denies that this power is from Christ, since all power in the Church is from Him, or that it is immediately from God in that God acts immediately in and with the action of all other causes. The question is of the immediate principle of this power—a power that is immediate in that any second cause between the first and principal cause and its effect is excluded.

There are some who suppose that the ordinary jurisdiction of bishops is received immediately from Christ. They use the arguments given above, by which we demonstrated the divine institution of the episcopate. They generally explain the immediate derivation of power from Christ by Christ's conferring this power in episcopal ordination itself, but however in first act only, and bound as to its exercise and not reduced to second act unless the Supreme Pontiff, confirming the bishop, assigns to him a territory and subjects. They believe that in this way the subordination of the bishops to the Roman Pontiff remains secure, for even if it is allowed that both pope and bishop receive their jurisdiction immediately from God, the bishop is still subject to the power of the Roman Pontiff; it is not necessary that every jurisdiction proceeding immediately from God be independent. As against this view, many others think that although Christ instituted the episcopate willing that His Church be ruled by bishops, ordinary jurisdiction is conferred by the pope on individual bishops, in such a way that, before this bestowal by the pope, in no way, even in first act, does the bishop possess jurisdiction in virtue of his ordination. The ordination of a bishop gives him only the aptitude to receive jurisdiction, in virtue of Christ's institution.

In the first hypothesis, it is asserted that the Roman Pontiff cannot licitly and validly remove or restrict the jurisdiction of a bishop without just cause: once the condition of the Roman Pontiff having assigned subjects to a bishop is satisfied, the jurisdiction received by bishops is given by God, for it is this jurisdiction of divine origin that is exercised. The Roman Pontiff may indeed regulate and modify this jurisdiction for reasons derived from just causes. He can even in certain cases declare that this jurisdiction has been lost, in virtue of his right to interpret divine law. He cannot however directly remove jurisdiction from a bishop, because this jurisdiction does not exist in its subject through him, but by divine law; and divine law takes precedence over papal authority.

Unresolved Tensions in Papal-Episcopal Relations

In the second hypothesis, the pope cannot indeed licitly remove a bishop without cause, but he can certainly validly do this, and his act will have force on its own; a bishop in this situation cannot claim jurisdiction for himself on the pretext that there is no just cause for his removal. It is apparent from what has already been stated that this is not a question of words, as will become more clear further on: it touches on the nature of the papal primacy and the whole economy of ecclesiastical jurisdiction. The jurisdiction of the bishop in his diocese is the question that is now being considered—the question of the jurisdiction held in ecumenical councils over the whole Church will be considered later in its proper place. The question under consideration is currently a subject of discussion among Catholic theologians. . . .

III. We therefore maintain that the plenitude of power of the Roman Pontiff in the Church is such that all power by which the Church is ruled either formally or virtually is included in it, and therefore that it is the immediate source from which the jurisdiction of bishops is derived.[137]

Mr. Ureta's mistaken characterisation of Palmieri's thesis makes his own position unclear. Is he advocating the positive, restricted sense of papal power that he attributes to Palmieri, but that Palmieri in fact rejects? This is incompatible with his defence of the papal right to remove bishops at will—a supposed right that, as Palmieri states above, depends on rejecting the positive sense of papal power and accepting what Palmieri terms the exclusive sense.

The consensus of all Catholic theologians is that the existence of a papal right to remove bishops at will depends on the claim that "the plenitude of power of the Roman Pontiff in the Church is such that all power by which the Church is ruled either formally or virtually is included in it," as Palmieri states. This understanding of papal power is the reason that is given for this supposed papal right to remove bishops, so there is no point in addressing the question of whether or not this supposed papal right can exist if the restricted—or, as I term it, the moderate—view of papal power is correct. Since the main goal of Mr. Ureta's argument is to defend the existence of this right, it will be assumed that given the choice between renouncing the existence of this right and accepting the exclusive sense of papal power, he would accept the exclusive sense—or the strong view, as I term it—of papal power.

Mr. Ureta points out that Palmieri maintains the following:

---

[137] Palmieri, *Tractatus de romano pontifice*.

In Defense of the Moderate Position on Papal Jurisdiction

> It is false that according to our position the bishops are the vicars of the pope. For bishops do not exist in the Church in right of papal authority, but in right of the authority of Christ, and the pope cannot abolish the episcopal dignity and authority; furthermore, the power and tribunal of the pope and of bishops are two different things, because Christ willed that besides the chair of Peter there should also be an episcopal chair. Nor are the bishops delegates of the pope, because they possess an ordinary jurisdiction through the power of the office that Christ has instituted. The bishops rule their flock as their own, for by Christ's institution they must be pastors of a portion of the sheep, over which they exercise the power of binding and loosing. And although the Roman Pontiff may remove jurisdiction from any and all, he is nonetheless bound to ensure that other bishops exist, in order that there may always be bishops in the Church; for he may not abolish episcopal authority itself.

I had characterised this passage as evasive, an evaluation that Mr. Ureta disputes.

Palmieri is required to hold the assertions made in this passage, because they are the teaching of the Council of Trent. The passage is however an incomplete description of the teachings of that Council on the episcopate. As I pointed out in the original article, Palmieri's assertion that "bishops do not exist in the Church in right of papal authority, but in right of the authority of Christ" evades the difficulty that the conciliar teachings raise for his position. The Council of Trent states not only that the episcopal order exists in right of the authority of Christ, as Palmieri says, but also that the individual bishop of a diocese has by divine right a power of jurisdiction over his diocese that is conferred on him by the Holy Spirit, and that he is one of the successors of the apostles. It is difficult to see how this can be reconciled with Palmieri's view that all power by which the Church is ruled is either formally or virtually included in the papal power of jurisdiction. Power that is virtually included in the papal power is power that is present in the papal power as the effect is present in the cause. How can a bishop have ordinary jurisdiction by divine right if his jurisdiction is the effect of the papal power, granted to him by the pope when he is given a canonical mission? Palmieri does not address this obvious difficulty.

Palmieri also holds that "ordinary jurisdiction is conferred by the pope on individual bishops, in such a way that, before this bestowal by the pope, in no way, even in first act, does the bishop possess jurisdiction in virtue of his ordination. The ordination of a bishop gives him only the aptitude to receive jurisdiction, in virtue of Christ's institution." A standard argument for the strong view of papal jurisdiction, made by Palmieri

Unresolved Tensions in Papal-Episcopal Relations

among others, is that men can and have received and exercised episcopal jurisdiction prior to their ordination as bishops; and since episcopal ordination is not necessary for the possession or exercise of episcopal jurisdiction, such jurisdiction cannot be conferred in any form by episcopal ordination. But if the ordination of a bishop only gives him the aptitude to receive jurisdiction, and this same aptitude exists in men who are not bishops—since such men can be given episcopal jurisdiction—then what is the connection between episcopal ordination and jurisdiction? This entails that there can be no intrinsic connection between jurisdiction and the episcopal character. But since the episcopal character makes its bearer one of the successors of the apostles, this consequence is absurd.

Mr. Ureta raises some questions about my describing the strong view of papal power as attributing the whole of the power of jurisdiction to the pope. For clarity, I will specify that when I talk about the pope having the whole of the power of jurisdiction, I mean that all power by which the Church is ruled is either formally or virtually included in the papal power of jurisdiction, as Palmieri states.

Mr. Ureta asserts that I mistranslate a passage from the *Dictionnaire de théologie catholique*, when I render the passage thus: "Others think, with St. Thomas, that the jurisdiction of bishops is directly connected to that of the vicar of Christ, to whom not only a portion but the whole of ecclesiastical power has been granted." He claims that the original French phrase, "la plénitude du pouvoir ecclésiastique," should be translated as "the fullness of ecclesiastical power," not as "the whole of ecclesiastical power." The complete passage is as follows, with the disputed phrase at the end:

> En effet, l'origine divine de la juridiction épiscopale est-elle immédiate, ou seulement médiate, de sorte que, s'appuyant sur le droit divin, elle découle immédiatement du souverain pontife? La question est controversée entre catholiques, comme on peut le voir dans Bellarmin, *De romano pontifice*, l. IV, c. XXII sq. Les uns soutiennent que la juridiction est conférée immédiatement par le Christ aux évêques dans l'acte même de la consécration épiscopale, quoique cette juridiction reste liée, quant à son exercice, jusqu'à ce que le souverain pontife ait assigné au nouvel évêque un territoire et des sujets. Parmi les théologiens qui défendent cette opinion, il faut citer, d'après Bouix, *De episcopo*, Paris, 1873, part. I, p. 61, François de Victoria, Alphonse de Castro, Vasquez, Tournely. D'autres pensent plus communément, avec saint Thomas, *Sum. theol.*, IIa IIae, q. xxxix, a. 3; *Contra gentes*, l. IV, c. 76; Suarez, *De legibus*, l. I, n. 12 seq.; *Defensio fidei*, l. IV, c. ix; Benoît XIV, *De synodo dioecesana*, l. I, c. iv, n. 2, que la juridiction des

In Defense of the Moderate Position on Papal Jurisdiction

évêques se rattache immédiatement à celle du vicaire du Christ, auquel a été confiée non seulement une portion, mais *la plénitude du pouvoir ecclésiastique.* Cf. const. *Pastor aeternus* du concile du Vatican, c. III.[138]

A translation of this passage was given in my article, omitting some of the references in the original. With the references restored, it runs:

> Is the divine origin of episcopal jurisdiction immediate or only mediate, so that, while resting upon divine law, it flows immediately from the sovereign pontiff? The question is a subject of controversy among Catholics, as can be seen in Bellarmine, *De romano pontifice*, 1. IV, c. XXII sq. Some maintain that jurisdiction is conferred immediately by Christ on bishops in the very act of episcopal consecration, although the exercise of this jurisdiction is bound until the sovereign pontiff assigns a territory and subjects to the new bishop. Among the theologians who defend this opinion, we can cite, (following Bouix, *De episcopo*, Paris, 1873, part. I, p. 61), Francisco de Vitoria, Alfonso de Castro, Vasquez, Tournely. More commonly, others think, with St. Thomas, *Sum. theol.*, IIa IIae, q. xxxix, a. 3; *Contra gentes*, l. IV, c. 76; Suarez, *De legibus*, l. I, n. 12 seq.; *Defensio fidei*, l. IV, c. ix; Benedict XIV, *De synodo dioecesana*, l. I, c. iv, n. 2, that the jurisdiction of bishops is directly connected to that of the vicar of Christ, to whom not only a portion but the whole of ecclesiastical power has been granted. Cf. the First Vatican Council, constitution *Pastor aeternus*, ch. III.

In this passage, the phrase "plénitude du pouvoir ecclésiastique," which I translated as "the whole of ecclesiastical power," is applied to the understanding of papal jurisdiction held by theologians who espouse the strong view of papal power. Since the strong view asserts that the pope does indeed have the whole of the papal power of jurisdiction, at least in the sense given above of including either formally or virtually all the power by which the Church is ruled, this translation does not give a misleading account of the French text.

Valton's use of the term "plénitude du pouvoir ecclésiastique" in the passage is somewhat disingenuous. The reference to the constitution *Pastor Aeternus* that immediately follows it gives the impression that the term "plenitudo potestatis," "plenitude of power/plénitude du pouvoir," which is applied in that constitution to the papal power of jurisdiction, was meant in the sense of the strong view of papal jurisdiction. But this is false. Palmieri's discussion above indicates that plenitude of power can be understood

---

[138] Valton, "Évêques: questions théologiques et canoniques," *DTC* 5, col. 1702.

Unresolved Tensions in Papal-Episcopal Relations

in more than one sense. As was pointed out in my original article, Palmieri and Valton himself, writing after the First Vatican Council, both acknowledge that the dispute between the strong view of papal jurisdiction and the moderate view of papal jurisdiction is an open question for Catholic theologians, and hence that the Council did not attribute the plenitude of power to the pope in the sense understood by the strong view.

Mr. Ureta asserts that I misrepresent the thought of Vitoria on papal jurisdiction:

> Furthermore, at the end of the passage from *Relectio II*, quoted by Dr. Lamont, Vitoria says, "It was said to Peter, 'Feed my sheep,' with no limitations or exceptions. Therefore all direction pertains to Peter without any exception, and in consequence even the creation of bishops falls under his power." He continues: "From this the corollary clearly follows that one cannot now become a bishop except according to the forms laid down by the supreme pontiff, and that *if anyone attempts to do otherwise, nothing will result; such an attempt will be null and void. I state this however about the authority of jurisdiction, for what pertains to consecration is different.* Secondly, it follows that all ecclesiastical power, whether of orders or of jurisdiction, depends mediately or *immediately* on the see of Peter."
>
> In this paragraph, Vitoria clearly distinguishes between the power of order (granted directly by Christ), whose transmission without a license from the pope renders it illicit but not invalid, and the power of jurisdiction, whose transmission without a canonical mission granted or recognized by the pope renders it null and legally invalid.

This flatly contradicts Vitoria's text. Vitoria states that the apostles had the power to name bishops to succeed them, and that those bishops themselves had the power to name their own successors. In the passages that immediately precede the one quoted by Mr. Ureta above, Vitoria asserts:

> Second proposition. Any of the apostles aside from Peter could leave a successor, not a universal one, but in any province that he wished, who would be the true bishop of that province. I know that this proposition will not please all the doctors, both theologians and canonists, and that it does not please the Cardinals Torquemada and Cajetan themselves. For all of them were once seized by the conviction that all power of jurisdiction so depends on the Roman Pontiff that no one can possess the most minimal spiritual power save by the command or law of that Pontiff: no one, that is, after the apostles, who by a

In Defense of the Moderate Position on Papal Jurisdiction

unique privilege had spiritual power granted to them by Christ, which no one else can receive save from Peter. . . .

Third proposition. Not only could the Apostles leave successors, but any of their successors could similarly do so. . . .

Last proposition. Any bishop, even without consulting the see of Peter, can establish a law stating that priests elect the bishop, or that bishops are instituted by some other form. This follows from the other points already made; the bishop can make appropriate laws for his province on this subject, as on others. This is the reason why the authority and dignity of a bishop can be derived successively from one bishop to the next until it reaches us, and through the bishop all other inferior power.[139]

Here Vitoria states that the bishops who succeeded the apostles could and did name their successors on their own authority, without having recourse to the pope. This is a rejection of the strong view of papal jurisdiction, since it asserts that episcopal jurisdiction can exist and has existed without having been received from the pope. Vitoria holds that the power of episcopal jurisdiction is received directly from God, citing Ephesians 4 to this effect. That is why Vitoria has always been cited by Catholic theologians as an opponent of the strong view of papal jurisdiction, as appears from the mention of him in the excerpt from the *Dictionnaire de théologie catholique* given above.

Vitoria allows that because of his supreme authority, the pope can establish other regulations for the appointment of bishops, and that any appointment of bishops to a see that violates these regulations will be null and void. The pope can therefore require bishops to have a canonical mission from himself prior to their appointment to a see.

---

[139] "Secunda propositio, Quilibet aliorum Apostolorum a Petro potuit relinquere successorum, licet non universalem, saltem in quacunque provincia voluisset, qui esset verus Episcopus illius provinciae. Hanc propositionem, scio non placituram omnibus doctoribus, tum theologis, tum iure consultis, quae nec ipsis Cardinalibus, Turrecremata et Caiet. placeret. Omnes enim illa persuasio semel invasit, omnem potestatis iurisdictionis ita dependere a Romano Pontifice, ut nullus possit habere, nec minimam quidem spiritualem potestatem, nisi ex mandato, vel lege ipsius: post Apostolos quidem, qui ex singulari privilegio habuerunt a Christo, quod nullus alius potest habere, nisi a Petro. . . .

"Tertia propositio, Non solum Apostoli hoc potuerunt, sed quilibet successorum similiter potuit relinquere sibi successorum. . . .

"Ultima propositio, Quilibet Episcopus in sua provincia potuit condere legem, ut presbyteri eligerent Episcopum, vel aliam formam institutionis dare, etiam inconsulta sede Petri. Haec sequitur ex aliis. Nam potuit leges convenientes provinciae facere de hac re, sicut de aliis. Ecce rationem, quomodo authoritas, et dignitas Episcopalis potuit derivari successive ad uno in alterum usque ad nos, et per Episcopos omnis alia potestas inferior." Vitoria, *Relectio II de potestate ecclesiae*.

Unresolved Tensions in Papal-Episcopal Relations

But this requirement follows from positive legislation that can be abolished, and that did not always exist. The pope has also always had *ex officio* the capacity to expel bishops from the Catholic Church by withdrawing from communion with them. This is the dependence of bishops on the pope that Vitoria refers to.

Mr. Ureta's mischaracterisation of Vitoria may be derived from his conviction that rejection of the strong view of papal jurisdiction is derived from "proposals based on claims and theories developed by neo-modernist theologians from before and after the Second Vatican Council." I know of no instance of neo-modernist theologians arguing for the moderate view of papal jurisdiction that Vitoria accepts. It is scarcely neo-modernist to assert that a pope needs to have some valid legal justification for removing a bishop from his diocese, which is the issue at the centre of this debate. This attribution of neomodernism would seem to originate in a tendency, formerly very prevalent, to identify orthodoxy with the greatest possible exaltation of the powers of the pope. One would have thought that Pope Francis (or even Pope John Paul II, or Pope Paul VI) would have cured Catholics of this tendency.

Magisterial teaching on papal jurisdiction

Mr. Ureta reproaches me with failing to give sufficient weight to the teaching of Pius XII in *Mystici Corporis* on papal jurisdiction. He cites the encyclical *Humani Generis* of Pius XII to justify this reproach:

> Nor must it be thought that what is expounded in encyclical letters does not of itself demand consent, since in writing such letters the popes do not exercise the supreme power of their teaching authority. For these matters are taught with the ordinary teaching authority, of which it is true to say: "He who heareth you, heareth me" (Luke 10:16); and generally what is expounded and inculcated in encyclical letters already for other reasons appertans to Catholic doctrine. But if the supreme pontiffs in their official documents purposely pass judgment on a matter up to that time under dispute, it is obvious that that matter, according to the mind and will of the pontiffs, cannot be any longer considered a question open to discussion among theologians.

However, Mr, Ureta inconsistently fails to apply the contents of this passage to the dogmatic constitution *Lumen Gentium*, which I cite in support of my view. *Lumen Gentium* is an official document in which the supreme pontiff passes judgment on theological questions. It is signed by the pope and by the bishops of the Catholic Church assembled in an ecumenical council.

In Defense of the Moderate Position on Papal Jurisdiction

Mr. Ureta appeals to the appendix to *Lumen Gentium* to justify his claim that its teachings are not authoritative. The appendix states:

> A question has arisen regarding the precise theological note which should be attached to the doctrine that is set forth in the Schema de Ecclesia and is being put to a vote.
>
> The Theological Commission has given the following response regarding the Modi that have to do with Chapter III of the de Ecclesia Schema: "As is self-evident, the Council's text must always be interpreted in accordance with the general rules that are known to all."
>
> On this occasion the Theological Commission makes reference to its Declaration of March 6, 1964, the text of which we transcribe here:
>
> "Taking conciliar custom into consideration and also the pastoral purpose of the present Council, the sacred Council defines as binding on the Church only those things in matters of faith and morals which it shall openly declare to be binding. The rest of the things which the sacred Council sets forth, inasmuch as they are the teaching of the Church's supreme magisterium, ought to be accepted and embraced by each and every one of Christ's faithful according to the mind of the sacred Council. The mind of the Council becomes known either from the matter treated or from its manner of speaking, in accordance with the norms of theological interpretation."

Mr. Ureta argues that *Lumen Gentium* did not intend to bind the Church to believe its contents:

> The manner of speaking of the First Vatican Council's constitutions *Dei Filius* and *Pastor Aeternus* clearly expresses the will to define and concludes with anathemas for those who deny its teachings. For example, the chapter on the primacy of the pope begins by saying "We *teach and declare* that . . ." It continues by saying "*We promulgate anew the definition of the ecumenical Council of Florence,* which *must be believed* by all faithful Christians." And it concludes by saying, "Therefore, we condemn and reject the opinions of those who hold that . . ." And, further, "So then, should anyone, which God forbid, have the temerity to reject this definition of ours; let him be *anathema*." Absolutely none of this can be found in *Lumen Gentium*'s manner of speaking or in any other document of Vatican II. Furthermore, at the close of Vatican II, Paul VI explicitly declared that in the Council, "the teaching authority of the Church . . . [did] not [wish] to issue extraordinary dogmatic pronouncements."

Unresolved Tensions in Papal-Episcopal Relations

All that this contrast with *Dei Filius* and *Pastor Aeternus* establishes is that *Lumen Gentium* did not solemnly define any dogmas and anathematise as heretical those who do not accept them. But binding magisterial pronouncements are not limited to extraordinary dogmatic pronouncements, as the passage from *Humani Generis* cited above asserts. The norms of theological interpretation must be used to determine whether *Lumen Gentium* binds the Church to believe its teachings on episcopal jurisdiction.

One of these norms is that the teaching of an ecumenical council is the highest form of magisterial teaching, and that a dogmatic constitution belongs to the most authoritative level of document issued by an ecumenical council. It is not the most authoritative kind of pronouncement of an ecumenical council; canons or other formulas giving definitions of the faith are more authoritative, becasue their entire content is infallibly true and must be accepted with the assent of faith. Some parts of a dogmatic constitution, if suitably formulated, may also demand the assent of faith, but the entire constitution does not require this assent. Nonetheless, the clear teaching of a dogmatic constitution of an ecumenical council concerning a matter of faith and morals is to be accepted by Catholics as final and binding. This is a straightforward rule of theological science. It is incorrect to say, as Mr. Ureta does, that a document's title is not enough to express the intention of teaching Catholic dogma in an authoritative fashion. The title of a document issued by an ecumenical council does express this intention. What else would the term "dogmatic constitution" mean, when applied to a document of an ecumenical council whose professed aim was to expound the nature of the Church of Christ?

Compare the text of *Lumen Gentium* on this subject to the text of *Mystici Corporis* that is cited to justify the strong view of papal jurisdiction. The relevant text of *Mystici Corporis* is emphasised below:

> 41. They, therefore, walk in the path of dangerous error who believe that they can accept Christ as the Head of the Church, while not adhering loyally to His Vicar on earth. They have taken away the visible head, broken the visible bonds of unity and left the Mystical Body of the Redeemer so obscured and so maimed, that those who are seeking the haven of eternal salvation can neither see it nor find it.
>
> 42. What we have thus far said of the Universal Church must be understood also of the individual Christian communities, whether Oriental or Latin, which go to makeup the one Catholic Church. For they, too, are ruled by Jesus Christ through the voice of their respective bishops. Consequently, bishops must be considered as the more illustrious members of the Universal Church, for they

In Defense of the Moderate Position on Papal Jurisdiction

> are united by a very special bond to the divine Head of the whole Body and so are rightly called "principal parts of the members of the Lord"; moreover, as far as his own diocese is concerned, each one as a true shepherd feeds the flock entrusted to him and rules it in the name of Christ. Yet in exercising this office they are not altogether independent, but are subordinate to the lawful authority of the Roman Pontiff, *although enjoying the ordinary power of jurisdiction which they receive directly from the same Supreme Pontiff.* Therefore, Bishops should be revered by the faithful as divinely appointed successors of the Apostles (cf. *Cod. Iur. Can.*, can. 329, 1), and to them, even more than to the highest civil authorities, should be applied the words: "Touch not my anointed one!"

The italicized text is inserted into a passage that teaches that neither individual Christians nor bishops can accept Christ as the Head of the Church while not adhering loyally to His Vicar on earth, and that bishops are subordinate to the lawful authority of the pope. The object of the passage is to teach this Catholic doctrine. The phrase about the reception of the power of jurisdiction from the pope is not even given as a reason for this teaching. It is included simply as an aside. It cannot reasonably be understood as having the intention or the effect of settling the long-standing dispute among Catholic theologians about the origin of episcopal jurisdiction. Papal statements intended to settle important and centuries-old theological disputes do not and cannot do so by adding a subordinate phrase to a text that deals with a different subject-matter. They must clearly state the resolution to such debates and clearly state that Catholics are bound to hold this resolution. This follows from the character of magisterial teaching as being, among other things, a legally binding norm for belief and utterance. In order for a legal norm to come into force, it must be manifestly promulgated; this is a basic principle of Catholic law. Manifest promulgation requires a clear and explicit statement of what must be believed and the obligation to believe it. It cannot be done by a subordinate phrase. Papal encyclicals are not divinely inspired documents whose every assertion is guaranteed to be true and must be believed by Catholics. The statement of *Mystici Corporis* on the reception of episcopal jurisdiction can have only the most minimal degree of authority, and is more reasonably believed to have no authority at all.

The strong view of papal jurisdiction is expressed more clearly and at greater length by Pius XII in the encyclicals *Ad Sinarum Gentem* (1954) and *Ad Apostolorum Principis* (1958), addressed to the Catholic bishops and people of China. But these encyclicals cannot be understood as binding Catholics to accept this position, because a binding teaching on this subject would have to be addressed to the universal Church. This is why I stated

Unresolved Tensions in Papal-Episcopal Relations

in my original article that the statements of *Mystici Corporis, Ad Sinarum Gentem* and *Ad Apostolorum Principis* on the subject of papal jurisdiction were improper and irresponsible uses of the papal teaching office. They give the impression to the uninitiated of settling a theological debate and making a binding pronouncement, while not in reality doing so.

Mr. Ureta criticises my remark that "one may speculate that these passages [sc. the passages supporting the strong view of papal jurisdiction] were included in the texts of these encyclicals by drafters at the Holy Office (of which Cardinal Ottaviani was the head at the time) in order to further the cause of a theological opinion that they accepted." He observes:

> Regrettably, in attributing this passage from *Mystici Corporis* to Cardinal Ottaviani or his staff, Dr. Lamont failed to check dates and made a historical error. The encyclical was published in 1943, but Cardinal Ottaviani was appointed secretary of the Congregation of the Holy Office—of which the pope was the prefect—only in 1959, sixteen years later.

I cite as an authority for my remark Msgr. Joseph Clifford Fenton, who was familiar with the workings of the Holy Office. Msgr. Fenton states:

> It was Pope John XXIII who appointed Cardinal Ottaviani to the position of Secretary of the Holy Office. It is important to remember, however, that the Cardinal has been the effective head of this most influential of the Roman Congregations since 1935, when he was appointed Assessor of the Holy Office, after having served with great distinction as the Substitute Secretary of State.[140]

I do not suggest that Cardinal Ottaviani introduced the strong view of papal jurisdiction into *Mystici Corporis* contrary to the will or belief of Pius XII, but that he introduced or caused to be introduced an inconspicuous mention of this view into the encyclical, with the intention of later being able to cite the passage as a definitive decison on the topic. Pius XII was a cautious man who tried to make reasonable accommodations to progressive opinion in the Church. It was most unlikely that he would have agreed to issue a clear and binding teaching requiring Catholics to accept the strong view of papal jurisdiction. That would not however prevent him from accepting the inclusion of an insinuation of this view in his encyclicals; he may not have given much thought to the matter when presented with a proposed draft.

---

[140] Msgr. Joseph Clifford Fenton, "Cardinal Ottaviani and the Council," *American Ecclesiastical Review*, vol. 148 (January–June 1963): 44–53, at 46.

In Defense of the Moderate Position on Papal Jurisdiction

Mr. Ureta objects that there was great resistance at the Second Vatican Council to the proposed teaching on the episcopate. We must however distinguish between two positions that faced opposition. One position was the assertion that the bishops shared in supreme power over the Church. Albert Kallio O.P., in a valuable study mentioned by Mr. Ureta, cites the objections of Cardinal Michael Browne to this proposal:

> A certain habitual participation in the supreme and full authority to govern the universal Church is attributed to the college of bishops, even though its exercise is said to depend on the Roman Pontiff who, as Vicar of Christ, already possesses full and supreme power in himself. This limitation with regard to the right to exercise it, although legally sufficient to save the fullness of the authority of the Roman Pontiff, does not, however, save it purely and simply (*simpliciter*), since the supreme authority to govern the universal Church, although under another title, namely by the right of collegiality, is also possessed by the body of bishops together with the Roman Pontiff, its head. Since this participation should be given by divine right, the Roman Pontiff would be obliged in all acts of his government to consult the thought and will of the whole episcopate, and this not only as a college of his brothers and counselors, but as participants with him in the supreme authority to govern the whole Church. We are thus in the position whereby the Roman Pontiff would have the greater share in the government of the universal Church, but not the fullness of this authority.[141]

Cardinal Browne plausibly objected that this position violated the solemn definition of the First Vatican Council, which pronounced anathema on anyone who asserted that the pope has "only the greater part but not the entire fullness of supreme authority" in

---

[141] Albert Kallio, "Collegialità nel Vaticano II," DeepL translation from the Italian, not from the original statement of Card. Browne. Fr. Kallio gives the orginal Latin (AS III/1, 629) as "Praedictis verbis Ordini, seu collegio episcoporum, attribuitur habitualis quaedam participatio supremae et plenae potestatis regendi universam Ecclesiam, etsi exercitium eiusdem ponitur dependere a Romano Pontifice qui, ut Vicarius Christi habet iam ex se eamdem plenam et supremam potestatem. Haec limitatio quoad ius exercitii, etsi mere iuridice aliquo modo sufficiat ad salvandam plenitudinem potestatis Romani Pontificis, simpliciter tamen loquendo eam non salvat. Potestas enim suprema regendi universam Ecclesiam, etsi sub alio titulo, iure scii, collegialitatis, possidetur quoque a corpore episcoporum una cum Romano Pontifice suo capite. Cum talis participatio ex parte corporis episcoporum sit, ut supponitur, divinitus largita, Romanus Pontifex moraliter ligaretur in omnibus suis actis gubernii ad habendam rationem mentis et voluntatis totius episcopatus et quidem non solum ut collegii suorum fratrum et consiliariorum, sed ut participantium cum eo in potestate suprema gubernandi totam Ecclesiam. Sumus exinde in positione illa secundum quam Romanus Pontifex haberet quidem potiores partes potestatis regendi universalem Ecclesiam non vero totam plenitudinem huius potestatis."

the Church. It is clear that it would severely limit papal power. This was the position that attracted the strongest opposition, as being a complete theological novelty and as contradicting the teaching of previous councils.

The other position was the question being addressed here, which is that of the origin of episcopal jurisdiction. This is concerned with the source and nature of the power of bishops over their own dioceses, not with the existence of some kind of participation by the bishops in the supreme government of the universal Church. It is the position of a well-established school in the Church. It is not clear that it limits papal power in any way at all. A ruler's authority is not *limited* by the requirement to follow natural and divine law, which is the requirement that the moderate view of papal jurisdiction imposes on the pope when dealing with bishops. Ruling authority is partially *constituted* by this requirement.

Two objections were raised to the text asserting that episcopal jurisdiction is conferred in consecration. The first was that it contradicts the texts of Pope Pius XII cited above. This objection has already been addressed.

The second objection was that the Church had for centuries considered that acts of jurisdiction by men appointed to a diocese, or elected to the papacy, were valid from the time of their appointment, even if they had not yet been consecrated as bishops. The case of the validity of the acts of jurisdiction of men who had been elected as pope but not yet consecrated as bishops does not cast light on our question, because it cannot be supposed that such men received their jurisdiction from the pope. It is a separate question, which seems only soluble by postulating that Christ supplies jurisdiction to the man elected pope prior to his consecration as bishop. In my original article, I addressed the question of men who exercised episcopal jurisdiction prior to their consecration as bishops by postulating jurisdiction supplied by the Church in such cases. Mr. Ureta objects to this proposal:

> Dr. Lamont... confidently suggests an alternative: "This jurisdiction can be explained as papal jurisdiction supplied to its possessor, which is replaced by properly episcopal jurisdiction when its possessor is consecrated." But in this hypothesis, the transitory jurisdiction would not be properly *episcopal*. It would not be *ordinary* but pontifically delegated, like that of any apostolic delegate or apostolic administrator. We would then have to conclude that many of the successive prelates who have governed some of the most important dioceses in Europe should be removed from the annals because they would not have been real bishops. For example, many bishops in the dioceses of the Holy Roman

In Defense of the Moderate Position on Papal Jurisdiction

Empire's Prince-Bishoprics remained simple tonsured clerics until the end of their lives and obtained from the Holy See the appointment of a "chor bishop" (a kind of auxiliary bishop) to carry out on their behalf all activities required by the episcopal *munus sanctificandi* they did not possess.

I agree that, on this hypothesis, the transitory jurisdiction would not be properly episcopal, but delegated (which may not imply that the delegated jurisdiction is in any way less extensive than properly episcopal jurisdiction). But this seems a natural consequence of the fact that the person possessing this jurisdiction is not in fact a bishop. I cannot see any objection to the assertion that men who governed important dioceses all their lives while remaining simple clerics were not real bishops. I think it correct to say that in order to be a real bishop, one must be consecrated a bishop.

The resistance of many Council Fathers to the statements of *Lumen Gentium* on collegiality was taken into account in the *Nota praevia* to the dogmatic constitution. This *Nota praevia* cannot be accused of having been composed under modernist influence, because it was drafted and included specifically to exclude modernist positions—a unique example of a responsible intervention and correction at the Council, prompted no doubt by Paul VI's concern to preserve his own authority. But the *Nota praevia* also confirms and explains the teaching that the power of jurisdiction is conferred by episcopal consecration. The difference between its treatment of the participation of bishops in supreme power over the Church and its treatment of the source of episcopal jurisdiction is worth noting. It qualifies the document's assertion about bishops sharing in supreme power over the Church in a way that takes into account Cardinal Browne's objections and rejects modernist understandings of collegiality:

> As Supreme Pastor of the Church, the Supreme Pontiff can always exercise his power at will, as his very office demands. Though it is always in existence, the College is not as a result permanently engaged in strictly collegial activity; the Church's Tradition makes this clear. In other words, the College is not always "fully active [*in actu pleno*]"; rather, it acts as a college in the strict sense only from time to time and only with the consent of its head.

Its description of the source of episcopal jurisdiction, however, simply gives the traditional account of the moderate view of papal jurisdiction:

> A person becomes a member of the College by virtue of episcopal consecration and by hierarchical communion with the head of the College and with its members. Cf. no. 22, § 1 *in fine*. In his consecration a person is given an ontological

participation in the sacred functions [*munera*]; this is absolutely clear from Tradition, liturgical tradition included. The word "functions [*munera*]" is used deliberately instead of the word "powers [*potestates*]," because the latter word could be understood as a power fully ready to act. But for this power to be fully ready to act, there must be a further canonical or juridical determination through the hierarchical authority. This determination of power can consist in the granting of a particular office or in the allotment of subjects, and it is done according to the norms approved by the supreme authority. An additional norm of this sort is required by the very nature of the case, because it involves functions [*munera*] which must be exercised by many subjects cooperating in a hierarchical manner in accordance with Christ's will. It is evident that this "communion" was applied in the Church's life according to the circumstances of the time, before it was codified as law.

This is a statement and confirmation of this traditional theological position, made after deliberate consideration and debate. It is binding on all Catholics.

St. Thomas on episcopal jurisdiction

Mr. Ureta contests my view that St. Thomas makes use of a Neoplatonic conception of causality when describing the power of jurisdiction of the pope. The passage in question from St. Thomas is the following:

> I answer that a superior power and an inferior power can relate to each other in two different ways. In one way, the inferior power originates entirely from the superior power; and in this case, the entire power of the inferior is founded on the power of the superior; and then the power of the superior is to be obeyed *simpliciter* rather than the inferior, and is so to be obeyed in all things, just as in natural causes, the first cause acts more on an effect produced by a secondary cause than the secondary cause itself does, as is stated in the *Liber de causis*. This is the way in which the power of God is related to all created powers; it is the way in which the power of the Emperor is related to the power of the proconsul; and it is the way in which the power of the pope is related to all other spiritual powers in the Church, since every dignity in the Church is distributed and ordered by the pope, whose power is in a certain manner the foundation of the Church, as is shown by Matthew ch. 16.[142]

---

[142] "Respondeo dicendum, quod potestas superior et inferior dupliciter possunt se habere. Aut ita quod inferior potestas ex toto oriatur a superiori; et tunc tota virtus inferioris fundatur supra virtutem superioris;

In Defense of the Moderate Position on Papal Jurisdiction

Here St. Thomas cites the *Liber de causis* as the source for his claim that "the first cause acts more on an effect produced by a secondary cause than the secondary cause itself does." The *Liber de causis* is a Neoplatonic work that is largely taken from the Neoplatonic philosopher Proclus, as St. Thomas observes in his commentary on it. There is no doubt that while St. Thomas was not a Neoplatonist, he accepted some Neoplatonist ideas, either through St. Augustine—whose philosophical formation was Platonist, and who was not familiar with Aristotle—or through Neoplatonist commentators on Aristotle such as Simplicius, with whom St. Thomas was familiar. In his commentary on the *Liber de causis*, St. Thomas states his agreement with its account of the causation of the first cause. Mr. Ureta asserts that according to Neoplatonism, secondary causes do not have an actual existence, and do not act with their own autonomy; they have only pseudo-being. This is not the case. It is a true characterisation of occasionalism, but it is not true of Neoplatonism.

In holding that episcopal authority derives from the pope in the way that the authority of a proconsul derives from the emperor, St. Thomas seems to deny to bishops a proper and ordinary authority that is derived from God. A proconsul does not have an authority that is proper to his office and is not derived from the emperor. The position of St. Thomas had not been definitively rejected by the Church in his time, but it has since been ruled out by the Council of Trent, which states:

> The holy Synod declares that, besides the other ecclesiastical degrees, bishops, who have succeeded to the place of the apostles, principally belong to this hierarchical order; that they are placed, as the same apostle says [Acts 20:28], by the Holy Ghost, to rule the Church of God; that they are superior to priests; administer the sacrament of Confirmation; ordain the ministers of the Church; and that they can perform very many other things; over which functions others of an inferior order have no power.

---

et tunc simpliciter et in omnibus est magis obediendum potestati superiori quam inferiori; sicut etiam in naturalibus causa prima plus influit supra causatum causae secundae quam etiam ipsa causa secunda, ut in Lib. de causis dicitur: et sic se habet potestas Dei ad omnem potestatem creatam; sic etiam se habet potestas imperatoris ad potestatem proconsulis; sic etiam se habet potestas Papae ad omnem spiritualem potestatem in Ecclesia: quia ab ipso Papa gradus dignitatum diversi in Ecclesia et disponuntur et ordinantur; unde ejus potestas est quoddam Ecclesiae fundamentum, ut patet Matth. 16."

St. Thomas continues: "Et ideo in omnibus magis tenemur obedire Papae quam episcopis vel archiepiscopis, vel monachus abbati, absque ulla distinctione. Potest iterum potestas superior et inferior ita se habere, quod ambae oriantur ex una quadam suprema potestate, quae unam alteri subdit secundum quod vult; et tunc una non est superior altera nisi in his quibus una supponitur alii a suprema potestate; et in illis tantum est magis obediendum superiori quam inferiori: et hoc modo se habent potestates et episcopi et archiepiscopi descendentes a Papae potestate." *In II Sent.*, D. 44, Q. 2, art. 3, expos.

Unresolved Tensions in Papal-Episcopal Relations

> CANON VI. – If any one shall say that in the Catholic Church there is not a hierarchy instituted by divine ordination, consisting of bishops, priests, and ministers; let him be anathema.
>
> CANON VII. – If any one saith, that bishops are not superior to priests; or, that they have not the power of confirming and ordaining; or, that the power which they possess is common to them and to priests; or, that orders, conferred by them, without the consent, or vocation of the people, or of the secular power, are invalid; or, that those who have neither been rightly ordained, nor sent, by ecclesiastical and canonical power, but come from elsewhere, are lawful ministers of the word and of the sacraments; let him be anathema.[143]

With his usual clarity, St. Thomas states:

> A superior power and an inferior power can relate to each other in two different ways. In one way, the inferior power originates entirely from the superior power; and in this case, the entire power of the inferior is founded on the power of the superior. . . . In another way, the power of a superior and an inferior are related by both of them having originated from a higher power, which subordinates the one to the other as it chooses; and in this way the one is superior to the other only in so far as it has been subordinated to the other by a higher power, and the superior is to be obeyed rather than the inferior only in so far as it has been given authority by the higher power.[144]

We have seen that the Church has rejected the first of these ways as an account of the relation between the power of the pope and the bishops. The second of these ways is preferable to the first for a reason that is independent of magisterial teaching on the connection between episcopal ordination and episcopal jurisdiction. This second way allows for the fact that it is Christ, rather than the pope, who is the head of the Church and the source of the power of both pope and bishops. It is in fact true to say that in the Church, "the power of a superior and an inferior are related by both of them having originated from a higher power, which subordinates the one to the other as it chooses." One cannot deny that Christ is the higher power in the Church, who is the source of the power of both pope and bishops, and who subordinates the one to the other as he chooses. The Church's rejection of the strong view of papal jurisdiction should be seen for what it is: a welcome acknowledgement of the headship of Christ over the Church.

---

[143] Council of Trent, Session XXIII, ch. 4.

[144] The Latin text for this quotation may be found on the preceding page.

In Defense of the Moderate Position on Papal Jurisdiction

The division of authority between pope and bishops postulated by the moderate view can also be seen to be suited to the situation of the Catholic Church. Absolute monarchy is proposed by Palmieri as the best form of government for the Church, because it is (he says) the best form of government for a state. But the Church, unlike temporal states, is intended to embrace the whole human race. She already exists on all the inhabited continents of the world. Even if absolute monarchy is the best form of government for a single state (an extremely dubious assertion), it is clearly unsuited to a polity that covers the whole human race. A division of authority between a supreme power and subordinate powers who are subject to this supreme power, but who have a real local authority of their own, is a better form of government for the Church.

7

Closing Remarks in My Debate with Dr. John Lamont

José Antonio Ureta

Much of what Dr. John Lamont includes in his response[145] to my previous reply[146] repeats what has already been seen. Thus, I will limit myself here to some brief remarks.

1. For Dr. Lamont, the fact that bishops have a power of ordinary jurisdiction is incompatible with the fact that this power was granted to them directly by the pope. As he sees it, if bishops were to receive their jurisdiction from the pope it would turn them into papal delegates. Grounded in this perspective of supposed incompatibility, Dr. Lamont then attributes to the defenders of the traditional theological position (from St. Thomas Aquinas to pre-conciliar theologians) a position they do not hold, namely, that bishops do not enjoy an ordinary power of jurisdiction and are mere delegates of the pope. He calls this mischaracterization of traditional thought "the strong view of papal jurisdiction." To build up this misrepresentation, he reinterprets what defenders of the traditional position state and he also forces a translation. But he does this in good faith, declaring it candidly.

For example, Palmieri maintains that the fullness of power belongs to the Roman Pontiff in the sense that the pope can, by his ordinary legal authority, carry out everything useful and necessary for the Church and the faithful "even though there are subordinate powers that, together with him and under him, exercise an authority that does not derive from him" (because it comes mediately from God). It could not be clearer. However, since Palmieri's real opinion does not fit into Dr. Lamont's "strong view" misrepresentation, Dr. Lamont stretches his thinking by claiming that, with this phrase, Palmieri is actually saying that the pope possesses *at least* this degree of power. However, the supposedly missing remainder of papal power cannot be found in Palmieri's writings.

Another example is the forced translation of the article from the *Dictionnaire de théologie catholique*, where Dr. Lamont translated "plénitude de pouvoir ecclésiastique" as "the whole of ecclesiastical power" instead of "the fulness of ecclesiastical power" or "the plenitude of ecclesiastical power." He defends the mistranslation candidly,

---

First published at *Rorate Caeli*, March 20, 2024.
[145] See the last chapter.
[146] See chapter 5.

affirming that he used "the whole" because that term "is applied to the understanding of papal jurisdiction held by theologians who espouse the strong view of papal power." In other words, since Dr. Lamont thinks that the traditional doctrine corresponds to his misrepresentation of it, he adapts the translation to correspond to the idea he has in his mind, even if it cannot be found in the text. He sees E. Valton, the author of the *Dictionnaire* article in question, as "somewhat disingenuous."

Francisco de Vitoria did not fare much better. He states that the apostles received their power of jurisdiction directly from Our Lord Jesus Christ and not from Saint Peter. However, Vitoria does not say that this continued to be the practice in the Church so that bishops today also receive their jurisdiction directly from God. (According to Vitoria, in the early Church, new bishops received jurisdiction from their predecessor.)

In my second reply, I quoted a passage from Cardinal Journet where he states: "It was by a special favor, as we have seen, that Christ Himself bestowed on the apostles a jurisdictional power which, normally, was to reach them through Peter as intermediary." That is why "as time went on, the jurisdictional power would devolve differently on the pope and on the other bishops. On the pope it is bestowed immediately by Christ as soon as he is validly elected. To the bishops it is given mediately, through the pope." Dr. Lamont does not refute Cardinal Journet. He doubles down by drawing from Vitoria's thoughts a consequence that Vitoria himself never drew.

2. Dr. Lamont attributes to the Second Vatican Council's dogmatic constitution *Lumen Gentium* a degree of magisterial authority it lacks. Based solely on the presence of the adjective *dogmatic* in the conciliar document's title, Dr. Lamont states that "the clear teaching of a dogmatic constitution of an ecumenical council concerning a matter of faith and morals is to be accepted by Catholics as final and binding." Consequently, the doctrinal novelties of *Lumen Gentium* would be, for him, irreformable teaching to which a *final and binding* assent of faith must be given. The paradox is that, in this case, we would be faced with a conciliar document that is rendered infallible against the express intent of its drafters and signatories, as well as the pope who confirmed it. As has been amply demonstrated, the Council Fathers and Paul VI decided not to exercise the charism of infallibility during the Second Vatican Council. In France, the poor Alsatians who were forcibly integrated into the German Army are known as the "*malgré nous*" ["despite ourselves"]. Similarly, if Dr. Lamont's casting of *Lumen Gentium* were correct, then this Council document would be magisterial dogma "malgré lui" [despite itself].

3. I am pleased to note that Dr. Lamont did not address Cardinal Journet's texts on the difference between the solely supernatural origin of the divino-ecclesiastical origin of power of order and the power of jurisdiction. It would seem that, through

Unresolved Tensions in Papal-Episcopal Relations

this silence, Dr. Lamont has implicitly abandoned his thesis that ordinary jurisdiction is a *gratia gratis data* that can be granted only by God.

4. Dr. Lamont added something in his rejoinder that needs to be addressed: "The distinction between a valid act and a licit act makes sense when applied to exercises of the power of order. For example, a sacrament such as the Eucharist can be celebrated validly but not licitly. The distinction does not however apply to exercises of the power of jurisdiction. The power of jurisdiction just *is* a power to give legally binding orders or permissions. Its object is the law and what is governed by the law. The distinction between valid acts and licit acts thus has no application when it comes to exercise of the power of jurisdiction. *If the exercise of such a power is valid, then it is licit*" (my emphasis).

From the perspective of Canon Law this is incorrect. In the 1983 Code, canons 124–128 indicate the conditions for the validity and licitness (or lawfulness) of every juridical act (including jurisdictional acts). They rest on four principles:

- ❖ *Validity*: the quality of the act that complies with the *essential requirements* that the legal system demands for its validity;
- ❖ *Nullity*: the quality of the act that does not meet these essential requirements;
- ❖ *Licitness*: the quality of the act that complies with *all legal requirements* and not just the essential ones;
- ❖ *Illicitness*: the quality of the act that meets only some of the legal requirements.

Consequently, *every lawful act is valid, but not every valid act is licit*. If an act is illicit (unlawful), this does not necessarily mean it is invalid. It may be valid, even if triggering a sanction or a need for compensation.

From a canonical point of view, the principle that "If the exercise of such a power is valid, then it is licit" is positivism and leads to arbitrariness. From the perspective of moral theology, this principle is an aberration because the common good requires that a general law or a particular precept be just, morally good, possible, and necessary or at least useful for achieving the common good. A law or precept that does not possess these qualities has no legal force.

I want to believe that Dr. Lamont was distracted when including this principle in his reply. As the old saying goes, "Quandoque bonus dormitat Homerus."

By way of conclusion, I adapt Dr. Lamont's good-natured invitation and append to it Prof. Plinio Corrêa de Oliveira's lifelong counsel to TFP members: the reader is best advised to compare both my arguments and Dr. Lamont's as to what the Church has always taught, then accept, love, and defend only those points that fully correspond to that traditional teaching.

8

Two Prelates Speak Out: Cardinal Müller and Bishop Schneider on Bishop Strickland

STATEMENT OF CARDINAL GERHARD LUDWIG MÜLLER[147]

What is being done to Bishop Strickland is terrible, an abuse of office against the divine right of the episcopate. If I could advise Bishop Strickland, he should absolutely not resign because then they can wash their hands of the affair.[148]

A bishop can be deposed by the pope in accordance with the dictates of justice only if he is guilty of something evil (heresy, schism, apostasy, a crime or totally unpriestly behavior)—for example, the pseudo-blessing of people of both or one sex in extramarital relationships, which offend God and defraud people of their salvation.

An arbitrary removal of a bishop of a diocese, over which he is appointed by Christ Himself as its own shepherd, undermines the authority of the pope, as happened historically with the unworthy bargaining for office under the Avignon papacy. This loss of trust was one of the main reasons for the secession of Reformation Christianity from the Catholic Church and its hatred of the pope, who had put himself in the place of God with his arbitrary actions.

According to Catholic doctrine, the pope is by no means the Lord of the Church, but only, as Christ's representative for the universal Church, the first servant of his Lord, who had to say to Simon Peter when newly appointed as the rock of the Church: "Get behind me (in Italian, *indietro*—the true *indietrismo*), for you have in mind not what God wants, but what men want" (Mt 16:23).

The pope has no authority from Christ to harass and intimidate good bishops modeled on Christ, the Good Shepherd, who, in accordance with the episcopal ideal of Vatican II, sanctify, teach, and shepherd God's flock in Christ's name, simply because false friends denounce these good bishops to Francis as enemies of the pope, while heretical and immoral bishops can do whatever they please, or disturb the Church of Christ every day with yet another stupidity.

---

[147] Given to and published by kath.net in German on September 21, 2023 (www.kath.net/news/82581), and also carried by many other sites in various languages.

[148] In fact, Bishop Strickland did not resign when asked to do so, and therefore he was summarily deposed.—*Ed.*

Unresolved Tensions in Papal-Episcopal Relations

STATEMENT OF BISHOP ATHANASIUS SCHNEIDER[149]

"The one charge which is now sure to secure severe punishment is the careful keeping of the traditions of the Fathers." These words of St. Basil (*Ep.* 243) can most aptly illustrate the deposition of the bishop of Tyler, Texas, His Excellency Joseph E. Strickland. The deposition of Bishop Joseph E. Strickland signifies a black day for the Catholic Church in our times. We are witnessing a blatant injustice towards a bishop who did his duty in preaching and defending with *parrhesia* the immutable Catholic faith and morals and in promoting the sacredness of the liturgy, especially in the immemorial traditional rite of the Mass. All understand—even the declared enemies of this confessor bishop—that the accusations brought against him are ultimately insubstantial and disproportionate and were used as a welcome opportunity to silence an uncomfortable prophetic voice within the Church.

What happened to certain bishops during the Arian crisis in the fourth century, who were deposed and exiled only because they intrepidly preached the traditional Catholic Faith, is again happening in our day. At the same time several bishops, who publicly support heresy, liturgical abuses, and gender ideology and openly invite their priests to bless same-sex couples, are not in the least importuned or sanctioned by the Holy See.

Bishop Strickland will probably go down in history as an "Athanasius of the Church in the USA," who however, unlike St. Athanasius, is not persecuted by the secular power, but, incredibly, by the pope himself. It seems that a kind of "purge" of bishops who are faithful to the immutable Catholic Faith and the Apostolic discipline, and which has been going on already for some time, has reached now a decisive phase.

May the sacrifice which Our Lord asked from Bishop Strickland bear plenty of spiritual fruits for time and eternity. Bishop Strickland and other faithful bishops who were already asked to resign, who are currently marginalized, or who will be the next in line, should say in all sincerity to Pope Francis: "Holy Father, why are you persecuting and beating us? We tried to do what all holy popes asked us to do. With fraternal love, we offer the sacrifice of this kind of persecution and exile for the salvation of your soul and for the good estate of the Holy Roman Church. Indeed, we are your best friends, Holy Father!"

---

[149] Published at many sites, including *OnePeterFive*, from which the text here has been extracted.

9

Pope Francis Has No Right to Dismiss Bishop Strickland Without Cause

Antonio Francés

On November 16, Raymond Arroyo conducted an excellent interview with Bishop Strickland.[150] The prelate demonstrated once more his love for Christ and for His Church and spoke like a prophet or a Church Father, as Bishop Schneider has pointed out recently. There was one point, however, that I think needs clarification.

Amidst many truths, the bishop stated that the pope is above canon law and therefore had the right to "dismiss" him without procedure and without just cause. But, of course, this is not accurate. The pope is the supreme human legislator of the Church and, therefore, he is, in a way, above the particular canons of the Code, although he is subject to them while they are in force. No bishop can find permanent protection from tyrannical acts of the pope merely by invoking canon number xx or yy of the Code of Canon Law, because the pope can change them. This is so because the Church is a monarchy.

However, the Church is no tyranny. The pope is the vicar of Christ the King, not of Satan the Tyrant. We, as Catholics, should not forget that above human law, and as its foundation, we find divine law and natural law. Canon law is not just a system of regulations established by Church authorities. It is an intelligible structure of the Bride of Christ and of her decisions and enactments. The Church was established by Jesus Christ with a canonical structure: Simon was the Rock whose faith will not waver; the Apostles are the columns with authority received directly from Christ. From the beginning we find the "Apostolic Canons," and from that foundation emanated particular structures and regulations through the ages. All this was established to preserve the deposit of Faith and to perpetuate the salvific mission. Without this structure and this end, the pope has no authority whatsoever.

First published at *LifeSiteNews*, November 23, 2023.

[150] See *The World Over* with Raymond Arroyo, November 16, 2023: "Bishop Strickland Speaks and the Strickland Dismissal."

Unresolved Tensions in Papal-Episcopal Relations

This is the reason for which the Second Vatican Council in the Dogmatic Constitution *Dei Verbum* (no. 10) stated very accurately that the Magisterium is not above divine revelation:

> But the task of authentically interpreting the word of God, whether written or handed on, has been entrusted exclusively to the living teaching office of the Church, whose authority is exercised in the name of Jesus Christ. This teaching office is not above the word of God, but serves it, teaching only what has been handed on, listening to it devoutly, guarding it scrupulously and explaining it faithfully in accord with a divine commission and with the help of the Holy Spirit, and it draws from this one deposit of faith everything which it presents for belief as divinely revealed.

This subjection of the magisterium to divine Revelation is analogous to the subjection of the supreme legislator to divine and natural law. The classic works of canon law presuppose this whole intelligible structure. Let's examine briefly the *Decretum Gratiani*.

In its Distinctio Prima, C. 1 the *Decretum* states that there are divine and natural laws that in Latin are denominated *fas*; and there are human laws that in Latin are denominated *mores* established according to *ius*. In C. 2 it is stated that *ius* is what is just. Notice well: not whatever the whim of a tyrant desires, but what is just. In C. 5 the law is understood as something recommended by reason. It must be coherent with religion, expedient to discipline, and fruitful for salvation. In C. 7–9 Gratian introduces natural law, civil law, and the law of peoples.

In Distinctio Quarta, C. 2, following authorities, Gratian declares that the law must be just, honest, possible, according to nature, according to customs, fit for the circumstances, needed, expedient, well known, clear, not directed to private interest but to the common good.

In the Second Part of the *Decretum*, Causa XXIV, Quaestio 2, C. 4, we find a very interesting passage. It is asked whether the pope can absolve a person who is dead based on Christ's assertion, "whatsoever you bind on earth," etc. The reply is clear: *"de eo, qui in diuino iudicio est constitutus, nobis fas non est aliud decernere preter id, in quo eum dies supremus inuenit."* That is to say, the pope does not have power to change what has been established by divine decree. In Causa XXV, Quaestio 1, C. 4 it is stated that it is not licit for anybody to contradict laws divinely established and that the higher the position of the person who does contradict the laws the graver the sin of contradicting them would be.

Pope Francis Has No Right to Dismiss Bishop Strickland Without Cause

The same was declared by John Paul II in *Ordinatio Sacerdotalis*: "I declare that the Church has no authority whatsoever to confer priestly ordination on women."

We can now apply these principles to the case of Bishop Strickland. It is true that the constant tradition, also in canon law, declares that the Apostolic See has the power to judge all other bishops. And we must confirm this universal power of jurisdiction. But it is a power of *jurisdiction*, not of issuing arbitrary and tyrannical orders. *"Ius"* is "what is just," and *"jurisdictio"* is "the saying of what is just."

Since the authority of the bishops does not come from the pope, but from Christ, and since that authority may not and cannot be justly removed except when there is just cause, the pope has no power to "dismiss" a bishop as if the bishop were his house servant. This decision, the dismissal of Bishop Strickland, should have been contested (and perhaps still could be contested). The case for this contestation rests not merely on the concrete canons of the Code that were violated (although they are obviously relevant, because canon law teaches that they oblige the pope as well: "when laws have been established, there is no freedom to subject them to judgment, but it is necessary to judge in accordance with them"),[151] but more fundamentally on the divine Constitution of the Church. This is especially apt now that it has become clear that the reason for the "dismissal" was Bishop Strickland's opposition to the heretical agenda of the pope and his allies, including the minions of no less than Theodore McCarrick.

The most basic principle we must keep in mind is that the Church is the monarchy of the vicar of Christ the King on earth, not the tyranny of the vicar of Satan the Tyrant. Therefore, the actions of the pope, under pain of nullity, must be subject to divine and natural law and to the laws he himself or his predecessors have enacted.

---

[151] Gratian, Distinctio IV, C. 2.

10

Bishop Strickland's Removal Was Against Canon Law

Gerald E. Murray

The Holy See Press Office's *Summary of Bulletin* on November 11 contained this announcement under the heading "Resignations and Appointments": "The Holy Father has removed Bishop Joseph E. Strickland from the pastoral care of the diocese of Tyler, United States of America, and has appointed Bishop Joe Vásquez of Austin as apostolic administrator of the same diocese, rendering it *sede vacante*." The placement of this announcement under this incorrect heading—the removal of a bishop is not a resignation—is noteworthy.

The same incorrect heading was used in the March 9, 2022 announcement of the removal of Bishop Daniel Fernández Torres from the pastoral care of the Diocese of Arecibo, Puerto Rico. The Press Office is obviously not accustomed to categorizing announcements concerning the removal of a bishop, which is a rare, but not unknown, act. Privation from office is provided for in the *Code of Canon Law*. It is the result of a judicial process, or of an administrative procedure initiated to examine and render judgment upon a well-founded suspicion that a canonical crime was committed by a particular bishop. In the cases of both Bishop Strickland and Bishop Fernández Torres neither of these two possible canonical proceedings was used by the Holy See.

Canon 416 states that the "episcopal see becomes vacant . . . by deprivation notified to the bishop." Canon 196 states that "deprivation of office, that is, as a punishment for an offence, may be effected only in accordance with the law. Deprivation takes effect in accordance with the provisions of the canons concerning penal law." The commentary in the *Code of Canon Law Annotated, Fourth Edition* states that "deprivation is the loss of an ecclesiastical office as a penalty for an offence; it is judicially or administratively imposed on the completion of a penal process or a penal administrative procedure (cf. can. 1336, §4, 1°). Therefore, privation is a special type of removal; its efficacy and limits are subject to penal law."

There was no judicial penal process or administrative procedure in the cases of Bishops Fernández Torres and Strickland. An apostolic visitation, which was done in

First published at *Daily Compass*, November 22, 2023.

both cases, does not qualify as either a judicial process or an administrative procedure. Thus, their removal was by means of an act of the pope apart from existing canonical procedures. Canon 331 states that the pope "by virtue of his office . . . has full, immediate and universal ordinary power in the Church, and he can always exercise this power." The pope is free to dispense himself from the binding provisions of merely ecclesiastical laws (can. 11) if he so chooses. Canon 12 states that "universal laws are binding everywhere on all those for whom they were enacted."

The pope is bound to observe the law of the Church unless for a "just and reasonable cause" (can. 90) he decides to dispense himself "in a particular case" from its provisions (can. 85). He is to issue a decree. If he dispenses himself either from the obligation to issue a written decree as required by canons 48 and 51, or from the obligation "as far as possible . . . to consult those whose rights could be harmed" (can. 50), that act of dispensation itself should be done by a written decree. The decree "should express, at least in summary form, the reasons for the decision" (can. 51). If he dispenses himself from expressing the reasons for his dispensation, that also should be by means of a written decree. None of this happened in the case of these two deposed bishops.

An earlier case of the removal of a diocesan bishop by Pope Francis was that of the late Bishop Rogelio Ricardo Livieres Plano of Ciudad del Este, Paraguay. A Holy See Press Office *Note* in the daily *Bulletin* (Italian) of September 25, 2014 called this deprivation of office an *"avvicendamento,"* which is translated as a rotation or succession or change.

The 2014 *Note* stated that the removal was an "arduous decision of the Holy See, determined by serious pastoral reasons . . . called for by the greater good of the unity of the Church in Ciudad del Este and the communion of the bishops in Paraguay." In this case, a judgement was made that Bishop Livieres Plano was guilty of offending the unity of his diocese and the communion of the bishops of Paraguay. No specific incidents of these alleged offenses are cited in the *Note*.

Why is the failure to follow canonical provisions a matter of concern? St. John Paul II, in the Apostolic Constitution *Sacrae Disciplinae Leges* promulgating the 1983 *Code of Canon Law*, described the nature and importance of the *Code* as follows: "The Code rather looks towards the achievement of order in the ecclesial society, such that while attributing a primacy to love, grace and the charisms, it facilitates at the same time an orderly development in the life of the ecclesial society and of the individual persons who belong to it." He further stated that "because it is based on the juridical and legislative heritage of revelation and tradition, the Code must be regarded as the essential instrument for the preservation of right order, both in individual and

Unresolved Tensions in Papal-Episcopal Relations

social life and in the Church's zeal." The emphasis is upon right order in the Church. A promulgated set of laws establishes the conditions for equitable and just relations among the faithful who all share a common obligation to cooperate with one another in obeying clearly spelled out rules of conduct that promote and safeguard the nature and mission of the Church.

St. John Paul went on to state that "a Code of Canon Law is absolutely necessary for the Church . . . It needs rules, so that its hierarchical and organic structure may be visible . . . that the mutual relationships of Christ's faithful are reconciled in justice based on charity, with the rights of each safeguarded and defined . . . " He also noted that "canonical laws by their very nature demand observance. For this reason, the greatest care has been taken that during the long preparation of the Code there should be an accurate expression of the norms and that they should depend upon a sound juridical, canonical and theological foundation."

Bishop Strickland has related that he was told by the Apostolic Nuncio, Cardinal Christophe Pierre, in Washington on November 9 that he was being asked to resign for various reasons, including that he lacked fraternity with his fellow American bishops, that he failed to implement *Traditionis Custodes*, and that there were problems with his social media presence and his criticisms of the Synod on Synodality. Strickland said that the nuncio did not mention any administrative problems in his diocese. Strickland declined to resign. None of these reasons for his removal, communicated to him in a private conversation, was stated in a papal decree of removal. In fact, no papal decree has been published.

From what we can judge from the evidence so far available in the public realm, Bishop Strickland was accused not of canonical crimes, but rather of public disagreements, at times in offensive terms, with various statements and decisions of Pope Francis, and of acting differently from his fellow American bishops. No canonical crimes were alleged, and no judicial process or administrative procedure was commenced. Consequently, the due process rights of the bishop to be given the opportunity to know and to answer any formal charges brought against him in a process regulated by law were not respected. He was not given access to the evidence that had been gathered to support the claim of wrongdoing, and thus had no opportunity for rebuttal or for the submission of further evidence in his favor.

The setting aside of the canonical procedural guarantees found in the *Code* to protect the right of a bishop to a fair process when his hierarchical superior, the pope, suspects wrongdoing goes against natural justice and ignores the teaching and the spirit of both the Second Vatican Council and the 1983 *Code*.

11

Was Bishop Strickland's Termination Invalid?

Carlos Esteban

Bishop Joseph Strickland was dismissed from his see of Tyler, Texas, by a Vatican mandate that contained no explanation, and it is not the first case of its kind in this pontificate. *La Nuova Bussola Quotidiana* argues that, with the Code of Canon Law in hand, such removals would be invalid.[152]

Throughout his pontificate, Francis has "removed" four diocesan bishops: the late Rogelio Ricardo Livieres Plano, in 2014, Martin David Holley, in 2018, Daniel Fernández Torres, in 2022 and, recently, Joseph Edward Strickland. But does the pope have the power to depose his brothers in the episcopate—to whom by a divine disposition a particular Church has been entrusted—without a legal procedure?

The episcopate is an institution of divine right, and canon law establishes eighteen immutable juridical facts of divine institution that exceed the will of the human legislator—among them the individual ecclesiastical offices (can. 145 §1), the bishops as successors of the Apostles (can. 375 §1), the fact that those who are constituted in the sacred orders of the episcopate or presbyterate receive the mission and the power to act in the person of Christ the Head (can. 1009 §3). No one, not even the pope, has the power to change what is established by divine disposition.

According to can. 183 §1 of the 1917 Code, ecclesiastical service is lost by resignation, deprivation, removal, transfer, and with the expiration of the pre-established time. The 1983 Code added a sixth reason: reaching a certain age defined by law. The common denominator of all these cases is the loss (*amissio*) of ecclesiastical office.

Canon 416 enumerates and exhaustively determines the definitive list (*numerus clausus*) of the four exclusive cases in which the episcopal see becomes vacant: (1) with the death of the diocesan bishop; (2) with resignation accepted by the Roman Pontiff; (3) with transfer; (4) with deprivation, communicated to the bishop.

First published in Spanish at *InfoVaticana*, January 29, 2024; translation by the editor.

[152] See the preceding chapter.

Unresolved Tensions in Papal-Episcopal Relations

In the daily bulletin of the Press Office of the Holy See, in relation to the dismissal of the above-mentioned bishops, it can be noted that there is *no reference to any canon*; that the pope has decided that the "pastoral management of the diocese," that is, the service of the local ordinary, should cease for these bishops; that no canonical process (penal, contentious, or administrative) is notified; that the pope has temporarily appointed apostolic administrators at the head of the mentioned dioceses; that he speaks of *sede vacante* (in three out of four cases), *ad nutum Sanctae Sedis* (in two cases out of four), *sede vacante et ad nutum Sanctae Sedis* (once out of four).

From the canonical point of view, the most relevant aspect of these communications is that the episcopal see, in these dioceses, has become vacant; in fact, an apostolic administrator has been appointed for as long as the chair remains vacant (*sede vacante*).

There is a canonical difference between removal (*amotio*) and deprivation (*privatio*). The former occurs for disciplinary or pastoral reasons, for the common good, often without malice or guilt on the part of the incumbent, while deprivation always has a penal meaning, it is always a kind of punishment for a crime or transgression of the office holder.

Canon Law establishes that one cannot be "separated from the conferred office for an indefinite time, except for grave reasons and respecting the procedure provided by law," and that "the decree of expulsion, in order to take effect, must be communicated in writing."

Since the official communications make no reference to any canon, employ terms foreign to canon law, not even consistent with each other, and the decisions themselves have not been published, it is not absurd to conclude that the office of these bishops, according to canon law, has not ceased at all, also because the Code does not provide that mere removal (*amotio*) is the way in which the episcopal chair can become vacant, for it must be by deprivation (if it is not by death, resignation accepted by the pope, or transfer).

If deprivation is involved, it must be communicated to the bishop and requires a canonical penal procedure. But the various deposed bishops claimed that no procedure was carried out and that they were not even informed of the reasons for the removal.

Moreover, deprivation of episcopal office could only be the consequence of a *numerus clausus* of specific crimes, such as apostasy, heresy, schism, blasphemy, participation in abortions, physical aggression against the pope, arbitrary consecration of bishops, attempt to confer Holy Orders on a woman, or violation of confessional secrecy. Francis has expanded the list of these offenses particularly in relation to cases of sexual abuse committed against minors and vulnerable adults, but there is no trace anywhere of a "speech offense."

Was Bishop Strickland's Termination Invalid?

And even in these cases, loss of office under canon law can occur only after a clearly prescribed canonical procedure has been carried out, guilt has been established, and the penalty pronounced in writing—all aspects that did not occur in the cases of the four "relieved" bishops.

Therefore, according to canon law, these four bishops have in fact suffered neither a dismissal nor a deprivation. How then can it be said that their office has ceased and that their episcopal see is vacant?

12

The Pope May Not Depose Bishops Without Grave Cause

Antonio Francés

Father Gerald Murray has excellently analyzed the canonical side of Bishop Strickland's removal.[153] He has demonstrated that the guarantee of due process has been violated. Canon 196 and other related canons were masterfully explained. I myself published a different article that I wrote *before* having read Father Murray's analysis.[154] I saw the issue from a different angle. But I find that now it is expedient to combine the two perspectives.

The first point that I think must be highlighted is that canon 196, concerned with "privation from office," is within a chapter of the Code concerning "Provision of ecclesiastical offices" in general. In addition to canon 196, one can read in the same chapter canons 192 and 193 concerning "removal" from office. According to canon 193, "A person *cannot* be removed from an office conferred for an indefinite period of time except for grave causes and according to the manner of proceeding defined by law." When applying these canons to a bishop of a particular Church one must have in mind the particularities of the office.

A bishop of a particular church, according to the very Code of Canon Law, "by divine institution succeed[s] to the place of the Apostles through the Holy Spirit who has been given to [him]" (can. 375 §1). Moreover, bishops receive the function of sanctifying, teaching, and governing "through episcopal consecration itself" (can. 375 §2). This means that, although according to current canon (human) law, the bishops of the Latin Church are appointed by the pope, their authority derives from divine institution and is received directly from God, not from the pope.

This fact is clear in the Gospel and in the documents of the Second Vatican Council, as we will briefly examine. But an important point that Father Murray has noted but not explored in depth is that "this new Code could be understood as a great effort to

First published at *OnePeterFive*, November 28, 2023.
[153] See chapter 10.
[154] See chapter 9.

translate... the conciliar ecclesiology into canonical language."[155] This obviously means that the Code must be understood and explained in the light of the documents of the Second Vatican Council.

Moreover, the Code must reflect "the distant patrimony of law contained in the books of the Old and New Testament from which is derived, as from its first source, the whole juridical-legislative tradition of the Church" (ibid.):

> Christ the Lord, indeed, did not in the least wish to destroy the very rich heritage of the Law and of the Prophets which was gradually formed from the history and experience of the People of God in the Old Testament, but He brought it to completion (cf. Mt 5:17), in such wise that in a new and higher way it became part of the heritage of the New Testament. Therefore, although St. Paul, in expounding the Paschal Mystery, teaches that justification is not obtained by the works of the Law, but by means of faith (cf. Rom 3:28; Gal 2:16), he does not thereby exclude the binding force of the Decalogue (cf. Rom 13:28; Gal 5:13–25; 6:2), nor does he deny the importance of discipline in the Church of God (cf. 1 Cor 5–6).

For this reason,

> besides containing the fundamental elements of the hierarchical and organic structure of the Church as willed by her divine Founder, or as based upon apostolic, or in any case most ancient, tradition, and besides the fundamental principles which govern the exercise of the threefold office entrusted to the Church itself, the Code must also lay down certain rules and norms of behavior.

Thus, we must examine what Revelation tells us concerning the authority of the bishops, and what the Second Vatican Council has taught us concerning the content of Revelation on this very point, in order to judge the removal of a bishop.

The Gospel teaches us that Christ gave to all the Apostles the right to judge: "whatever you bind on earth will be bound in heaven, and whatever you loose on earth will be loosed in heaven" (Mt 18:18). Simon received this power first and above all, but as Scripture shows, the other Apostles received it as well. Moreover, when the dispute at Antioch took place, in the Council of Jerusalem, Peter and James spoke almost as equals because, although Peter has power over the whole Church,

---

[155] John Paul II, Apostolic Constitution *Sacrae Disciplinae Leges*.

Unresolved Tensions in Papal-Episcopal Relations

James was then the bishop in Jerusalem (see Acts 15:6–21). Again, in Corinth the jurisdiction of Peter and Paul seems to have overlapped, perhaps because Corinth was a Roman colony (1 Cor 1:12).

The Apostolic Canons contain a similar teaching: the local bishop has his own authority distinct from that of the Metropolitan, although in important matters he needs the approval of the Metropolitan.

According to both Scripture and Tradition, then, and according to the Second Vatican Council, the bishop has a native jurisdiction that cannot be taken away by the pope, except in a case where the bishop has committed a grave crime and must be punished by the universal visible head of the Church, as Father Murray indicates. The difference with other ecclesiastical offices is that by the very nature of the bishop's office he *cannot* be removed unjustly because he is free to use his native jurisdictional power to oppose an arbitrary and openly tyrannical act of the pope. No other ecclesiastical office enjoys this native power of divine institution besides the pope. In that way it would be better to see the pope as a special case of what is true of all bishops than to see the pope as radically other than they, and thus, to empty bishops of their Christ-conferred apostolic authority, which the canons of the Church acknowledge and must respect by natural and divine law.

The Second Vatican Council sheds further light on this issue in its Dogmatic Constitution *Lumen Gentium*:

> Bishops, as vicars and ambassadors of Christ, govern the particular churches entrusted to them by their counsel, exhortations, example, and even by their authority and sacred power, which indeed they use only for the edification of their flock in truth and holiness, remembering that he who is greater should become as the lesser and he who is the chief become as the servant. This power, which they personally exercise in Christ's name, is proper, ordinary and immediate, although its exercise is ultimately regulated by the supreme authority of the Church, and can be circumscribed by certain limits, for the advantage of the Church or of the faithful. In virtue of this power, bishops have the sacred right and the duty before the Lord to make laws for their subjects, to pass judgment on them and to moderate everything pertaining to the ordering of worship and the apostolate.
>
> The pastoral office or the habitual and daily care of their sheep is entrusted to them completely; nor are they to be regarded as vicars of the Roman Pontiffs, for they exercise an authority that is proper to them, and are

The Pope May Not Depose Bishops Without Grave Cause

quite correctly called "prelates," heads of the people whom they govern. *Their power, therefore, is not destroyed by the supreme and universal power, but on the contrary it is affirmed, strengthened and vindicated by it,* since the Holy Spirit unfailingly preserves the form of government established by Christ the Lord in His Church.[156]

This long citation is necessary in order to make it clear that, whatever else may be the case, the Code of Canon Law may not be interpreted in a way that changes the divine constitution of the Church. *A fortiori,* the pope, even if in some sense he is above canon law as the one who promulgates it, has no right to act against the principles of natural and divine law that the Code embodies and particularizes. When he acts against the provisions set forth in the Code, he demonstrates his unwillingness to be bound by the deeper and immutable law that canon law exists to serve. He demonstrates, in short, contempt for rights and duties, which is the definition of an unjust ruler or, in the ancient title, a tyrant.

For all these reasons, the universal power of jurisdiction possessed by the pope cannot annul and destroy the native power of the local bishop, as would be the case if the pope could whimsically remove any bishop without due process, stated grave cause, and the opportunity for defense, as Francis has now done with many successors of the Apostles. It is tragic that these men have not exercised their God-given rights and duties by resisting the false and injurious exercise of the primacy of Peter.

The time has come when bishops have to withstand the current arbitrary use of power by the Roman See, because this resistance is required by the need to preserve divine Revelation, as the case of Bishop Strickland has made exceedingly clear. This means that no bishop should comply with a "dismissal" that is not the result of a canonical procedure in which a grave crime committed by the bishop himself (not any of his inferiors) has been fully proved. And "grave crime" is not a concept that the pope can manipulate *ad libitum*: it must be connected with the fundamental tenets of the revealed divine Laws (of the Old and New Testaments) and/or with the keeping of divine Revelation and the office of sanctification.

Jesus Christ Himself is calling the faithful bishops to be brave and to withstand this most subtle attack against the divine constitution of the Church. What is at stake here is not just the "guarantee of due process." This attack is directed against the structure that the Lord Himself established. It is an attack that is perhaps fulfilling the prophecy transmitted in a prayer by Leo XIII:

---

[156] *Lumen Gentium*, no. 27, emphasis added.

Unresolved Tensions in Papal-Episcopal Relations

Most cunning enemies have filled with bitterness and drenched with gall the Church, the Spouse of the Lamb without spot, and have lifted impious hands against all that is most sacred in it. Even in the holy place where the See of Blessed Peter and the chair of truth was set up to enlighten the world, they have raised the abominable throne of their impiety . . . [157]

---

[157] *The New Raccolta, or Collection of Prayers and Good Works to which the Sovereign Pontiffs Have Attached Holy Indulgences*, from the third Italian ed. (Philadelphia, PA: Peter F. Cunningham & Son, 1903), 365.

13

The Removal of Strickland: An Act of the Arrogance of Power

Stefano Fontana

The removal of Bishop Joseph Strickland from the Diocese of Tyler, Texas, is a highly symbolic act and certainly marks a turning point. Why do I speak of a highly symbolic act? Because Strickland had distinguished himself on many occasions, and consistently, in reiterating truths of Catholic faith and morality precisely concerning those matters in which changes are desired and implemented by Francis.

His were not generic interventions on the need to maintain tradition; generality bothers no one. Instead, they were very pointed stances on abortion, the admission of pro-abortion politicians to communion, the blessing of same-sex couples, gender, and the new synodality. All the points of the "Bergoglio agenda" were being challenged in the name of what the Church has always taught. If we think of Francis as the speaker at a conference, we must see Strickland as someone sitting in the lecture hall who continually raises his hand and intervenes to contradict the speaker. The act of removing the heckler is equivalent—in the example now given—to calling security and having him ejected from the conference room.

This punitive choice by Francis thus marks a new phase, as had happened with the appointment of Victor Manuel Fernández to the Dicastery for the Doctrine of the Faith. In that case, Francis had appointed the one least deserving of being named, or nameable only with an act of great bravado and contempt. With that appointment, the future agenda was already being mapped out, as we see punctually happening before us. The nomination was meant to make it definitively clear that there would be no "going back," and it also ruled out a certain political caution that Francis has exercised in other areas in which he has held back the achievement of outcomes that he had certainly planned but for which the time had not yet proved ripe.

We refer, for example, to the Synod on the Amazon, which, according to prior planning, should have approved far more innovations than those actually decided upon; the

First published at *La Nuova Bussola Quotidiana*, November 13, 2023; translation by the editor.

Unresolved Tensions in Papal-Episcopal Relations

same holds for the recent Synod on Synodality that was downgraded to a big gab-session among groups of friends. Fernández's appointment and the defenestration of Strickland, on the other hand, are the same sort of event: highly symbolic acts that look very much like a declaration of war in the Church. There is no going back; the schism is in place.

Speaking of schism: returning from his visit to Mozambique, Madagascar, and Mauritius on September 10, 2019, Francis had said he would pray for the unity of the Church—but *he would not be afraid of schism*. As for the American bishops, he declared that "criticism helps, and when one receives criticism, immediately one must be self-critical. I always see the benefits of criticism . . . I like it when one has the honesty to say it. I don't like it when criticism is done under the table, maybe smiling at you with all their teeth and then stabbing you in the back. Criticism is a building block and can start a dialogue. Instead, arsenic-pill criticism is like throwing a stone and hiding your hand." Certainly Strickland had the honesty to "say the criticisms," but he was struck down anyway, and the act undoubtedly helps accelerate the schismatic process. But who is pushing for this outcome—Strickland or Francis?

One could say that the suspension of a bishop is a disciplinary act, while the Church is held together by faith and thus by doctrine as the revealed truth we believe. But Francis has now accustomed us—and *Compass* has been talking about this for a long time—to the implementation of changes by way of *praxis*, as this latest case exemplifies. Those waiting for formal revolutionary statements will wait in vain. At most, we can read ambiguous and deliberately bungled statements, as in the case of the recent responses of the Dicastery for the Doctrine of Faith. This confirms that the removal of Strickland is an act of ecclesiastical politics, an act of the arrogance of power, the exercise of a political "sovereignty" that asserts itself not by statements or documents but by acting in accord with its agenda. By now, these Leviathanic acts are coming out more and more into the open—a sign that there is a desire to speed things up, that changes must be implemented quickly and enemies eliminated without taking prisoners.

After the "Strickland affair," which was followed in short order by the "Fernández affair," one must ask what attitude to adopt in the face of this new phase, characterized by the acceleration of forcibly imposed innovation. Until now, those who disagreed with the trends and processes opened up and led by Francis managed to get away with distinguishing carefully between the things he said and did and the things he expressed in official documents. Except that even in the latter, there are several highly objectionable aspects: think of the Exhortation *Amoris Laetitia*, where the aforementioned distinction ended up hiding behind the phrase, "But this is not magisterium anyway." The removal of a bishop? "But this is not magisterium anyway."

The Removal of Strickland: An Act of the Arrogance of Power

Hence, we have seen a kind of abstention and silence by many commentators until serious doctrinal novelties were expressed not only by deeds but also in official documents. After the appointment of Fernández and after the dismissal of Strickland, such a hesitant position is no longer sufficient (even assuming it was before). The wait-and-see opposition must come out of the woodwork. We will see how many bishops, besides Schneider who has already intervened, and how many lay people, will do so. Conscientious objection must be exercised not only tacitly but actively.

14

May a Pope Fire a Bishop?
What Is Bishop Strickland to Do?

BRIAN M. MCCALL

November of 2023 witnessed the disturbing news that after attempting to obtain Bishop Joseph Strickland's resignation as bishop of Tyler, Texas, Pope Francis removed the bishop from the See and declared it vacant.[158]

This is not the first time Francis has removed a bishop after a refusal to resign. In March of 2022, Francis removed Bishop Daniel Fernández Torres of Arecibo, Puerto Rico. What were the serious crimes and malfeasances of these Successors of the Apostles that merited removal? Financial corruption? Sexual abuse? Heresy? In fact, neither bishop has been convicted nor even accused of any crime, ecclesiastical or secular. Bishop Fernández Torres made this statement about his firing: "I feel blessed to suffer persecution and slander for proclaiming the truth."[159] The *National Catholic Reporter* described the reason for his removal thus:

> Bishop Fernández has long defended the traditional family and, publicly distancing himself from the position of the president of the Puerto Rican bishops' conference, opposed a bill that would have banned "conversion therapy" for homosexuals. But he has been best known recently for his support of people who conscientiously objected to the COVID-19 vaccine, although the Puerto Rican government required many people in health care and the public sector to be vaccinated.[160]

Likewise, Bishop Strickland characterized the reasons for his removal as being his adherence to the truth:

> I really can't look to any reason except I've threatened some of the powers that be with the truth of the Gospel. . . . The only answer I have to that is because

---

First published in *Catholic Family News*, January 2024, pp. 1, 18–19.
[158] See "Bishop Strickland relieved of pastoral governance of US diocese," *Vatican News*, November 11, 2023.
[159] See "Pope removes Puerto Rican bishop from office," *National Catholic Reporter*, March 9, 2022.
[160] Ibid.

May a Pope Fire a Bishop? What Is Bishop Strickland to Do?

forces in the Church right now don't want the truth of the Gospel. They want it changed. They want it ignored.[161]

To either bishop's claims that he was removed for speaking the truth, the Vatican has not responded by pointing to any evidence of another reason. These extraordinary acts of removing bishops for no sound reason beg the obvious question: "May a pope just 'fire' a bishop for simply speaking the truth?"

Can vs. may

The difficulty for us in answering this question is that we labor under the influence of centuries of Liberalism. Although we may not be liberals ourselves, consciously adhering to its erroneous ideas, we live in an entirely liberal world, and our minds cannot help but be infected in some way by it. Even Archbishop Lefebvre (in the early twentieth century) was surprised to realize upon arrival at the French Seminary in Rome that he had absorbed some liberal ideas.[162]

Liberalism, and a form of political liberalism known as Legal Positivism, fundamentally confuses the concepts of "can" and "may." The distinction can be grasped by considering a hypothetical conversation that a mother rooted in true Catholic principles would have with her child to teach the distinction. "Mother, can I eat a cookie?" "Yes, son, you *can* eat a cookie, but you *may* not because we are about to eat dinner." The verb "can" indicates a physical ability, a potentiality for action. The verb "may" indicates a legal and/or moral permission to turn a potentiality into action. For Liberals, there is no distinction between, to use Leo XIII's terms, "physical liberty" and "moral liberty."[163] Physical liberty refers to a potentiality or capacity for actions which one is physically capable of performing. Moral liberty refers to actions that one is free to perform under the natural and divine law and their instantiation in legitimate positive law. Thus, one is physically free to murder the baby in one's body by taking poisons, but one is not morally free to do so. Yet, for Liberals, there is no distinction. One is free to do whatever one can.

Now, most liberals cannot live with the full implication of their philosophy—that would be anarchy. Thus, to varying degrees, they will admit that the State can place some restrictions on liberty, but they will see these as artificial constraints on liberty

---

[161] Steven Ertelt, "Catholic Bishop: Pope Francis Ousted Me Because I Spoke Truth to Power," *LifeNews*, November 13, 2023.

[162] Bernard Tissier de Mallerais, *Marcel Lefebvre: The Biography* (Kansas City, MO: Angelus Press, 2004), 35–37.

[163] Leo XIII, Encyclical *Libertas Praestantissimum*.

imposed when necessary. The most common restraint they use is the harm principle. The State can restrain a person's use of liberty to the extent that it prevents another person from exercising *his* liberty. Yet, even those liberals who admit that constraint find it less than ideal. Their mythical "state of nature" has no constraints on physical liberty. People mythically agreed to surrender some of their liberty when they formed the equally fictitious social contract to protect their remaining liberties from interference. The starting premise of Liberalism is, therefore, if I can do something, then I *may* do it. There is no law above physical liberty and the social contract to prevent me from doing what I can. For Catholics, the starting point is different: if there is something I *can* do, I must determine if I *may* do it before acting.

The implications of this error of Liberalism are manifold since it has spread throughout society. I can mutilate my body as created by God; therefore, I should be allowed to do so if I want to, since mutilating my own body does not stop others from exercising their own liberty. Any questions of "may this be done" are dismissed as irrelevant to the desires of the person who wants to do what he can. Power to act means permission to act.

Tyrannical authority

Liberalism is the most amiable philosophy to tyranny. Even before examining this claim philosophically, modern history proves it. The world has seen more tyrannical governments since the advent of Liberalism: the French Revolutionary Directorate, Napoleon, the National Socialists, Russian Communism, Chinese Communism, Latin American dictators, etc. The reason this is true is the same as the may/can error on the individual level. If a ruler has the power to act, then the ruler may so act. This is the jurisprudence of Legal Positivism: whatever the sovereign commands must be obeyed.

The *Stanford Encyclopedia of Philosophy* explains that the main insight of legal positivism is that "the conditions of legal validity are determined by social facts," and therefore, "the basic source of legal validity resides in the facts constituting political sovereignty."[164] For them, law is "basically the command of the sovereign."[165] Positivism rejects the existence and legally binding nature of eternal, divine, and natural law. The human lawmaker—be it a dictator, king, congress, or the Party—is unconstrained by any law higher than human law. They may enact any laws they have the political power to enact. Citizens may protest and object to laws that seem unfair, but the laws are binding regardless, and punishments meted out for civil disobedience of such laws are legally

---

[164] Andrei Marmor and Alexander Sarch, "The Nature of Law," *The Stanford Encyclopedia of Philosophy* (Fall 2019 edition), ed. Edward N. Zalta, https://plato.stanford.edu/archives/fall2019/entries/lawphil-nature/.
[165] Ibid.

justified. If citizens do not like the laws, they can try to seize political power themselves. If they succeed, then they can change the laws as they wish.

Constrained human authority

In contrast to Legal Positivism's unconstrained human authority, the perennial Catholic philosophy has always held that no human governor wields unlimited power. First, we can compare St. Thomas Aquinas's definition of law, which is much more complex than "the command of the sovereign." Law is "an ordinance of reason for the common good, made by him who has care of the community, and promulgated." Notice that in addition to being an act of the will (promulgated) by one vested with authority (with care of the community), to be a law, the command must be (1) an ordinance of reason and (2) for the common good.[166]

The first requirement indicates that legal acts must be judged by their substance, not merely their procedure. For Positivists, the only relevant question is, "Did the actual sovereign issue this command?" If the answer is yes, it is a law. For St. Thomas, we must inquire beyond this question to ask if the promulgated command comports with reason as expressed in natural and divine law, which are rooted in God's eternal law or eternal reason. Human lawmakers are only permitted to make reasonable determinations (more specific precepts) of laws made by God, both natural and divine. In addition to being reasonable, all human laws must be oriented to a purpose, the common good. The nature of that common good will depend on the nature of the community for which the law is made: a city, a nation, the Church. To be a law, a command must be for the applicable common good.

Unlike Positivists, St. Thomas makes clear that not all purported commands are laws. Simply because a lawmaker can command does not mean that he may. He explains:

> Laws framed by man are either just or unjust. If they be just, they have the power of binding in conscience, from the eternal law whence they are derived. . . . Now laws are said to be just, both from the end, when, to wit, they are ordained to the common good; and from their author, that is to say when the law that is made does not exceed the power of the lawgiver; and from their form, when, to wit, burdens are laid on the subjects, according to an equality of proportion and with a view to the common good . . . so that on this account, such laws as these . . . are just and binding in conscience, and are legal laws.[167]

---

[166] *Summa theologiae* I-II, Q. 90, art. 4.
[167] *Summa theologiae* I-II, Q. 96, art. 4.

Unresolved Tensions in Papal-Episcopal Relations

Not all "laws" are binding. Only *just* laws are binding. Laws are just if they are (1) within the scope of authority of the one issuing them, (2) derived from the eternal law, i.e., are an ordinance of reason, (3) oriented to the common good, and (4) proportioned fairly on subjects. Clearly, for Aquinas, what a superior can do is not equivalent to what he may do.

What to do about illegal laws

Although St. Thomas clearly states that unjust laws are "no law at all" but rather "acts of violence" that "do not bind in conscience," he offers nuanced advice on how we are to react to unjust laws.[168] Although objectively, these purported laws are only acts of violence and need not be obeyed, St. Thomas is very practical about how we should react. He considers our reaction a matter of prudence. We must discern if the unjust law requires that we act contrary "to the divine good."[169] If so, we are obligated in conscience to disobey and to refuse to conform to the law. He gives the example of a command to commit idolatry. Such an illegal law may never be obeyed.

In contrast, a certain law might not compel action contrary to the divine good but merely persecute unjustly a person who has committed no wrong. A core principle of the natural law is that evildoers should be punished; it is entrusted to human authorities to determine how evildoers should be punished in such and such a case, subject always to the punishment being just (reasonable and for the common good).[170] It is, under natural law, unjust to punish an innocent person. Human lawgivers are only permitted to determine the particular punishment of wrongdoers. To punish the innocent is the definition of persecution.

In a case where the unjust law does not require us to act contrary to the divine good but in which we are persecuted unjustly, we are not obligated in justice to obey the illegal law, but we must discern in prudence if we should resist or not. St. Thomas advises that we must endure the persecution "perhaps in order to avoid scandal or disturbance, for which cause a man should even yield his right."[171] Being a matter of prudence, the persecuted must weigh the effects of resistance against the consequences of "yielding his right" to refuse to obey. Such considerations include the likelihood and consequences to oneself of succeeding in resistance and the effects on others (especially those under our care) of complying or resisting.

---

[168] Ibid.
[169] Ibid.
[170] *Summa theologiae* I-II, Q. 95, art. 2.
[171] *Summa theologiae* I-II, Q. 96, art. 4.

May a Pope Fire a Bishop? What Is Bishop Strickland to Do?

But isn't the pope different?

Having established these principles, we can turn directly to the matter at hand. Do these principles of jurisprudence constrain the pope, or is he above them? In response to the removal of Bishop Strickland, some commentators have simply stated that the pope has supreme and universal jurisdiction and, therefore, can remove any bishop. Within the Church, the pope possesses the highest authority on earth, and there is no appeal from his judgments.

Nevertheless, that does not mean that the pope is unbound by the principles of law. The pope is not Christ; he is the *vicar* of Christ on earth. He exercises supreme authority, yet like all legal authority, his must be exercised in accordance with reason and for the common good (which, in the Church, is the salvation of souls). It is insufficient to state that the pope has the legal power to remove a bishop. That prompts the further question, *may* he do so in accordance with the requirements of natural and divine law and justice? Like Legal Positivists, those who blindly defend Pope Francis's ability to remove a bishop do so by arguing he is the pope and, therefore, can do it. If he can, he may. But as we have seen, possessing legitimate authority is only one criterion for assessing the legality of commands. Essentially, the ecclesiastical Legal Positivists argue that it is never permissible to refuse the pope because he is the pope and must always be obeyed. St. Thomas's principles indicate the contrary.

St. Robert Bellarmine explicitly stated that it was permissible to resist the pope, i.e., to refuse to obey unjust commands and to impede his will. The saint writes, "Just as it is licit to resist the Pontiff who attacks the body, so also is it licit to resist him who attacks souls or destroys the civil order or, above all, tries to destroy the Church. I say that it is licit to resist him by not doing what he orders and by impeding the execution of his will."[172] In accordance with St. Thomas, St. Robert is careful not to say, "must resist." He says "it is licit" to resist. Once again, we are faced with a matter of prudence. One persecuted by the pope may licitly refuse to do what he orders when it is not for the common good of the Church. By this statement, St. Robert makes clear that all the principles that govern our reaction to unjust laws also apply to the Supreme Pontiff.

Thus, we must conclude that although the pope *can* remove any bishop in the world from any diocese since his jurisdiction is universal, he *may not* remove any bishop when doing so is not an ordinance of reason and not for the common good or when it is inequitable. What does this distinction mean in practice? Clearly, the pope can remove any bishop who is complicit in crimes, although Francis has usually refused to

---

[172] *De Romano Pontifice*, Bk. II, ch. 29.

Unresolved Tensions in Papal-Episcopal Relations

do so. When all the Chilean bishops as a group offered to resign for their complicity in covering up sexual abuse, Francis refused to accept their resignation and left them all in office.[173] In addition, the pope may remove a bishop in order to reassign that bishop to another diocese to fill a pastoral need.

Yet even such administrative movements were viewed very skeptically before modern times. For most of Church history, the relationship between a bishop and his diocese was considered analogous to a marriage. In the absence of extraordinary circumstances, bishops were not supposed to be moved. Notwithstanding the errors of avaricious men, ideally the hierarchy was not considered to be like a corporate bureaucracy through which a bishop rises. Once appointed to their Sees, bishops were presumed to remain there until death, absent extraordinary need. They did not take a small diocese to prove their loyalty so as to merit a promotion. Although the pope could transfer bishops, it would only be done when the common good of the Church, the salvation of souls, required it. Transfer and removal were not considered legitimate if the pope merely wanted to persecute a bishop not guilty of any serious fault. In any event, Bishop Strickland is not being transferred for a pastoral need elsewhere. He has been fired, benched.

So what is Bishop Strickland to do?

In light of the foregoing, what should Bishop Joseph Strickland do in response to his summary firing from Tyler, Texas? Based on our evidence, there appears to be no justification for the removal. Bishop Strickland has not been found guilty of any canonical or civil crime, nor has he even been accused of one. His diocese is in sound financial shape relative to the rest of the country. He has a large crop of seminarians by postconciliar standards (low as they are). According to Bishop Strickland himself, he was removed solely for speaking the truth. In an interview with Raymond Arroyo, Bishop Strickland claimed that Francis's Apostolic Nuncio told him that the problem was he talked about the "Deposit of Faith" too much.[174] That is like saying that a priest is saying Mass too many days each week. How can a bishop, who is required by virtue of his episcopal ordination to preach the Deposit of Faith, talk "too much" about it? Bishop Strickland has exhibited the fortitude, virtually alone among bishops, to do what St. Robert Bellarmine says is licit—impede the execution of Francis's will to remake the Catholic Church. Bishop Strickland has made clear that he believes Pope Francis has attempted to destroy the Church by certain of his acts of governance (*Traditionis Custodes*

---

[173] See, e.g., Junno Arocho Esteves, "All of Chile's bishops offer resignations after meeting pope on abuse," *National Catholic Reporter*, May 18, 2018.

[174] See *The World Over* with Raymond Arroyo, November 16, 2023: "Bishop Strickland Speaks."

May a Pope Fire a Bishop? What Is Bishop Strickland to Do?

and the Synod on Synodality, for example) and has therefore refused to execute Francis's will. The Vatican has not contradicted Strickland's claims regarding the reasons for his dismissal nor charged him with a canonical crime for this resistance. If Francis had just reasons for his removal, why would he not make them known, and thus settle the matter once and for all?

Thus far, it seems clear that Strickland has acted justly in claiming the right to resist Francis in actions that are harmful to the common good of the Church. It also seems clear that without further proof from the Vatican, his removal was unjust (not being an act of reason to punish wrongdoing, nor for the sake of the common good). Thus, Bishop Strickland is not obligated to recognize this command as a legal law, but rather, he should regard it as an act of violence.

Yet, should he act following the example of Archbishop Marcel Lefebvre or Bishop Antonio de Castro Mayer, each of whom refused to comply when "removed" by the pope? Lefebvre concluded that complying with the unjust command of Paul VI to close the seminary and abandon the seminarians was unjust and that he must not comply because there was nowhere for these seminarians to go to be formed as priests in the traditional faith. De Castro Mayer refused to leave his flock in Campos, Brazil as he knew they would be subjected to postconciliar modernism. Although scandal and disturbance did arise from their actions, they were careful to minimize that scandal by explaining clearly the reasons for their disobedience. In addition, they both had a reasonable likelihood of success in resisting. The vast majority of the seminary professors, seminarians, and benefactors remained with Lefebvre in his persecution. A large portion of the priests and thousands of faithful remained with Bishop de Castro Mayer in Campos.

The assessment of similar considerations lies within the purview of Bishop Strickland. He, more than I or any other outside commentator, is the one who must weigh these factors. He must make the prudential judgment, aided by an invocation of the Holy Ghost the Counselor, as to whether the danger to souls in his diocese and beyond is greater than the scandal and disturbance that would result from a refusal to leave the episcopal office. As shepherd of his diocese, he is most knowledgeable about whether the clergy and laity would support such resistance. The point is that in justice, Strickland is not required to *refuse* to acquiesce and to surrender the diocese. It is a matter of prudence about which he must decide. From the weeks that have followed, it appears that Bishop Strickland has concluded that although his removal is unjust, he will not resist in the manner of Lefebvre or de Castro Mayer. Just as it is inappropriate for those not in their position to judge their decision to resist, we should be equally careful not

Unresolved Tensions in Papal-Episcopal Relations

to judge Strickland for his endurance of the persecution without direct resistance to impede the appointment of a new bishop.

That does not mean that Bishop Strickland has no role to play as a Successor of the Apostles. One of the other confusions of the murky Vatican II theology on the nature of the bishop is the blurring of the distinction between the power of order and legal jurisdiction. One of the reasons that modernists could not understand the distinction Archbishop Lefebvre carefully drew in consecrating four bishops in 1988 is that the postconciliar understanding of episcopal consecration is that it confers both the fullness of sacramental orders (the ability to confirm as ordinary minister and the ability to ordain) as well as jurisdiction. Thus, from this postconciliar point of view, consecrating a bishop without papal mandate is in and of itself a claim to confer jurisdiction on a bishop. From this muddled perspective, modern churchmen cannot comprehend Lefebvre's claim that he consecrated so as to preserve the priesthood. He chose to consecrate four men so that there would be bishops with the sacramental ability to ordain when his imminent death arrived. He explicitly disclaimed giving them any jurisdiction over a portion of the Church.

This same confusion leads many to fear that Strickland can no longer act as a Successor of the Apostles. They are mistaken. He still possesses the fullness of orders and the ability and duty to preach the Gospel to all nations and to administer the sacraments. He has no jurisdiction over a particular church (as is the case with the bishops ordained by Lefebvre). He can, in this sense, continue to resist the unjust and illegal acts of Francis by talking about the Deposit of Faith "too much," denouncing errors, and administering the sacraments (in the traditional rites, we should insist). Perhaps this persecution is permitted by God to help His Excellency realize that he must move from privately celebrating the traditional Mass to publicly and exclusively embracing the Traditional Mass and Sacraments. As Tertullian told us, the blood of the martyrs is the seed of the Church. Perhaps the persecution of bishops like Strickland will be a seed of even more universal resistance to the errors of Vatican II and its aftermath. We can pray it may be so.

15

In What Sense Is the Pope Above Canon Law?

PHILLIP CAMPBELL

A common refrain from hyperpapalists when the pope disregards canon law by his actions is, "So what? He can do that. The pope is not bound by canon law."

It is, of course, true that the pope is not bound by any human law, including ecclesiastical law. This is due not only to the pope's status as the supreme juridical authority within the Church, but also to the pope's being himself a source of canon law. Since canon law is subject to the authority of the Supreme Pontiff, it is clear that he cannot be bound by it in any coercive sense.

Does this mean, however, that the pope can break canon law at will as a normal exercise of his authority? When the pope violates canon law, is this to be understood as a legitimate exercise of his juridical authority?

Cicognani's five powers of the pope vis-à-vis canon law

To answer this question, let us turn to the commentary of Amleto Cardinal Cicognani (1883–1973), Professor of Canon Law in the Pontifical Institute of Canon and Civil Law at St. Apollinare in Rome and one of the mid-twentieth-century's most noted canonical jurists. Cicognani's career began under St. Pius X and culminated in becoming Cardinal Secretary of State under John XXIII (1961–1969) and Dean of the College of Cardinals under Paul VI from 1972 until his death.

In 1934, Cicognani published an exhaustive commentary on the 1917 code, simply called *Canon Law*.[175] Cicognani addresses the pope's relation to canon law in his section on the sources of human ecclesiastical law, where he lists the Supreme Pontiff as one of four sources of such laws (the other three being purely Apostolic Law, the Apostolic See, and the Councils, both ecumenical and particular). He begins by summarizing the traditional formulation of the pope's jurisdiction over the Church and his exemption from all human restraint:

First published at *Unam Sanctam Catholicam* on November 23, 2023.

[175] I will be working from the second edition, translated by Joseph M. O'Hara and Francis Brennan (Philadelphia, PA: Dolphin Press, 1935).

Unresolved Tensions in Papal-Episcopal Relations

The Roman Pontiff is, by the will of Christ, the Vicar of Christ on earth, the foundation, the head of the entire Church, and is endowed with primacy of jurisdiction, which from the very institution of the Church was established and determined by the Divine Founder Himself as supreme and universal power to rule others....

The pope's plenary, absolute, and strictly monarchical jurisdiction, manifesting itself in the exercise of judicial, administrative, and especially legislative power, is restricted by no human authority. Accordingly, the pope's primacy of jurisdiction over the Church of Christ is not circumscribed by General Councils, by the College of Cardinals, by any group of bishops, nor, for stronger reason, by the faithful, or by civil rulers, or by any human power whatsoever.[176]

Well and good, but what does this imply *vis-à-vis* canon law? Cardinal Cicognani says that the pope's universal jurisdiction is exercised through five specific powers. This enumeration can be found on pages 72–73 of Cicognani's *Canon Law*. According to Cicognani, the pope's supreme jurisdiction over canon law gives him the authority:

1. To make new laws, both universal and particular

The pope's jurisdiction implies legislative power, which means the pope can make new laws, binding upon the universal Church or upon particular churches or institutes. "Hence," says Cicognani, "the fact that a pope enacts new laws, according to the circumstances and necessities of the times, should not be regarded as something strange." And hence we see popes regularly exercising this authority by making amendments to the Code of Canon Law.

Does the pope's legislative authority extend to the content of tradition? Yes and no. Cicognani of course exempts divine traditions (whether dominical or apostolic) from the purview of the pope's powers. Regarding other traditions, however, he says "purely apostolic and ecclesiastical traditions, since they form part of human law, may indeed be changed, but since they have some relation to divine law, they are not easily subject to change; in point of fact, they have always been held in great esteem."[177] He then cites St. Paul and St. John Chrysostom on the value of preserving tradition intact.[178]

Essentially, Cicognani says the pope is the supreme lawgiver in the Church and can alter law as he pleases, although he should do so with extreme reticence in the case of

---

[176] Cicognani, *Canon Law*, 71.
[177] Cicognani, 103.
[178] Specifically, 2 Thess 2:15, and *Hom. in 2 Thess*, IV, no. 2 (*PG* 42:488).

laws hallowed by tradition because "they have some relation to divine law." In other words, he rightfully recognizes that the separation between so-called "big T" and "small t" tradition is not as cut-and-dried as is popularly believed. Even "small t" traditions are interwoven with the larger branches of divine law and should not be recklessly changed.[179] For this reason, there is a strong institutional resistance to their alteration, and this resistance is fitting.

2. To interpret the laws, both ecclesiastical and divine

As the supreme juridical authority in the Church, the pope enjoys the prerogative of interpreting the sense and meaning of the Church's law, "for he is the Universal Doctor and Supreme Teacher." The pope may do this directly, or through the various dicasteries and official organs of the Holy See, such as the Roman Rota.

3. To safeguard laws and to enforce them

For the Church's canonical legislation to have integrity, its supreme lawgiver must insist on observance of the Church's laws, "for he must be their defender against attacks." In Western democracies where we have divided branches of government, we are not accustomed to thinking of the legislative authority as being tasked with enforcing and defending law, but such has always been the case in every monarchical system. In fact, one of the most frequent gripes against poor monarchs of the past (such as King John) was that they failed to defend the laws; royal coronation liturgies frequently included promises to defend the laws. Papal coronation oaths, too, contained promises to defend the Church's customary laws and usages.[180]

4. To abrogate, derogate, and change human ecclesiastical laws

While the first point pertains to the pope's ability to create new law, this point concerns his relation to preexisting laws. Cardinal Cicognani specifies that the pope is not bound to the prior legislation, "whether they be the laws of his predecessors (since 'an equal has no dominion over an equal') or the laws of ecumenical or particular Councils, or even those of the apostles." The pope can abolish previous legislation (indeed, almost all papal legislation contains explicit clauses repealing prior decrees); he can modify the procedural methods by which legislation is understood or enforced, and he can make alterations to the legislation of his predecessors.

---

[179] See my article "The Church as a Barnacle-Encrusted Ship," *Unam Sanctam Catholicam*, March 5, 2023.
[180] See chapter 1 above; Kwasniewski, "The Pope's Boundedness to Tradition," in *From Benedict's Peace to Francis's War*.

5. To grant dispensations, privileges, and indults

This flows from the third point concerning the pope's role as enforcer of ecclesiastical law. It is within his purview to issue relaxations of law to persons or entities in view of special circumstances. Here Cicognani quotes an interesting passage from Boniface VIII, that "the Roman Pontiff has all laws in the archives of his heart."[181]

The pope ought not to violate canon law

Thus are the five powers of the pope which flow from his status as the Church's supreme lawgiver. The discerning reader will note something conspicuously absent from Cicognani's list, however: the ability to *break* canon law. Cicognani ascribes to the pope the powers of creating laws, interpreting laws, altering laws, enforcing laws, abrogating laws, or dispensing from them, but not breaking them. This is because it would be ridiculous to assert that one of the prerogatives the pope enjoys as supreme lawgiver is the power to break the law. Rather, when we speak of the Supreme Pontiff as "above the law" or "not bound by the law," it simply means that the pope has the authority to change the law if he wishes. As St. Thomas Aquinas says, "the sovereign is above the law, in so far as, when it is expedient, he can change the law, and dispense from it according to time and place."[182] If the pope is unhappy with some aspect of canon law, he should amend the code; but *changing* the law is fundamentally different from *breaking* it.

From the perspective of simple logic, it is a contradiction to assert that the breaking of law is an exercise of judicial authority. It would be akin to saying that adultery is an exercise of marital fidelity, or embezzlement is an aspect of fiscal responsibility. Simply considered terminologically, the phrases "breaking the law" and "judicial authority" cannot be deduced from one another. This is not to say someone in judicial authority can't break the law; we see that all the time, just like people who pledge marital fidelity still commit adultery and people in positions of fiscal responsibility still embezzle. We may certainly say that people do things contradictory to the spirit and demands of their state; but we cannot say that law-breaking is *derived* from judicial authority, that it flows from juridical authority as a consequent. In other words, if the pope breaks canon law, we cannot appeal to his supreme juridical authority as the justification for his violation. He violates canon law *despite* his juridical authority, not by virtue of it.

Furthermore, to assert that one of the pope's powers is breaking the Church's law would undermine the integrity of canon law itself. If the pope can simply violate canon law whenever he wishes, we are justified in asking what is the point of having canon

---

[181] *in scrinio sui pectoris*; c. 1, "De Const."

[182] *Summa theologiae* I-II, Q. 96, art. 5, ad 3.

In What Sense Is the Pope Above Canon Law?

law at all? The rules would exist only until the rule-giver gets tired of them and sweeps them away by sheer force of will. The whole concept of law would become a charade, a façade of legitimacy erected to mask what is ultimately an exercise of raw, arbitrary power. We know that papal authority was never meant to be wielded arbitrarily,[183] but this is the reality we are left with if we grant that the pope is justified in violating canon law on a whim. The integrity of any law suffers when the lawgiver breaks his own laws.

Let us recall, as well, that one of Cicognani's five juridical prerogatives of the Supreme Pontiff is the obligation to defend and enforce law. If the pope does not uphold the law by his actions, he undermines not only the law but his own role as its defender and enforcer. This would result in a nonsensical situation where two different purported exercises of the pope's juridical power undermined each other (i.e., if the pope is obligated to uphold the law, then he undermines law by acting against it; but if the pope can act against law as he pleases, then he cannot effectively uphold it). In that case, in what sense could the pope's power be "plenary and absolute" if it could not even be exercised *in toto* without undermining its own legitimacy?

That the pope should obey canon law is a principle well enshrined in the Church's canonical tradition. We find this in the *Decretum* of Gratian. Gratian's *Decretum* was the supreme authority for legal opinions in the Church throughout the Middle Ages,[184] much of it surviving into the modern codes. It is the most authoritative canonical text in the Church other than the official codes promulgated by the pontiffs. In the *Decretum*, we find the maxim of Pope Gelasius that, "It befits no See more than the first to carry out an enactment of the universal Church."[185] The import of the passage is that the dignity befitting the Apostolic See demands that the pope and his church should be the *first* in obeying the laws of the universal Church, by way of modeling obedience to Christians everywhere and honoring the special dignity of the Roman See.

St. Thomas Aquinas says the same. In the *Summa theologiae* he presents the assertion that rulers are free from the law in the form of an objection: "The sovereign is exempt from the laws. But he that is exempt from the law is not bound thereby. Therefore all are not subject to law." In his response, Aquinas explains why this line of reasoning is deficient:

> The sovereign is said to be "exempt from the law," as to its coercive power; since, properly speaking, no man is coerced by himself, and law has no coercive power

---

[183] See my article "Strict Consistency with the Past," *Unam Sanctam Catholicam*, November 12, 2023.
[184] See "Twelve Notable Decretists of the Middle Ages," *Unam Sanctam Catholicam*, March 5, 2023.
[185] Causa 25, q. I, c. I.

save from the authority of the sovereign. Thus then is the sovereign said to be exempt from the law, because none is competent to pass sentence on him, if he acts against the law. . . . But as to the directive force of law, the sovereign is subject to the law by his own will, according to the statement that "whatever law a man makes for another, he should keep himself. And a wise authority [Dionysius Cato, *Dist. de Moribus*] says: 'Obey the law that thou makest thyself.'" Moreover the Lord reproaches those who "say and do not"; and who "bind heavy burdens and lay them on men's shoulders, but with a finger of their own they will not move them" (Mt 23:3–4). Hence, in the judgment of God, the sovereign is not exempt from the law, as to its directive force; but he should fulfil it by his own free-will and not by constraint. Again, the sovereign is above the law, in so far as, when it is expedient, he can change the law, and dispense from it according to time and place.[186]

In other words, while canon law cannot bind the pope in a *coercive* manner, he is not exempt from its *directive* force, that is, as a guiding principle dictating how the pope should act. He who does otherwise risks the reproach of Lord levelled against those who "say and do not" (cf. Mt 23:3–4).

The same principle is cited by the great Thomas Cajetan in his 1514 anti-conciliar tract *De comparatione auctoritatis papae et concilii* ("The Authority of Pope and Council Compared"). Cajetan appeals to the responsibility of the pope to obey the laws of the universal Church specifically as a response to the Conciliarist assertion that the pope's power is arbitrary and unchecked.[187] The rhetorical use of Cajetan's argument is important—the Conciliarists claimed that an Ecumenical Council must be above the pope, otherwise the pope's power is unchecked and he will have license to ruin the Church. Citing Gratian, Cajetan responds by noting that the pope's freedom from coercion does not mean the pope disregards law, for it is fitting that the Holy See be the first and most exemplary model of canonical observance.

Cajetan reinforces this argument in another work, the *Apologia*, in which he takes up the same theme against the Conciliarist Jacques Almain of Paris. Here again he says that the pope's superiority from the coercive power of ecclesiastical law does not mean he is free to discard it. Even if they don't bind the pope legislatively, they bind him on pain of mortal sin. Therefore, given his exalted station, it is especially fitting for the Roman Pontiff to observe the laws of the Church:

---

[186] *Summa theologiae* I-II, Q. 96, art. 5, ad 3. For further discussion of this text, see above, pp. 7–8.
[187] *De comparatione*, ch. 8.

In What Sense Is the Pope Above Canon Law?

It is obvious that it is improper [for a pope] to annul the decisions of a council, even a provincial one: how much more those of a general council, whose decrees bind even the pope in the forum of conscience no less than his own do. Therefore, according to the sacred canons, it behooves the Roman pontiff especially to observe the statutes of the fathers.[188]

These two works of Cajetan are excellent references for this discussion. I am not aware of an unabridged English online version of *De comparatione* or *Apologia*, but I recommend the text *Conciliarism and Papalism*,[189] which also contains the *responsa* of Cajetan's adversaries, Jacques Almain and John Mair.

When the pope violates canon law

Neither Cajetan nor Cicognani, nor any of the other authorities I am familiar with, suggests that a pope's acts in violation of canon law lack juridical force or become *ipso facto* invalid. In a coercive sense, the pope is bound only by divine law in his government of the Church, and hence his actions—even outside of canonical norms—still possess binding power so long as they do not contravene divine law. But we need not argue such acts are invalid to rebut the hyperpapalist claim, for the original statement we set out to examine is that the pope can legitimately contravene canon law when he wishes *by virtue of his supreme authority*. This is manifestly false. The sources suggest that when a pope violates canon law, it is not an exercise of his authority but an abuse of it. When a police officer brutalizes an innocent civilian, we would never say he was acting by virtue of his law-enforcement responsibilities, but in violation of them. Similarly, when a pope violates canon law, he is not acting by virtue of his supreme juridical authority, but in violation of it. He not only abuses his juridical authority, but undermines the integrity of canon law and degrades his own role as *defensor legis*. He fails to lead by example, brings the Holy See into disrepute, and (according to Aquinas) merits the reproach of Our Lord. The pope possesses all power necessary to revise canon law as he wishes; that he wields such a plentitude of power and would still choose to simply disregard the law makes it that much worse, like King David killing Uriah to take Bathsheba when he could have had any woman in Israel.

What is the proper response when the pope violates canon law? We should be gravely concerned. We should strongly but charitably remind any who would listen that

---

[188] *Apologia*, ch. 6.
[189] Thomas Cajetan, *Conciliarism and Papalism*, ed. J.H. Burns and Thomas Izbicki (Cambridge: Cambridge University Press, 1998).

Unresolved Tensions in Papal-Episcopal Relations

ecclesiastical law exists for a reason and that breaking the law is not one of the prerogatives of papal authority. It certainly is not an exercise of his supreme juridical authority, but an abuse thereof, which the faithful should not only *not* defend, but should pray to be delivered from, as one prays to be delivered from a tyrant.[190] And we should certainly not celebrate it, nor make apologies for it by arguing, "So what? The pope is not bound by canon law." The pope's exemption from the coercive power of canon law was never understood to mean that the pope can violate it at will, and those who argue otherwise are undermining the very foundations of ecclesiastical law by doing so.

---

[190] See my article "The Context of Cajetan's Comments on Praying for a Pope's Death," *Unam Sanctam Ecclesiam*, March 29, 2024.

16

May a Bishop in Extraordinary Circumstances Ordain Another Bishop Without Papal Consent?

Antonio Francés

That the Church of Christ is Apostolic and that among the Apostles the primacy belongs to Peter and to his successors is a truth clearly established in Scripture and Holy Tradition. Nevertheless, the understanding of the exact *content* of such primacy is something that has developed in history. It is when a special crisis arises that the Holy Spirit gives light to the Church so as to clearly distinguish what is true from what is false in this as in other matters.

Right now we are enduring one of the most dangerous crises in ecclesiastical history. Let us invoke the Holy Trinity so that we may be able to distinguish the right path from the wrong one.

(1) No one can claim to be Catholic if he is not in communion with all definitive prior magisterial teachings of the popes and the college of bishops, and with the canonical declarations of past councils. Our communion is such that it is based primarily on our union with Christ, the Head of the Church, and with the Apostles. Public Revelation ended with the death of the last Apostle. Afterward we grow in our understanding of what has been revealed. If anyone claims that he has a new truth not contained in the deposit of revealed truth that Jesus the Christ bequeathed to us, or a "development" that contradicts a truth already attained and clarified, that person and his doctrine must be rejected as heretical. We know that this is so even if the person in question were "an angel from heaven," as St. Paul says (Gal 1:8).

(2) When trying to reflect on the nature and limits of papal prerogatives, theologians point out that any society, including the Church, needs a leader in order to have unity. They add, however, that this sociological argument is not sufficient; "there must be a theological justification." And here they teach that the pope is a sign:

> If the general system of the People of God is that of a union of the heavenly and the earthly that is simultaneously the translation of the heavenly in the

First published at *OnePeterFive*, October 23, 2023.

Unresolved Tensions in Papal-Episcopal Relations

earthly and the service of the heavenly by the earthly, in short, a system in which the earthly is "symbol," "icon," "sacrament" of the heavenly, are we not then authorized to look for an icon, a *"viceregens"* of . . . the Shepherd of the one flock in a supreme bishop who is steward and major-domo and therefore *claviger* [key-bearer] of the whole house of God?[191]

In this context, Soujeole adds: "This clearly does not specify right away the different causalities that the sign manifests, and the Church has unceasingly progressed in the understanding of this reality. . . . We have not yet arrived at definitive results."[192]

(3) The main reason for which the primacy exists is for the preservation of the deposit of faith.[193]

(4) The solemn magisterium of the Church did not make formal systematic pronouncements concerning this subject—i.e., the primacy of Peter and its relations to other bishops—until the Constitution *Pastor Aeternus* of the First Vatican Council.[194] Here, only the position of the pope is clarified; there is no treatment of the episcopate because the Council was suspended and there was no time to discuss this part of the schema of the Constitution on the Church. So, Pius IX published just chapter 1 of that schema. Only the Second Vatican Council elaborated a systematic treatment of the episcopacy.[195]

(5) In *Pastor Aeternus*, many important points concerning the primacy are clarified.

(a) The end of the primacy is the following, according to the Prologue:

> That the episcopacy itself might be one and undivided, and that the entire multitude of the faithful through bishops closely connected with one another might be preserved in the unity of faith and communion . . . [Christ] established in him [Peter and his successors] the perpetual principle and visible foundation of both unities.

If there is an end, then of course there is a limit too. Soujeole comments:

---

[191] Yves Congar, O.P., "De la communion des Églises a une ecclésiologie de l'Église universelle," in *L'Episcopat et L'Eglise universelle* (Paris: Cerf, 1962), cited by Benoît-Dominique de la Soujeole, O.P., *Introduction to the Mystery of the Church* (Washington, DC: The Catholic University of America Press, 2014), 605–6. The original French edition was published in 2006.

[192] Soujeole, *Introduction to the Mystery of the Church*, 606–7.

[193] See Soujeole, 607.

[194] Notice well that the claim is not that there are no previous pronouncements on the primacy of the Pope, but that there are no previous *systematic* pronouncements on the primacy of the Pope *in its relation to the authority of other bishops*.

[195] See Soujeole, 608.

May a Bishop Ordain Another Bishop Without Papal Consent?

The pope has no privilege in the usual sense of the word. . . . He possesses a ministry, a service, the ministry of the unity of faith and charity. . . . He is measured by something other than himself. . . . There is no room here for the papolatry that considers the pope as an end and not as a means.[196]

As *Dei Verbum* declares (no. 10), the Magisterium, and therefore the pope, is not master of Revelation and faith, but its servant. Yves Congar had previously dealt with this subject in his *Tradition and Traditions*, Vol. 1, Excursus C.[197] I will copy here three of the authorities he cites, but I will point out that he states explicitly another aspect of this issue: "The care of ecclesiastical authority must be to keep and observe the doctrinal and disciplinary decisions of the past." Here are some of the authorities cited by Congar:

> For a pope can make an article of faith, if "article of faith" be taken not in a proper sense but broadly for that which must be believed, when earlier it did not have to be believed by a necessary precept of the Church; but from the aforesaid, do not believe that a pope can make a *new* article through which a new faith may be introduced or that anything of the truth of the faith may be taken away or may be added to as regards its substance.[198]

Saint Thomas Aquinas:

> The apostles and their successors are God's vicars as far as governance of the Church constituted through faith and the sacraments of faith is concerned. Whence, just as they may not institute another Church, so neither may they deliver another faith, nor institute other sacraments.[199]

Pope Zosimus, writing to the bishops of Gaul on March 22, 417:

> Not even the authority of this Holy See can grant anything against the statutes of the Fathers or change anything in them. Because among us, with roots unshaken, lives the old tradition [*antiquitas*] for which the decrees of the Fathers ordain reverence.[200]

---

[196] Soujeole, 609.
[197] Yves Congar, O.P., *Tradition and Traditions: An Historical and a Theological Essay* (New York: The MacMillan Company, 1966), 222–28. The original French edition was published in two parts, dated 1960 and 1963.
[198] John XXII, *Lettres communes*, vol. VI, ed. G. Mollat (Paris, 1912), 483; letter of March 18, 1327.
[199] *Summa theologiae* III, Q. 64, art. 2, ad 3.
[200] *Regesta Pontificum Romanorum*, ed. Philip Jaffé (Leipzig: Veit, 1885), 50; repeated in Gratian C. 7, C. XXV, q. 4, col. 1008–9.

Unresolved Tensions in Papal-Episcopal Relations

(b) According to chapter 1 of *Pastor Aeternus*, the pope was given a universal jurisdiction over the entire Church. In chapter 3 it is declared that "the Roman Church . . . holds sovereignty of ordinary power over all others, and . . . this power of jurisdiction . . . which is truly episcopal, is immediate . . . " So, the faithful are subject to obedience "not only in things which pertain to faith and morals, but also in those which pertain to the government of the Church." Yet immediately the text adds the purpose: "so that the Church of Christ, protected not only by the Roman Pontiff but by the unity of communion as well as of the profession of the same faith, is one flock under the one highest shepherd." Again, the true Shepherd is Christ Himself and the main unity to be preserved is unity in professing the same faith.

(c) Soujeole clarifies that in the above quotation "discipline" has to do with the liturgy and "government" has to do with canon law. He states immediately after: "The totality of these rules forms a whole that is extremely variable according to the place and time."[201] This jurisdiction of the pope is ordinary and could be exercised always and everywhere, "but it [such exercise] would not be justified per se because of the existence of the diocesan bishop, except in the case of the latter's failure, and for the duration of that failure."[202]

(d) *Pastor Aeternus* adds that this jurisdiction is possessed as a *full and supreme* power. "This means that it cannot be limited by any human authority because no human authority is superior to it. *Only natural law and the divine law limit it, but that is already a considerable limitation.*"[203] That is to say, the Church is a monarchy, not a tyranny. Only a tyrant wills his power to be unlimited by divine and/or natural law. But, of course, natural and divine law require that the deposit of faith be preserved for the salvation of souls. As our current Code of Canon Law states: "*salus animarum suprema lex*" (can. 1752).

(e) Soujeole adds that if there is a pope who fails to fulfill his office, there is no recourse or redress, although his power is limited as we have seen.[204] But he means that there is no way to *remove* the heretical pope. (On this point there is disagreement among the theologians, as some of them argue that a pope could be deposed by God, or "self-deposed," if he is adjudged to be a notorious or public formal heretic or apostate, since it is impossible for such a man to remain pope. In any case, even a pope who very

---

[201] Soujeole, *Mystery of the Church*, 611.
[202] Ibid.
[203] Soujeole, 612, emphasis added.
[204] "Cajetan says that the only remedy in the case of a heretical pope is to pray and to have others pray that he will die!" (Soujeole, 612). See Phillip Campbell, "The Context of Cajetan's Comments on Praying for a Pope's Death," *Unam Sanctam Ecclesiam*, March 29, 2024; Peter Kwasniewski, "Can We Legitimately Pray for a Pope's Death," *Tradition and Sanity*, April 8, 2024.

May a Bishop Ordain Another Bishop Without Papal Consent?

likely is a heretic, or whose heresies cannot be denied, continues to hold the papacy canonically unless his fall from office is declared by one who would have the authority to do so.[205]) However, Soujeole neglects to address what course of action an orthodox bishop should adopt when the pope is a heretic. The bishop has no power over the pope, but he has his own power that the pope cannot take from him, except based on canon law and the powers given to him by Christ. But Christ did not appoint the pope tyrant over the Church, and therefore, not over the bishops singly or collectively.

(f) In fact, chapter 3 of *Pastor Aeternus* adds:

> This power of the Supreme Pontiff is so far from interfering with that power of ordinary and immediate episcopal jurisdiction by which the bishops, who, "placed by the Holy Spirit" [see Acts 20:28], have succeeded to the places of the apostles, as true shepherds individually feed and rule the individual flocks assigned to them, that the same (power) is asserted, confirmed, and vindicated by the supreme and universal shepherd.

Soujeole observes that the same adjectives used for the pope's power are used in the case of the bishops, except for "full and supreme." This subject, however, was left incomplete by the First Vatican Council and was taken over at the Second Vatican Council in the Dogmatic Constitution *Lumen Gentium*. The implications of this text (especially no. 27) concerning the episcopal power have previously been explored.[206]

(6) The bishop has received his power not from the pope, but from Christ. And he has the power to ordain other bishops when the good of his sheep so requires it. This power is severely limited in the Latin Church, as we shall see, for the good of unity in the faith. But the power has existed since the beginning and *could* be exercised without the pope's consent *in extraordinary situations, if the good of unity in the faith required it.*

Of course, in such situations, the unity of jurisdiction should be preserved as much as possible. This means that, in principle, each extraordinary ordination should be somehow recorded[207] and communicated to the Roman Church in due time, that is to say, when it is not dangerous for the souls of the faithful.

St. Cyprian, for example, ordained Fortunatus without notifying Rome. He thought this was normally inappropriate, unless there was a grave reason.[208]

---

[205] For discussion of these complex questions, see Kwasniewski, ed., *Ultramontanism and Tradition*, 3–15 and 111–48.

[206] See chapters 2, 4, and 6.

[207] As circumstances allow; in places like China, secrecy is essential.

[208] Quasten, *Patrology*, 2:373–78.

Unresolved Tensions in Papal-Episcopal Relations

In 2002, Pope John Paul II erected the Apostolic Administration of St. John-Mary Vianney at Campos in Brazil, and it was Cardinal Castrillón Hoyos who furnished it with a bishop as its superior, by ordaining Bishop Fernando Rifan. This was an important step made in the direction of those who are close to Archbishop Lefebvre and to the Society of St. Pius X (SSPX). Indeed, the bishop at Cardinal Hoyos's side during Bishop Rifan's episcopal consecration, acting as co-consecrator, was Bishop Licinio Rangel, the successor of Bishop de Castro Mayer, who had participated as co-consecrator in Archbishop Lefebvre's consecrations of the SSPX bishops in 1988. Bishop Rangel had himself been consecrated bishop by three of those bishops: Bishop Tissier de Mallerais, assisted by Bishop de Galarreta and Bishop Williamson. The links, then, between this Apostolic Union of St. John Mary Vianney and Archbishop Lefebvre's Fraternity were strong, and rooted in a common combat dating back many years.[209]

(7) However, current Canon Law (CIC 1917, can. 329; CIC 1983, can. 377) establishes that it is the pope who appoints the bishops in the Latin Church. In this respect, the 1983 Code did not change in the light of the Second Vatican Council's texts. This is a *human* norm, not a norm of divine law, established for the good of unity in the faith and due to the historical development of the Latin Church, emanating from the Roman center as a Metropolitan. For this reason, matters were not always this way. We have seen that in the time of St. Cyprian it was not so; and for most of the history of the Church, bishops were elected either by popular acclaim, by the local chapter of canons, or by political rulers with the permission or the tolerance of the Church.

(8) Even today in the Eastern Catholic Churches, it is not the pope who appoints the bishops or even the metropolitans. It is the Patriarch who appoints them and has to notify the pope afterwards, in order to preserve unity (see canons 86 and 87 of the Code of Canons of the Oriental Churches). The Patriarch, moreover, is elected by the Synod of bishops of the Patriarchal church (can. 63).

(9) As can be seen in the case of the Eastern Catholic Churches, the lack of centralization of appointments in the hand of the Roman Pontiff is compatible with the

---

[209] Shaw, ed., *The Latin Mass and the Intellectuals*, 239–40. In other words, here is an example of a bishop who was (according to canon law) illicitly ordained, who later was not only reconciled but chosen as co-consecrator of his successor. The chain was: de Castro Mayer and Lefebvre consecrated de Mallerais, de Galarreta, and Williamson; de Mallerais, de Galarreta, and Williamson consecrated Rangel; Rangel (now reconciled) with Castrillón Hoyos consecrated Rifan; and today Rifan is a bishop in full communion with the Holy See. That is an example of where things that were done *praeter legem* turned out, ultimately, to be not only for the good of the local church in question but also for the good of the universal Church. The initial rupture was healed later on when the situation was better—and when Rome was willing to make appropriate concessions.

May a Bishop Ordain Another Bishop Without Papal Consent?

unity of the Catholic Church. Of course, even those Eastern Churches are subject to the universal jurisdiction of the Roman Pontiff in agreement with *Pastor Aeternus*, but they show their own innate divine power according to *Lumen Gentium*.

(10) We see, then, that *the preservation of the traditions* concerning the jurisdiction of the Patriarchs has led the Roman Church to acknowledge that they can appoint and ordain bishops for themselves. Much more important than such traditions, however, is the preservation of the unity of the Catholic Faith. If the Vatican were to side with the German bishops in some heretical opinions or, astutely, were to declare that each local Church is free to adhere or not to adhere to the Faith received from Christ or to any of the dogmas that have been defined during the history of the Church, then an orthodox bishop could be authorized in extreme circumstances to ordain a man whom he knows well and can trust to be a bishop who will transmit the true Faith.

(11) In the recent past we have seen extreme cases in which cardinals have appointed and ordained presbyters and even bishops against Roman prohibition and/or without Roman authorization.[210] Today we are clearly approaching the point at which ensuring the preservation of the Faith in the face of the Vatican's attempt to corrupt it will require the ordination of bishops by orthodox bishops, without papal consent. I would say that in China very clearly we have reached this point, since the Vatican capitulated to the Communist Party.

Of course, to act like Cyprian, that is, without papal mandate, is not to act against the pope's will. Even this could be licit, however, in extreme circumstances, since the pope's power exists just for the preservation of the unity of Faith and of discipline, and must be exercised within the limits of canon law.[211] The pope as legislator may change the canons, but always within the limits of natural and divine law and within the margin required by the goal to which his power is divinely directed. If he acted against that goal or end he would be abusing his power and his decisions could be canonically void.[212]

---

[210] See "Clandestine Ordinations Against Church Law," in Kwasniewski, *Bound by Truth*, 167–77. I would just say that these ordinations should not be viewed as being *"against"* church law," because standing above the human law that specifies the last details of papal jurisdiction is the principle *salus animarum suprema lex* and also the preservation of the Faith.

[211] There is no doubt that an episcopal consecration by a bishop with the intention of ordaining the minister able to ordain the ministers capable of offering the sacrifice of the Mass and using the appropriate words and matter is valid even if it could be illicit. Leo XIII declared that the Anglicans had lost the Apostolic succession not because they ordained bishops without papal mandate but because for a long period of time they lost the faith in the Mass as a sacrifice and therefore did not have the intention really of ordaining bishops. Moreover, it is clear that the Eastern Orthodox churches, while being schismatic, have Apostolic succession.

[212] See chapters 1, 14, and 15.

Unresolved Tensions in Papal-Episcopal Relations

This includes his decision about who should or should not be ordained. Indeed one may act according to what the will of the pope *ought* to be, namely, the preservation of the true Faith; and in that sense one may say that certain actions are against the will of the man who is pope, but not against the duty of the papacy as Christ instituted it (and which the pope should embrace).

(12) But there are other problems that must be considered. "Episcopal consecration, together with the office of sanctifying, also confers the office of teaching and of governing" (*Lumen Gentium*, no. 21). Therefore, the bishop, who has jurisdiction over one local church, may not invade the jurisdiction of a different one without usurping the authority of another. But since the care of his own flock has been truly entrusted to him, it follows that in extreme circumstances—that is, if he seriously and soberly judges that preserving the Faith in his local church demands it—he may ordain his successor or, as need demands, an auxiliary bishop.[213]

(13) It must be added here that as long as an apostate, a heretic, or an infiltrated person holds the office of pope and has not been lawfully removed, he must be obeyed in anything that does not clash with divine or natural law. If the extreme step of ordaining bishops without Roman consent is taken, then canonical measures must be put in place to ensure that full unity can be regained as soon as the tyranny ceases.

---

[213] In very extreme circumstances the good of souls might require that a bishop embrace anew the original commandment of Christ to the Apostles: "go to the whole world and preach the gospel to every creature!" (Mk 16:15), so that "Jesus Himself sent out through them from the East to the West the holy and incorruptible proclamation of everlasting salvation" (Mark, short ending). Then the bishop might have to act like Thomas who travelled far to India or like James who travelled to Spain.

17

The Responsibility of the Bishops for the Universal Church in a Time of Confusion

Pro Ecclesia Universali

A bishop is a shepherd and guardian of God's sheep. His ministry stems not only from the human legislation of Church institutions, but also from a supernatural appointment. Bishops are successors of the Apostles, and in their mission, Christ's mission is to be fulfilled for the sanctification and salvation of souls. This creates the most important obligations, and especially in situations in which it is necessary to face the fact that a heresy has come into being.

Today, many Catholics have become increasingly convinced that heresy has forced its way into the Church. Some of the faithful think that *de facto* we are already facing a schism, although it has not been *de jure* legitimized. In many parts of the Church, doctrines are being preached which are, or could at least be interpreted as, contradictory to the deposit of faith. There are some bishops who favor far-reaching changes in the doctrine and morality of the Church. These bishops represent a significant part of the episcopal college who consistently enjoy the support of the Bishop of Rome, or at least the lack of a reaction which would correct their actions.

For this reason, a bishop who is concerned about the deposit of faith finds himself in a difficult situation. When the faith is under threat, it is he who is the first guardian of the faith and who is accountable for it before the One who appointed him. However, a bishop might fear that if he openly acted against these revisionists, he would be perceived to be in opposition to episcopal collegiality, and in turn, accused of schism.[214]

What should a bishop do when a heresy arises—not only in his own particular church, but also in a wider ecclesial context?

In such a difficult situation, there is a temptation for a bishop to protect the deposit of faith only in his diocese, leaving doctrinal problems beyond his diocese to the pope to

---

See the Preface for information about this chapter.

[214] This fear is justified in itself; a lack of fear could indicate the shepherd's lack of prudence or incomprehension of his own power which was given to him by Christ in the Church, through the Church and for the benefit of the Church. This authority loses its plenipotentiary power when he opposes the Church.

Unresolved Tensions in Papal-Episcopal Relations

address. However, if he gives in to this temptation, he will neglect the task of guarding the deposit of faith of the universal Church to which he is obliged. Moreover, if he acquiesces to changes in doctrine or morality in other particular churches, he also does so in the universal Church. This in turn, in a real way, affects his own diocese, which is a part of and expression of that universal Church.[215]

Legal-canonical solutions concerning those aspects of a bishop's ministry that are included in the voice of the Magisterium do not give clear instructions for how to act at a time of crisis.[216] Meanwhile, the history of the Church teaches us that despite the Holy Spirit's assistance and protection enjoyed by the Church and despite the assurance that the Church will survive while preserving intact the deposit of faith until the second coming of the Savior, individual bishops might fall into error (even a majority of them, as was the case during the Arian crisis). In some statements, excluding *ex cathedra* statements, even Saint Peter's successor, whose particular task is to guard the deposit and to strengthen his brothers in the faith, might fall into error. This was, for example, the case of Pope Honorius I, who was condemned after his death, at the Third Council of Constantinople, for his support of the heresy of Monothelitism.[217]

In such situations, a series of necessary questions arise. The answers might provide a possible way of reacting to a state of crisis.

First of all, we must consider what the Church is; meaning, what the mystery of the Church is. This should be done in the context of the interrelationship between the Church and the Magisterium, since the interrelationship seems to be more ambiguous than may be commonly understood. The voice of the Magisterium is rightly considered to be the voice of the Church, but there is no absolute identity between the Magisterium and the Church.

Next, we will consider the role and authority of the Magisterium of the Church.

Finally, we will examine the practical application of these considerations: the intervention of bishops who are concerned about the Church, so as not to shrink from the task of protecting the people of God in their own dioceses and to care for the deposit of the whole Church, while at the same time not disrespecting the college of bishops which sanctions their authority. It is important to present criteria which should be the touchstone of the proper, ecclesiastical reaction of a shepherd against threats in the Church.

---

[215] Congregation for the Doctrine of the Faith, Letter to the Bishops of the Catholic Church on Some Aspects of the Church Understood as Communion *Communionis Notio*, no. 7.
[216] See the Supplement at the end of this chapter.
[217] Third Council of Constantinople, *Exposition of Faith*, no. 8.

The Responsibility of the Bishops for the Universal Church

The main conclusions of our analysis are as follows:
- ❖ A diocesan bishop should guard the unity of the whole Church;
- ❖ When an error is publicly proclaimed in a different particular church than his own, a bishop is obliged to react;
- ❖ Silence toward a heresy or other error that has arisen in another part of the universal Church is tantamount to a consent to a manifestation of this error in his own diocese;
- ❖ When the integrity of the deposit of faith is violated, both in his own diocese and in the forum of the universal Church, an intervention is a bishop's responsibility resulting from the mandate given by Christ Himself.

The mystery of the Church

The Church is a complex reality. The Second Vatican Council introduces this mystery using diverse images.[218] The most solemn name given to the mystery of the Church is to call it the Mystical Body of Christ, as this term best expresses the interrelationship between the human and divine elements, "For this reason, by no weak analogy, it is compared to the mystery of the incarnate Word. As the assumed nature inseparably united to Him serves the divine Word as a living organ of salvation, so, in a similar way, does the visible social structure of the Church serve the Spirit of Christ, who vivifies it, in the building up of the body."[219]

This complexity does not allow the Church to be reduced either to a merely human institution or to a merely spiritual reality:

> It is not enough that the Body of the Church should be an unbroken unity; it must also be something definite and perceptible to the senses as Our predecessor of happy memory, Leo XIII, in his Encyclical *Satis Cognitum* asserts: "the Church is visible because she is a body." Hence they err in a matter of divine truth, who imagine the Church to be invisible, intangible, a something merely "pneumatological" as they say, by which many Christian communities, though they differ from each other in their profession of faith, are united by an invisible bond.[220]

And then:

> From what We have thus far written, and explained, Venerable Brethren, it is clear, We think, how grievously they err who arbitrarily claim that the Church

---

[218] See Vatican II, *Lumen Gentium*, ch. 1.
[219] *Lumen Gentium*, no. 8.
[220] Pius XII, Encyclical *Mystici Corporis*, no. 13.

is something hidden and invisible, as they also do who look upon her as a mere human institution possessing a certain disciplinary code and external ritual, but lacking power to communicate supernatural life.[221]

This teaching is also confirmed by the Second Vatican Council:

> Christ, the one Mediator, established and continually sustains here on earth His holy Church, the community of faith, hope, and charity, as an entity with visible delineation through which He communicated truth and grace to all. But the society structured with hierarchical organs and the Mystical Body of Christ are not to be considered as two realities, nor are the visible assembly and the spiritual community, nor the earthly Church and the Church enriched with heavenly things; rather, they form one complex reality which coalesces from a divine and a human element.[222]

It is exactly the Catholic Church itself which has the aforementioned status and character that the declaration *Dominus Iesus* reminds us of:

> Therefore, there exists a single Church of Christ, which subsists in the Catholic Church, governed by the Successor of Peter and by the Bishops in communion with him. . . . The Christian faithful are, therefore, not permitted to imagine that the Church of Christ is nothing more than a collection—divided, yet in some way one—of Churches and ecclesial communities; nor are they free to hold that today the Church of Christ nowhere really exists, and must be considered only as a goal which all Churches and ecclesial communities must strive to reach.[223]

A deep awareness of and rootedness in this truth raises a justified fear in the hearts of many shepherds, of coming out against this true Church and its rulings. Taking into consideration the nature of the unity of the divine and human elements in the Church, it is difficult to oppose the purported voice of the Magisterium, while taking a stand of fidelity to the Church. There is a fear of separating the spiritual Church from its visible structures. A strict identification of the voice of the Magisterium with the voice of Christ himself might seem a safer course—regardless of the content that may be given by the Magisterium at a given moment.

---

[221] *Mystici Corporis*, no. 64.
[222] *Lumen Gentium*, no. 8.
[223] Congregation for the Doctrine of the Faith, Declaration *Dominus Iesus*, no. 17.

The Responsibility of the Bishops for the Universal Church

This fear of separating these two elements of the Church is connected with two errors that are common in our times. First, the Church is equated with the hierarchy; or, alternatively, with the Church's Magisterium; second, a perhaps unconscious tendency to equate the hierarchy and the Magisterium. However, the Church teaches that "one must not think... that this ordered or 'organic' structure of the body of the Church contains only hierarchical elements and with them is complete; or, as an opposite opinion holds, that it is composed only of those who enjoy charismatic gifts—though members gifted with miraculous powers will never be lacking in the Church."[224]

The one who becomes a bishop does so as a member and fruit of this Mother Church—as a member of this community of faith that gave birth to him, has led and chosen him. This "line of ascension," proper to a bishop, should never be omitted and silenced nor crossed out by the dimension of power, sanctification, or Christological birthmark, which are given to him by the power of consecration. Therefore, it is necessary to remember that a bishop is a man of the Church first of all, born of the Church and called by the Church to build, to govern, and to serve, and first and foremost, to be a good father in it.

This distinction and hierarchical submission of the bishops to the primacy of the Church allows us to avoid the error of equating the divine and human elements without distinguishing them. This distinction is rooted in the biblical image of the Body and Head, which, although inseparable, are not identical: "And thus, just as the head and members of a living body, though not identical, are inseparable, so too Christ and the Church can neither be confused nor separated, and constitute a single 'whole Christ.' This same inseparability is also expressed in the New Testament by the analogy of the Church as the *Bride* of Christ."[225]

For this reason, the Church is called the "Mystical Body of Christ" and not a physical Body of Christ, so as to avoid equating either the rulings of the Magisterium or the way of life of the members of the Church with the expression of Christ's divine existence in the Church. Although he is united with Christ through the Sacraments, a Christian exercising his own will and reason can act in a way that does not befit, or even opposes, Christ's will; and similarly, a shepherd, who by Christ's will manifests His authority and dignity, might—apart from when he overtly exercises the charism of infallibility—express himself in a way contrary to Christ. Pius XII reminds us of this in a synthetic way:

---

[224] Pius XII, *Mystici Corporis*, no. 17.
[225] Congregation for the Doctrine of the Faith, *Dominus Iesus*, no. 16.

Unresolved Tensions in Papal-Episcopal Relations

For there are some who neglect the fact that the Apostle Paul has used metaphorical language in speaking of this doctrine, and failing to distinguish as they should the precise and proper meaning of the terms the physical body, the social body, and the Mystical Body, arrive at a distorted idea of unity. They make the Divine Redeemer and the members of the Church coalesce in one physical person, and while they bestow divine attributes on man, they make Christ our Lord subject to error and to human inclination to evil. But Catholic faith and the writings of the holy Fathers reject such false teaching as impious and sacrilegious; and to the mind of the Apostle of the Gentiles it is equally abhorrent, for although he brings Christ and His Mystical Body into a wonderfully intimate union, he nevertheless distinguishes one from the other as Bridegroom from Bride.[226]

In consequence, the teaching of the Magisterium cannot be accepted or rejected at will. The exposition of the Church's Magisterium must not be treated as something discretionary and loosely associated with the revealed objective truth. The Magisterium, while not identical with Christ and thereby lacking His prerogatives and nature, by its unity with Him and in His power, is equipped with the charism that allows His will to be carried out.

In a precise way, the charism of infallibility, which is a particular gift to guard the deposit of faith, belongs to the Church. The College of Bishops and the pope enjoy this charism, not as their own, but as a form of the particular realization of the infallibility of the Church.[227]

To summarize:

1) A shepherd's concern not to criticize the Magisterium or the pope's rulings is justified because of the sense of fidelity to the Church and because of the collegiality of the episcopal office.

2) The Church is not merely a human institution, but human and divine.

3) The shepherds are called to protect the people of God through Christ's mandate and are able to fulfill this task through the Holy Spirit.

4) The Magisterium of the Church is equipped with gifts and charisms which serve to guard the deposit of faith.

5) Except for solemn doctrinal and moral rulings which are guaranteed to be true, the voice of the Magisterium may not always be identical to the revealed objective truth.

---

[226] Pius XII, *Mystici Corporis*, no. 86.
[227] See Vatican I, *Pastor Aeternus*, ch. 4, no. 9.

6) It does not follow from this fallibility that the Magisterium can be disregarded in issues other than dogmatic rulings.

7) This imposes on individual bishops the duty of seeking the purity and unity of Church doctrine in such a way as not to go beyond the Magisterium, while not withdrawing from the defense of the good of the whole Church.

The practical applications of this defense seem to be particularly problematic. To determine this, it is first of all necessary to remember what authority the following have in the Church: the pope, the college of bishops and individual bishops. It is necessary to decide in which cases and to what degree it is possible for each to fall into error. Then we will be able to specify what interventions are possible and to what degree, and what interventions each one is obliged to make if an error occurs. We are going to treat these three issues synthetically.

The role and the competence of the Magisterium

"The task of authentically interpreting the word of God, whether written or handed on"[228] belongs to the Magisterium of the Church, which is constituted by the bishops in communion with the pope. The Magisterium carries out this task in an authoritative way on behalf of Christ, which does not mean that it is equal to or above the Word of God and Church Tradition, but rather, that it is to serve the task of preserving the purity and immutability of the deposit of faith.[229]

For this reason, the faithful are obliged to be submissive to the Magisterium. However, as was shown above, neither the divine delegation of authority to the college of Apostles with Peter at its head, nor the continuation of the apostolic mission by the college of bishops in union with the pope, nor the assistance of the Holy Spirit in equipping the Church with the charism of infallibility, guarantee that each statement by a part of the college or by the pope enjoys infallibility by its nature.

Competence and the scope of papal authority

The Bishop of Rome is the visible head of the Church. He has ordinary, proper, and immediate authority. The Holy See is not subject to anyone, nor can it be judged by anyone. However, history shows that a pope can also commit an error in his ordinary teaching. The infallibility of the pope is assured only when his teaching has the character of *ex cathedra* teaching. Moreover, the charism of papal infallibility is a way of fulfilling the infallibility of the Church and is meant to serve as a guardian of the deposit of faith.

---

[228] Vatican II, *Dei Verbum*, no. 10.
[229] Ibid.

Unresolved Tensions in Papal-Episcopal Relations

Therefore, this charism does not extend to the creation of new doctrine. It is applied in cases where the pope resolves a disputed issue concerning the immutable teaching of the Church which has not been definitively formulated before. Thus, all the faithful owe obedience of supernatural faith to *ex cathedra* pronouncements by the pope. Questioning such a ruling is *de facto* a schismatic act.

We also owe the obedience of faith to the ordinary papal Magisterium. Nevertheless, in a case in which reason enlightened by faith perceives a doubt concerning the preservation of continuity between the perennial deposit and the present teaching, or at least its interpretation, the faithful are obliged to reveal these doubts to their shepherds in a spirit of responsibility for the Church:

> Conscious of their own responsibility, the Christian faithful are bound to follow with Christian obedience those things which the sacred pastors, inasmuch as they represent Christ, declare as teachers of the faith or establish as rulers of the Church ... According to the knowledge, competence, and prestige which they possess, they [viz., the Christian faithful] have the right and even at times the duty to manifest to the sacred pastors their opinion on matters which pertain to the good of the Church and to make their opinion known to the rest of the Christian faithful, without prejudice to the integrity of faith and morals, with reverence toward their pastors, and attentive to common advantage and the dignity of persons.[230]

Such an act is authorized by the binding authority of conscience:

> Conscience is a law of the mind; yet [Christians] would not grant that it is nothing more; I mean that it was not a dictate, nor conveyed the notion of responsibility, of duty, of a threat and a promise. ... [Conscience] is a messenger of him, who, both in nature and in grace, speaks to us behind a veil, and teaches and rules us by his representatives. Conscience is the aboriginal Vicar of Christ.[231]

The college of bishops and individual bishops are especially obliged to react should doubts arise concerning the ordinary teaching of the pope that might not preserve continuity with previous teachings. While no one in the Church is superior to the pope as an authority, the pope's teaching takes place at various levels of authority, and questioning or rejecting a problematic teaching in no way violates the duty of bishops to

---

[230] *CIC*, can. 212, §1 and §3.
[231] *CCC*, no. 1778, citing St. John Henry Newman.

The Responsibility of the Bishops for the Universal Church

remain in communion with the pope. It is permitted and actually a duty to ask questions and request clarification of doubtful matters, as it might occur that a bishop's or the faithful's discernment that there is a rupture of continuity is inaccurate. The Holy See is obliged to resolve the doubts of bishops and the faithful in such cases (although he has the supreme authority, the Bishop of Rome exercises it with the college of bishops).

In the absence of explanations, and if doubts persist and the conscience continues to entertain a conviction that a new teaching is contradictory to the previous deposit, a bishop has the right to refrain from implementing the teaching and to point out the existing conflict to the faithful, as long as the bishop continues to remain in unity with the pope and the college. In other words, it is precisely for the sake of collegiality and the unity of the Church that a bishop has the right to express doubt and keep watch over the immutable deposit of faith.

The competence and scope of the authority of the College

As stated earlier, the college of bishops maintains its validity by always acting in unity with the pope. The college of bishops can teach in a solemn way, as is done at councils. Such a gathering also preserves its own validity by acting in unity with the Bishop of Rome. Although the college of bishops must maintain doctrinal and moral unity with the Holy See, this is always on condition that the Holy See itself maintains fidelity and continuity with the doctrinal and moral teaching of the Church.

Thus, if an episcopal body (a conference of bishops or a local synod) gave rulings which provoke doubt about their orthodoxy, their continuity or unity with the previous deposit, etc., the first one who should react and point out an error is the Bishop of Rome. If he does not condemn such an error or even approves of it, then the bishops, both collectively and individually, are obliged to react.

For example, such a situation might arise with the Synodal Path in Germany, or with the introduction of the ritual of blessing for homosexual couples by the Episcopate of Belgium. In such situations, the orthodox bishops should admonish the bishops who have introduced erroneous teachings and appeal to the Holy See, asking for an unambiguous resolution for the good and unity of the Holy Church and for the salvation of souls.

The authority and competence of bishops

A bishop has ordinary, proper, and immediate authority in his own diocese. This means that, although the validation of his authority is connected with exercising it in union with the whole College and its head, his authority in the diocese is not a delegated power. The bishop, therefore, while exercising his authority to govern his diocese in an ordinary way, does the task of the Magisterium of the Church.

This results from the fact that a diocese is not only an element of the universal Church, but the realization of the Church with all its essential elements.[232] Particular churches are both part of the people of God and make the universal Church present, and as particular churches, they are entrusted to a diocesan bishop's care and to the priests who work with him.[233] Therefore, a bishop who has been entrusted with a particular church can exercise his pastoral office only in reference to this part of the people of God. He has no authority to govern either other Churches or the universal Church. However, this does not release him from his duty of taking care of the whole Church together with other bishops.[234]

For "bishops as members of the episcopal College, which is the successor of the Apostolic College, are intimately united to Jesus Christ, who continues to choose and to send out his Apostles. As a successor of the Apostles, by virtue of his episcopal ordination and through hierarchical communion, the bishop is the visible principle and guarantee of unity in his particular Church" (the Congregation for Bishops, Directory for the Pastoral Ministry of Bishops *Apostolorum Successores*, Introduction), but at the same time each bishop is responsible for the whole universal Church and owes it care and help:

> For it is the duty of all bishops to promote and to safeguard the unity of faith and the discipline common to the whole Church, to instruct the faithful to love for the whole mystical body of Christ, especially for its poor and sorrowing members and for those who are suffering persecution for justice's sake.[235]

If a diocesan bishop, for example, opposes the blessing of homosexual unions, seeing in this act a rupture with the traditional anthropological teaching of the Church and with the teaching about the gravity of sin and about the dignity of marriage, but fails to issue a public correction because he sees the Holy See's approval of the Belgian Church that introduced such a rite as normative and binding, then such a silent bishop has *acquiesced to a possible fulfillment of this norm in his own diocese* and he is *responsible for this act of blessing*.

Even if now he hopes that his diocese will not be affected by such an error while he exercises the pastoral office, he is responsible for the introduction of this norm in

---

[232] See the Congregation for the Doctrine of the Faith, *Communionis Notio*, no. 7.
[233] See Decree Concerning the Pastoral Office of Bishops in the Church *Christus Dominus*, no. 11.
[234] See Vatican II, *Lumen Gentium*, no. 23.
[235] *Lumen Gentium*, no. 23.

The Responsibility of the Bishops for the Universal Church

the future—possibly while his successor is exercising the office—because it is he, not his successor, who maintained silence when such an error arose in another part of the universal Church.

Considering then the nature of collegiality and the structure of the universal Church, it is necessary to point out that collegiality is not intended to submit bishops to liberal errors approved by higher authority, but is supposed to serve to secure unity. Collegiality is broken not by a bishop who opposes German bishops or Belgian bishops' new ideas, but by these German and Belgian bishops themselves. As a corollary, the particularity of churches cannot serve to build up a false conviction of security on "their own" territory. A particular church is a real manifestation of the universal Church, not a detached and autonomous part. Therefore, it is erroneous to set in opposition or dichotomy the particularity and universality of the Church. The care of a particular church is always the care of the universal Church and vice versa.

The duty of a bishop to preach true doctrine in his own particular church is also an obligation to uphold the purity of the doctrine of the whole Church. Therefore, guarding the doctrine and intervening when the integrity of the deposit of faith is broken, both in his own diocese and in the forum of the universal Church, is not only a right resulting from the divine mandate to exercise the episcopal office, but also an obligation because of Christ's mission.

To sum up, in an exceptional situation in which the pope or part of the College of Bishops (even a larger part), in unity with and under the open or tacit approval of the pope, expresses views that break with the settled doctrine of the Church—or at least have every appearance of breaking with it—then if they desire to fulfill the duty of guarding the doctrine in their own dioceses and to care for the universal Church, the bishops stand before the problem of taking care of preserving collegial unity with the Church and with its Magisterium. When in response to the ensuing problems in the above-mentioned areas, despite their own perception concerning the real preservation of the deposit of faith, they submit to some doubtful statements or at least maintain reserved silence, they preserve a "unity" which is only external and ostensible. A reaction that would directly question the pope's and the college's errors would be treated as leading towards a schism.

Given these realities, the ideal solution would be to preserve unity with the pope and the college of bishops, while not abdicating responsibility for guarding the deposit of faith in each diocese, nor the care of the good of the universal Church. Such a solution would entail several steps: (1) a clear and unambiguous expression of doubt, maintaining respect towards the pope and the college; (2) a clear recollection and expression of the perennial teaching of the Church; (3) a demonstration of the lack of continuity and cohesion in the proposed policies or reforms, and (4) if necessary, for the sake of collegiality and fidelity to the Church, a refusal to put them into effect, while expressing the reasons for taking such a stance; namely, the preservation of fidelity to the Church and to the deposit of faith that was given to the Church by Christ and that the Church has no right to change. This is not only the right but also the duty of every bishop, which stems from his supernatural vocation and from episcopal collegiality itself.

Situations that require intervention

The above analysis demonstrates that bishops are responsible for guarding the deposit of faith both in their own dioceses and in the forum of the universal Church. This should be carried out in different spheres in different ways. In an exceptional situation an admonition of a brother bishop is necessary and could even be made to the head of the college of bishops.

It remains to indicate situations in which intervention is necessary for the sake of preserving fidelity to the mission and service of the successors of the Apostles.

An intervention of the highest priority is required in any situation in which errors are propagated which stand in glaring contradiction to the deposit of faith. Of course, this concerns not only situations in which dogmas are directly challenged, which are not usually encountered; but also, for example, those in which dogmas are re-interpreted in a way which breaks with the traditional understanding of dogmatic formulations (or of non-dogmatic teachings which are directly or indirectly connected to or result from the immutable deposit). One example of the latter is the demand to ordain women as priests or deacons. The subject of female ordination was formally closed by St. John Paul II, albeit not dogmatized, based on the truth about the nature of holy orders, which is richly documented and has been repeatedly confirmed in Church teaching.

Ambiguous expressions in magisterial documents also require intervention. The ambiguity of a doctrinal or moral expression or even a pastoral postulate should not automatically be deemed to make it somehow conformable to orthodoxy. Indeed, the perceived possibility of an orthodox interpretation is often put forward as an argument for relieving the bishop from his duty of intervention, even though the corresponding possibility of heterodox interpretation by that fact invalidates any attempt to fit such an expression into orthodoxy, while practically creating a real threat of legitimizing an error.

A clear example of the poisonous fruit which results from a teaching that breaks with existing Church practice can be seen in the thesis of the exhortation *Amoris Laetitia*, on the possibility of admitting to Communion the divorced living in non-sacramental unions. The Vatican approved, via endorsing the Buenos Aires statement, the offering of Communion to people remaining in mortal sin or in an objectively disordered situation. Scandalously, this went unchallenged by many orthodox bishops who chose to remain silent.

Another category of such situations comprises erroneous customs that spread without meeting with disapproval or correction by the shepherds. The most common situations of this type are various liturgical experiments which are incompatible with the gravity of, and are connected with the essence of, the Blessed Sacrament. Customs, rites, or moral norms in the Church have always resulted from, and are reflections of, the revealed truth. Sanctioning customs which are detached from and do not express the revealed truth leads to erroneous conceptions about the very essence of the truth which is supposed to be expressed. Celebrating Mass in a way that makes it resemble a concert or a memorial meal, over time non-verbally and naturally forms such a trivializing perception in those who attend.

Also requiring intervention are serious errors which concern not so much particular articles of faith as a global way of understanding the whole supernatural reality of the Church, for example, speaking and acting as if the primary mission of the Church is not eternal salvation, but building up worldly well-being, whether economic, ecological, social, etc.; an erroneous understanding of synodality in opposition to hierarchism; an erroneous understanding of the sense of faith in which each baptized person has the same competence in discernment of spiritual and ecclesiastic matters; identification of the collective opinions of the faithful with the voice of the Holy Spirit; and so on. These kinds of systematic errors result from an inversion in which, instead of the deposit of faith forming the understanding of the faithful, the understanding of the faithful (formed by the spirit of this world) becomes a criterion of understanding the deposit of faith.

Also, demands which open up room for new errors coming into existence and being given approval require intervention. One such demand is, for example, a falsely understood theological pluralism. We have always had a kind of pluralism which means we can understand individual truths of faith in different but complementary ways; e.g., the truth about the redemptive meaning of the Sacrifice of the Cross can be understood in the principles of atonement, propitiation, fulfillment, unification, etc. Theological pluralism, however, is increasingly understood as a justification of the co-existence of various theological propositions which not only contradict each other, but also do not maintain integrity with the deposit of faith.

Unresolved Tensions in Papal-Episcopal Relations

The last issue which should be addressed is awareness of the difference between intentions and their validity. The fact that decision-makers in the Church may have good intentions is not an argument for the validity or proper direction of changes made. Just as the end does not justify the means, good intentions (means) do not guarantee the rightness of the end (an improper solution).

Summary

The consequences of a shepherd's actions—or the consequences of his inaction—are of the greatest importance for the spiritual well-being of the faithful. They can affect them for decades, and in special cases for even longer periods. In history, there are plenty of examples of the perpetuation of exceptionally good or exceptionally bad customs in a particular church. Even if a bishop himself does not introduce any reformist solutions in his diocese, he cannot be content with passively watching how the faith and morals of the faithful are shaped from the outside, by the example of others. In hindsight, it is easy to prove that the problems which appear throughout the Church today have their origin in the negligence or erroneous decisions of the past. Each bishop awaits the judgment of history, which shows holiness or the opposite better than the judgment of his contemporaries. Each shepherd, however, will have to give an account of his rule before yet another court—the fearful judgment seat of Christ himself, as the One who entrusted him with authority in his diocese. While one can hide his own actions or lack thereof from people, sometimes even successfully by using the principle of collegiality, it will not be possible before this Judge. His judgment will be on each shepherd's personal responsibility for how, if at all, he cared of the souls of the faithful entrusted to his authority.

SUPPLEMENT

Theological-historical outline

The word "bishop" derives from the Greek term ἐπίσκοπος (*episkopos*), which means guardian, caretaker, administrator, guard, sentry, shepherd. In this term, the Christian tradition recognizes the functions of prophet, priest, and king assigned to Church superiors. The Council of Trent teaches that "bishops, who have succeeded to the place of the apostles, principally belong to this hierarchical order; that they are placed, as the same apostle says, by the Holy Ghost, to rule the Church of God."[236] This teaching has been confirmed and repeated many times by the Magisterium of the Church.

---

[236] Council of Trent, Session XXIII, ch. 4; cf. CCC 861.

The Responsibility of the Bishops for the Universal Church

By the will of Christ, bishops, as successors of the Apostles, are witnesses and continuators of the mystery of the Church.[237] Thus, even as Christ's life and actions were reflections of the presence of the Father and the Holy Spirit in the world, so bishops are signs of the presence and actions of the Holy Trinity.

> Because of this Trinitarian shaping of his existence, every Bishop in his ministry is committed to keeping watch over the whole flock with love, for he has been placed in their midst by the Spirit to govern the Church of God: in the name of the Father, whose image he represents; in the name of Jesus Christ his Son, by whom he has been established as teacher, priest and shepherd; in the name of the Holy Spirit, who gives life to the Church and by his power strengthens us in our human weakness.[238]

From this trinitarian constitution of the bishop's office, it follows that a bishop appears in the Church and emerges from the Church as the one who expresses the redemptive vitality continuously activated by the Holy Spirit and as the one who is supposed to teach, sanctify, and lead the people of God who were entrusted to him by God until the return of Christ.[239]

St. Augustine comments in the same spirit when he explains St. Paul's words:

> It is to this the apostle refers when he says, "He that desireth the episcopate desireth a good work." He wished to show that the episcopate is the title of a work, not of an honor. It is a Greek word, and signifies that he who governs superintends or takes care of those whom he governs: for ἐπί means *over*, and σκοπεῖν, *to see*; therefore ἐπισκοπεῖν means "to oversee." So that he who loves to govern rather than to do good is no bishop.[240]

In the same way St. Augustine explains the meaning of the elevated position of a bishop:

> This is exactly Jerusalem. It has guardians. As it has workers who build, who labor in order to build it, so it also has guardians. Since the Apostle's words refer to the guardianship: "But I am afraid that, as the serpent deceived Eve by his cunning, your thoughts may be corrupted from a sincere [and pure] commitment to Christ" (2 Cor 11:3). He protected, he was a guardian, he did his best to take

---

[237] See John Paul II, Post-Synodal Apostolic Exhortation *Pastores Gregis*, no. 1.

[238] John Paul II, *Pastores Gregis*, no. 7.

[239] See Acts 13:1-3; John Paul II, Encyclical *Ecclesia de Eucharistia*, no. 28.

[240] Augustine, *De civitate Dei contra paganos* XIX, 19, CCL 48, ed. B. Dombard and A. Kalb (Turnhout: Brepols, 1955), 686–87; translation from *Nicene and Post-Nicene Fathers*, ed. Philip Schaff, from ccel.org.

Unresolved Tensions in Papal-Episcopal Relations

> care of those he led. Bishops do the same. Because of that a higher place was prepared for bishops so that they could look from above and watch over people. What in Greek is expressed by the word "bishop," in Latin means "guarding"; for he guards, they look down from above at their people. . . . From this elevated place they realize in great detail that there is danger, unless in their hearts they stand in such a way as to be with humility under your feet.[241]

Hence, St. Augustine after St. Paul the Apostle (Tit 1:9) points out that only he can be chosen as a bishop who in the Church hands down healthy doctrine (*doctrina sana*) which builds up the faith of all the listeners and convinces those who oppose it.[242] However, in the negative dimension, the preaching of the word of God should protect and guard Catholics against teachings contrary to Church doctrine which are propagated by heretics whom St. Augustine called mind-deceivers (*vaniloqui et mentium seductores*).[243]

Therefore, a bishop cannot be made equal with other members of the Church. His duty, commissioned by Christ, places him as the leader of the people of God. Speaking more vividly, the establishment of the bishop's office is the establishment of the hierarchical order in the Church which cannot be replaced or made equal with the synodal order in its new, modern understanding:

> For in the Church there is such an order: some go ahead and some follow them. Those who go first set an example to those following them. Those who follow them imitate those who go first. Do those, who set an example to those going behind them, follow nobody? If they followed nobody they would lose their way. They follow somebody: Christ himself. Well, those who are better in the Church and who have nobody among people to imitate because by making progress they have outdistanced everybody, they have only Christ as an example and will follow him to the end. And you have seen steps presented by Paul the Apostle one by one, "Therefore, I urge you, be imitators of me" (1 Cor 4:16). Therefore, let those who put their feet strongly on a rock be an example to the faithful.[244]

This hierarchical order is supposed to serve the whole Church; therefore, bishops are particularly obliged to seek exemplary holiness and to examine if they are not in some way a scandal to the faithful, even anti-witnesses. Already Origen asks:

---

[241] Augustine, *Enarratio in Ps.* 126, 3, ed. V. Tarulli (Rome, 1977), 140–42.
[242] See Augustine, *Enarratio in Ps.* 67, 39; Augustine, *Sermo* 178, 1, PL 38:961.
[243] *Enarratio in Ps.* 67, 39.
[244] Augustine, *Enarratio in Ps.* 39, 6.

The Responsibility of the Bishops for the Universal Church

> Do you think that they who fill the priestly office and boast of their priestly rank [*ordo*] "advance according to their order" and do all that is worthy of this order? Do you think likewise that the deacons "advance according to the order" of their ministry? Why then do we often hear people blaspheme and say: "Behold, what a fine bishop!" Or, "What a fine priest!" Or, "What a fine deacon!" Are not such things said when either a priest or a minister of God has been seen going *contrary* to his order in some matter?[245]

Thus, the office gives a certain power over the people of God but does not guarantee its automatic realization. Among hierarchs who have been placed as leaders of the people of God, there are those who do not guard their sheep.

The bishop's care of the people of God especially concerns the particular church entrusted to him. The Second Vatican Council teaches:

> The individual bishops, who are placed in charge of particular churches, exercise their pastoral government over the portion of the people of God committed to their care, and not over other churches nor over the universal Church. But each of them, as a member of the episcopal college and legitimate successor of the apostles, is obliged by Christ's institution and command to be solicitous for the whole Church, and this solicitude, though it is not exercised by an act of jurisdiction, contributes greatly to the advantage of the universal Church. For it is the duty of all bishops to promote and to safeguard the unity of faith and the discipline common to the whole Church.[246]

The mutual care of all the bishops for the Church is realized in their collegiality: "And the Sacred Council teaches that by episcopal consecration the fullness of the sacrament of Orders is conferred, that fullness of power, namely, which both in the Church's liturgical practice and in the language of the Fathers of the Church is called the high priesthood, the supreme power of the sacred ministry. But episcopal consecration, together with the office of sanctifying, also confers the office of teaching and of governing, which, however, of its very nature, can be exercised only in hierarchical communion with the head and the members of the college."[247]

On the one hand, collegiality for a bishop means that in terms of power he has competence regarding his own diocese, but always and only in unity with the whole

---

[245] Origen, *Homilies on Numbers* 2, 1, 4, trans. Thomas P. Scheck (Downers Grove, IL: IVP Academic, 2009).
[246] Vatican II, *Lumen Gentium*, no. 23.
[247] Vatican II, *Lumen Gentium*, no. 21.

Unresolved Tensions in Papal-Episcopal Relations

Church. He has no jurisdictional power or power of teaching regarding the whole Church. On the other hand, he is obliged to care for the faith of the whole people of God. Thus, a bishop, although he has no power to judge his other brother bishops and no power to correct them in an authoritarian way, is obliged to keep watch over the purity of doctrine and of the welfare of the whole Church and must react to errors appearing in other bishops' teaching.

This action, which comes down to brotherly correction, constitutes a state of emergency in pastoral care, which is sanctioned by both Scripture and the tradition of the Church. Already St. Paul reminds Timothy of this duty:

> I charge you in the presence of God and of Christ Jesus, who will judge the living and the dead, and by his appearing and his kingly power: proclaim the word; be persistent whether it is convenient or inconvenient; convince, reprimand, encourage through all patience and teaching. For the time will come when people will not tolerate sound doctrine but, following their own desires and insatiable curiosity, will accumulate teachers and will stop listening to the truth and will be diverted to myths. But you, be self-possessed in all circumstances; put up with hardship; perform the work of an evangelist; fulfill your ministry.[248]

In the same spirit, St. Gregory the Great directs his teaching to pastors:

> For, as incautious speaking leads into error, so indiscreet silence leaves in error those who might have been instructed. For often improvident rulers, fearing to lose human favour, shrink timidly from speaking freely the things that are right; and, according to the voice of the Truth, serve unto the custody of the flock by no means with the zeal of shepherds, but in the way of hirelings; since they fly when the wolf comes if they hide themselves under silence.[249]

This correction applies not only to subordinates but also to those equal to them in terms of exercised power and also to their superiors, which is evidenced by St. Paul's admonition of St. Peter in the Epistle to the Galatians (cf. Gal 2:11-14) and the tradition of the interpretation of this text. St. Thomas Aquinas comments on it in the following way:

> If the faith were endangered, a subject ought to rebuke his prelate even publicly. Hence Paul, who was Peter's subject, rebuked him in public, on account of the

---

[248] 2 Timothy 4:1–5.

[249] Gregory I, *Liber Regulae Pastoralis*, pars II, cap. 4, trans. James Barmby, *Nicene and Post-Nicene Fathers*, Second Series, vol. 12 (Buffalo, NY: Christian Literature Publishing Co., 1895).

The Responsibility of the Bishops for the Universal Church

imminent danger of scandal concerning faith, and, as the gloss of Augustine says on Galatians 2:11, "Peter gave an example to superiors, that if at any time they should happen to stray from the straight path, they should not disdain to be reproved by their subjects."[250]

Legal-canonical outline

Collegially, the order of Bishops is, "together with its head, the Roman Pontiff, and never without this head, the subject of supreme and full power over the universal Church." As is well known, in teaching this doctrine the Second Vatican Council likewise noted that the Successor of Peter fully retains "his power of primacy over all, pastors as well as the general faithful. For in virtue of his office, that is, as Vicar of Christ and pastor of the whole Church, the Roman Pontiff has full, supreme and universal power over the Church. And he can always exercise this power freely."[251]

These words quoted from a 1998 apostolic letter by John Paul II remind us of the unity of the whole college of bishops, headed by the pope as the Bishop of Rome (the Bishop of the Diocese of Rome). He leads the Church in cooperation with the rest of the bishops, in a continuation of the College of the Twelve Apostles (Apostolic College) which was headed by St. Peter the Apostle. The authority of the College was expressed by Christ this way: "Whatever you bind on earth shall be bound in heaven, and whatever you loose on earth shall be loosed in heaven" (Matt 18:18).

The Fathers of the Second Vatican Council emphasized:

> Individual bishops who have been entrusted with the care of a particular church—under the authority of the supreme pontiff—feed their sheep in the name of the Lord as their own, ordinary, and immediate pastors, performing for them the office of teaching, sanctifying, and governing.[252]

This truth expressed by the Fathers of the Council was developed by the present code of canon law when it states:

> Bishops, who by divine institution succeed to the place of the Apostles through the Holy Spirit, who has been given to them, are constituted pastors in the Church, so that they are teachers of doctrine, priests of sacred worship, and

---

[250] Thomas Aquinas, *Summa Theologiae*, II-II, Q. 33, art. 4, ad 2.
[251] John Paul II, Motu Proprio *Apostolos Suos*, no. 9; cf. Vatican II, *Lumen Gentium*, no. 20.
[252] Vatican II, *Christus Dominus*, no. 11.

ministers of governance. Through episcopal consecration itself, bishops receive with the function of sanctifying also the functions of teaching and governing.[253]

Thus, a bishop's duty as a teacher of the faith is to guard the deposit of faith (*depositum fidei*) in his particular church, which means the revealed truths of the faith and morality (contained in the Bible and Apostolic Tradition). St. Paul presented this task when he wrote to the bishop St. Timothy, "Guard this rich trust with the help of the holy Spirit that dwells within us" (2 Tim 1:14). In the aforementioned motu proprio, St. John Paul II described the duty of sanctification this way:

> The individual Bishop too, as "steward of the grace of the supreme priesthood," in the exercise of his office of sanctifying contributes greatly to the Church's work of glorifying God and making men holy. This is a work of the whole Church of Christ, acting in every legitimate liturgical celebration carried out in communion with the Bishop and under his direction.[254]

Thus, a diocesan bishop after the Second Vatican Council is perceived more as a shepherd than as an administrator, although his administrative activity was precisely specified in Church documents. The Holy See underlined the scope and responsibility of this service in different documents including the Council Decree *Christus Dominus* of 1965 and the Instruction *Ecclesiae Imago* of 1973 by the Congregation for Bishops. Then, the pastoral service of bishops was articulated in the 1983 Code of Canon Law, in the post-conciliar apostolic exhortation *Pastores Gregis* by John Paul II in 2003, and above all in the Directory *Apostolorum Successores* of 2005 issued by the Congregation for Bishops.

The Code legislator also specified that "a diocesan bishop in the diocese entrusted to him has all *ordinary, proper, and immediate* power which is required for the exercise of his pastoral function."[255] Under the notion of *ordinary* power the Church understands the one associated with the office (and not delegated to a particular person) which for a diocesan bishop is *proper* and not vicarious.[256] Therefore, a diocesan bishop as a successor of the Apostle in the particular church entrusted to him acts in his own name, not in the name of the pope. He should, however, maintain unity with the Bishop of Rome. The *immediate* power is joined with the right to immediate action towards the

---

[253] Can. 375 of the *CIC*.
[254] John Paul II, *Apostolos Suos*, no. 11.
[255] Can. 381 §1.
[256] Can. 131.

The Responsibility of the Bishops for the Universal Church

fold entrusted to him and not only through one-man or group organs which function within a diocese (a vicar general, an episcopal vicar, a diocesan synod, a diocesan curia, an ecclesiastical court, etc.). Likewise, each of the faithful of the particular church has the right to turn to his bishop directly.

The diocesan bishop, as a successor of the Apostles, receives a triple power: legislative, executive, and judicial. "The bishop exercises legislative power himself." He exercises executive and judicial power himself or through the aforementioned organs.[257] The Code specifies that "in exercising the function of a pastor, a diocesan bishop is to show himself concerned for all the Christian faithful entrusted to his care."[258] The Code also lists the pastoral duties of a bishop, such as: care of presbyters; care of priestly and monastic vocations; preaching the whole of Christian doctrine and morality, and care of "the homily and catechetical instruction"; care of the spiritual growth of the faithful "through the celebration of the sacraments"; supporting "various forms of the apostolate in the diocese"; visitations.[259] The wide scope of the power of dispensation from the Church law entrusted to bishops should also be mentioned.[260] Moreover, a diocesan bishop

> must protect the unity of the universal Church; a bishop is bound to promote the common discipline of the whole Church, and therefore, to urge the observance of all ecclesiastical laws. He is to exercise vigilance so that abuses do not creep into ecclesiastical discipline, especially regarding the ministry of the Word, the celebration of the sacraments and sacramentals, the worship of God and the veneration of the saints, and the administration of goods.[261]

Therefore, his is the care of the unity of the Church expressed in the unity of the faith, sound discipline, and worthy celebration of the sacraments.

Bishops exercise their power in unity with other bishops. The Code specifies that:

> A conference of bishops, a permanent institution, is a group of bishops of some nation or certain territory who jointly exercise certain pastoral functions for the Christian faithful of their territory in order to promote the greater good which the Church offers to humanity, especially through forms and programs of the

---

[257] Can. 391.
[258] Can. 383.
[259] Can. 384–87, 394, 396–98.
[260] See Vatican II, *Christus Dominus*, 8b; Can. 87.
[261] Can. 392; Vatican II, *Lumen Gentium*, no. 23.

apostolate fittingly adapted to the circumstances of time and place, according to the norm of law.[262]

The role of the conference of bishops or episcopal conference was theologically elaborated in the motu proprio *Apostolos Suos* by John Paul II in 1998. Clause 15 of this document reads as follows:

> The Council clearly highlighted the need in our day for harmonizing the strengths deriving from the interchange of prudence and experience within the Episcopal Conference, since "Bishops are frequently unable to fulfill their office suitably and fruitfully unless they work more harmoniously and closely every day with other Bishops." It is not possible to give an exhaustive list of the issues which require such cooperation but it escapes no one that issues which currently call for the joint action of Bishops include the promotion and safeguarding of faith and morals, the translation of liturgical books, the promotion and formation of priestly vocations, the preparation of catechetical aids, the promotion and safeguarding of Catholic universities and other educational centers, the ecumenical task, relations with civil authorities, the defense of human life, of peace, and of human rights, also in order to ensure their protection in civil legislation, the promotion of social justice, the use of the means of social communication, etc.

The Code's clarification is also important: "A conference of bishops can only issue general [and executive] decrees in cases where universal law has prescribed it or a special mandate of the Apostolic See has been established." In other cases, e.g., with issued resolutions, "the competence of each diocesan bishop remains intact" in his particular church.[263]

Apart from diocesan bishops, other bishops (the so-called titular bishops) are also obliged to distinguish themselves by their care for the particular and universal Churches. A coadjutor bishop (a bishop with the right of succession in the post of a diocesan bishop) and auxiliary bishops have the task of "assist[ing] the diocesan bishop in the entire governance of the diocese and take his place if he is absent or impeded."[264] They can have special tasks entrusted to them and exercise executive power in the diocese in the role of vicars general and episcopal vicars.[265] Bishops who presented their

[262] Can. 447.
[263] Can. 455.
[264] Can. 405.
[265] Can. 406.

The Responsibility of the Bishops for the Universal Church

resignation from office and had it accepted by the Bishop of Rome, retain the title of bishop emeritus and, in the various works they may undertake, such as offering the sacraments, continue to serve the common good of the Church.[266]

At the end of the aforementioned Instruction *Ecclesiae Imago*, the Congregation of Bishops summed up the pastoral mission of a bishop:

> To take the first place means to reach out, to preside means to serve, to govern means to love, while respect corresponds to duty (burden). The office of a bishop does not constitute a foundation of temporary honors any more but it is a *burden* which weighs down the shoulders of a bishop, purifying his dignity from any kind of filth of exterior vanity and secular reign.

Similar words are contained in the Directory for the Pastoral Ministry of Bishops by the Holy See in which the responsibility the bishops hold for their office is mentioned: "The Lord Jesus always assists his Church and his ministers, especially the Bishops to whom he has entrusted the governance of the Church. With the office, He imparts grace; together with the burden, He provides the strength to carry it."[267] These words from the documents fit into the mold of the observation by Pope Boniface VIII, "*Rationi congruit, ut succedat in onere, qui substituitur in honore,*" which can be translated as: "It is fitting that the one who assumes the office has also assumed the burden associated with it."

---

[266] Can. 401–2.
[267] Directory for the Pastoral Ministry of Bishops, *Apostolorum Successores*, no. 231.

Epilogue

The following set of petitions is prayed daily by this anthology's editor, who invites others to adopt the same prayers if they find them useful.

O Lord, remember in Your kingdom
all religious, clergy, and laity throughout the entire world
who are dedicated or drawn to the *usus antiquior*.
Bless us, govern us, defend us, purify us, and multiply us
for the good of souls, for the restoration of your Church,
and for the glory of Your Holy Name. Amen.

Have mercy on all those for whom I am accustomed to pray;
all who have asked for my prayers;
all for whom I have promised my prayers.

Have mercy on all good bishops,
    that they may be strengthened and exalted.
Have mercy on all wicked bishops,
    that they may be converted or confounded.
Have mercy on all mediocre bishops,
    that they may be awakened and stirred into action.
Have mercy on all the cardinals,
    that they may elect a worthy successor of St. Peter.
Have mercy on all the Holy Souls in Purgatory.
Have mercy on all who are most desperately in need
    of Your mercy at this very moment.

Have mercy on us and save us,
for You are gracious and You love mankind,
and to You we render glory,
Father, Son, and Holy Spirit,
now and always and forever and ever,
Amen.

Appendix 1

Is the Pope the Vicar of Christ or CEO of Vatican, Inc.?

Peter A. Kwasniewski

By now, many will have heard of the arbitrary removal, by Pope Francis, of a young (57-year-old) bishop of Puerto Rico—Daniel Fernández Torres of the Diocese of Arecibo—because, apparently, he wasn't "sufficiently in union" with the pope and his fellow bishops on the island. By all accounts and by the bishop's own testimony, no objective canonically-classifiable wrongdoing or even hint or claim of wrongdoing has been pressed against him, as *The Pillar* summarizes in its article "Can the pope just fire a bishop?"[268] Rather, the bishop exercised a certain freedom of judgment by which he took a more conservative line than his fellow bishops: he would not send his seminarians to a new interdiocesan seminary; he would not enforce vaccinations; he would not collaborate in the suppression of the traditional Latin Mass; he would not buckle to the agenda of the lavender mafia.[269] This was enough to make him hated and feared. He had to be terminated, just like that. One might say his crime was to be a Catholic in the mold of the pope, Benedict XVI, who had appointed him.

Bishop Torres passionately and articulately defended himself in a crystal-clear statement on March 9, part of which reads (my translation):

> I regret very much that in a Church where mercy is so much preached, in practice some lack a minimal sense of justice. No process has been made against me, nor have I been formally accused of anything and simply one day the Apostolic Delegate verbally communicated to me that Rome was asking me to resign. A successor of the apostles is now being replaced without even undertaking what would be a due canonical process to remove a parish priest. I was informed that I had committed no crime but that I supposedly "had

---

Extract from Peter A. Kwasniewski, *The Road from Hyperpapalism to Catholicism: Rethinking the Papacy in a Time of Ecclesial Disintegration* (Waterloo, ON: Arouca Press, 2022), vol. 2: *Chronological Responses to an Unfolding Pontificate*, 266–71.

[268] Published March 9, 2022.

[269] See Inés San Martín, "Pope removes Puerto Rican bishop from office after he refused to resign," *Crux*, March 9, 2022.

Unresolved Tensions in Papal-Episcopal Relations

not been obedient to the pope nor had I been in sufficient communion with my brother bishops of Puerto Rico." It was suggested to me that if I resigned from the diocese I would remain at the service of the Church in case at some point I was needed in some other position—an offer that in fact proves my innocence. However, I did not resign because I did not want to become an accomplice in a totally unjust action, one that even now I am reluctant to think could happen in our Church.[270]

The Pillar article, which is quite revealing in itself, competently explains that removing a bishop is an extremely grave matter: he is, after all, a successor of the apostles who receives his authority *from Christ*, even if through the pope's appointment; he is not a middle manager appointed by the CEO of Vatican, Inc.[271] *The Pillar* treats us to fascinating historical details of the considerable pains taken by earlier popes *not* to fire bishops, because it would have been considered unthinkable to act that way toward one of the "high priests" in the Church of Christ: "*Ecce Sacerdos magnus*," as the old antiphon for the entrance of a bishop exclaimed.

A telling example of this reverential attitude towards the episcopate comes to us from the reign of Pope Pius XII. As Yves Chiron narrates in his biography of Giovanni Battista Montini, the government of France at the end of World War II wanted to punish all the bishops who openly supported Marshal Pétain and the Vichy regime. Understandable enough. But when individuals in the new French government like Hubert Guérin, Pierre Bloch, René Massigli, and Georges Bidault made it known to the Vatican that they wished not only to swap out the papal nuncio but to see a slew of hierarchs removed from their offices—three cardinals and thirty bishops, to be exact—Pius XII responded indignantly:

> On the 27th [of November 1944], Pius XII received Msgr Théas. Concerning the change of the nuncio, the pope "stated his displeasure with the attitude of the French government, which he regards as offensive, discourteous, injurious. He will change the nuncio because he has become *persona ingrata*, but he will not do it without pain or protest." As for purging the episcopacy, he declared: "There can be no question of changing the bishops. That has never been done.

---

[270] "Declaración del Obispo Daniel Fernández Torres," www.diocesisdearecibo.org/2022/03/09/declaracion-del-obispo-daniel-fernandez-torres/, accessed March 21, 2022.

[271] See Phil Lawler's take: "The Pope's arbitrary actions belie his call for 'synodal' governance," *CatholicCulture.org*, March 9, 2022.

Is the Pope the Vicar of Christ or CEO of Vatican, Inc.?

That will not be done. That would be an injustice. That would be without precedent. That is inadmissible."[272]

Pius XII, who knew and hated the Nazis like few others, had the instinct of a pope who also knew that even when a successor of the apostles has behaved dishonorably, one doesn't just fire him "at will"; he's not an employee of a corporation or a government official. Pius XII would not remove bishops who bore the real guilt of collaborating with Vichy, while Francis removes Bishop Torres who seems to have done nothing grievously wrong.

Let us return now to *The Pillar*. In glorious hyperpapalist fashion, we are told that *of course* the pope can remove a bishop *ad libitum* because the pope's the boss, with no limits to his power:

> Notwithstanding the absence of any evidence of a canonical crime, or the reticence of previous popes to remove diocesan bishops by papal fiat, Francis does have, according to canon law, "supreme, full, immediate, and universal ordinary power" in the Church, and specifically the "primacy of ordinary power over all particular churches [dioceses]."

The Pillar sidesteps the million-dollar question of what all these words—"supreme, full, immediate, universal, ordinary, power"—actually *mean*: if their interpretation were self-evident, they would not have been the object of canonical and theological scrutiny for centuries.[273] Scholastics famous and obscure all took the position that there are limits to *any* human authority's exercise of power, even the pope's. It is astonishing that anyone could adhere to an interpretation that makes the pope a mortal god on earth, before whom every bishop must quake for fear that he will be arbitrarily removed from his office at the pope's next whim.

The Pillar's simplistic ecclesiology (and would that it were limited only to journalists!) makes an utter hash of the episcopacy as part of the inherent constitution of the Church. If bishops have zero rights in the possession of their office—that is, if they can be "fired at will"—they are not actually governing the Church with divine authority in collegial communion with the vicar of Christ. They are, as the nineteenth-century caricature had it, "vicars of the pope" who govern their dioceses simply because the pope can't practically be everywhere at all times. According to that ecclesiology (if one may dignify it with such a name), the pope would be the real bishop of each and

---

[272] Yves Chiron, *Paul VI: The Divided Pope*, trans. James Walther (Brooklyn, NY: Angelico Press, 2022), 93.
[273] [See chapter 1 above.—*Ed.*]

Unresolved Tensions in Papal-Episcopal Relations

every diocese, who has delegated some of his authority, *pro tempore* and *ad hoc*, to these various individuals.

On this view of papal authority, no one in the Church has any objective rights except by papal sufferance. That is, as long as the pope is willing to let you have the appearance of rights, then you can live according to those appearances, and you might even be permitted to conduct a canon law case in reference to them; but the moment he says "Okay, enough of that make-believe; I deprive you of XYZ," then we must bow our heads and submit. Not only (on this view) does canon law have no say over the pope himself, it possesses force only by his continually willing it to have force, as if he were sustaining it in being. The pope is not the protector and promoter of the Church and her members, but the source and measure of all that belongs to them qua members of the Church. He *makes* and *unmakes* the members of the Church. In short, he is the sole actual possessor of authority and standing in the Church, while everyone else possesses it from his implicit grant, which may at any time be revoked.

Such is the *reductio ad absurdum* of a certain vein of ultramontanism. Thanks be to God it is not Catholicism, but only a rotten and sickly parody of it.

Let's explore this matter further. Who, in the Church, *has* absolute and unlimited power? Who is the source of all authority, all rights and duties? The answer is obvious: *Christ Himself*, the Head of the Church. The pope as *vicar* of Christ is one who stands in His place, exercising certain duties (and only those duties) that have been entrusted to him; but the pope is by no means the *equal* of Christ. Perhaps the chafing pain of this inherent limit explains Pope Francis's curious removal of the title "Vicar of Christ" from the list of titles in the *Annuario Pontificio*, where he had it relegated to the category of "historical titles": he no longer wants to be or to be seen as just a representative of Christ. Rather, in some sense, he wishes to be His *equal*, to rule and control and remake the Church as if it were his own possession, his own bride. To be "friend of the bridegroom" (cf. Jn 3:29) is not enough.

In spite of its democratic outward appearance, the synodal process fits snugly into this ultimate grab for power. Inasmuch as the Church could be described as monarchical in her papacy, aristocratic in her episcopacy, and democratic in the common access of all her members to the full treasury of Redemption poured forth in the liturgy and sacraments, the Church is by no means "synodal" in the newspeak sense of the term, where synodality is a process of "consultation" and "decision-making" emanating from the top down, and seeking to elicit and impose a progressivist vision of perpetual doctrinal and moral evolution validated by the will of the pope, who, taking the place of the "God of surprises," presides over the autodemolition of historic confessional

Is the Pope the Vicar of Christ or CEO of Vatican, Inc.?

Catholicism. That kind of synodality serves as both a smokescreen for and an engine of modernism.

The pope as *servus servorum Dei* who receives and hands on what he has received, the bishops as successors to the apostles who do the same, and the faithful as recipients of tradition and subjects of the *sensus fidei* have no place in this Rousseauian vision of a "general will" that emerges as if spontaneously from human meetings and human decisions. We might even say that the Bergoglian ecclesiology combines the worst features of the three social contract philosophers: it has Hobbes's autocratic Leviathan in the person of the pope who is not Christ's vicar but Christ's replacement; it has Locke's relativism about truth claims and the subordination of religion to political power; and it has Rousseau's inescapable regime masquerading as the people's will and voice.

There are those who celebrate the "reconciliation" of the Catholic Church with Enlightenment philosophy. We who recognize, in keeping with Vatican I, that the divine constitution of the Church is unchanging and unchangeable, should not be among them.

The Pillar concludes its article thus:

> Bishop Torres may not like, or even understand the reasons for his removal. And it may be true that he has committed no canonical offense, and received no kind of due process. Torres might believe the decision to be entirely unjust, and it very well might be unjust. The Church does not hold that the charisms of the Holy Spirit protect popes from bad decisions in governance—and every pope in history has made some. But does the pope have the power to do it? He does.

Catholic journalism is not meant to be theology, granted, but it should at least try to avoid trumpeting absurdities. Here is a suggested alternative conclusion:

> When a pope wields his power arbitrarily, against the rights of his subjects (for they do retain their rights, which come to them from sources above and beyond the pope), he sins in doing so, harms the common good of the Church, and deserves to be resisted in any way possible, such as non-compliance. Such a pope would be in a state of mortal sin and would have to seek absolution for it.

After all, Karl Rahner—no traditionalist he—argued the same about a pope who should dare to obliterate an Eastern Rite.[274]

---

[274] Fr. John Zuhlsdorf cites the text in "What the mighty Jesuit Karl Rahner would say, said, about suppressing *Summorum Pontificum*," *Fr. Z's Blog*, July 1, 2021.

Appendix 2

Why a Bishop Should Ignore His Unjust Deposition by a Pope[275]

Peter A. Kwasniewski

Servideus: Paulinus, Pope Francis has "relieved" Bishop Joseph Strickland of his office (what a euphemism!), even as he went after Bishop Daniel Fernández Torres in Puerto Rico, whom he removed from office at the age of only fifty-seven. That bishop allowed for conscientious objection to the Covid vaccines, and he was summarily dismissed from his diocese by the pope. The same thing happened with the less-well-known case

---

First published at *OnePeterFive*, September 18, 2023; incorporated into Peter Kwasniewski, *Bound by Truth: Authority, Obedience, Tradition, and the Common Good* (Brooklyn, NY: Angelico Press, 2023), 178–193.

[275] The following dialogue is based on a real interview that took place between John-Henry Westen and me, the video of which can be seen at *LifeSiteNews*. The transcript has been edited for brevity, clarity, and literary effect—changing names of the speakers, dividing up the speeches, adding interjections, etc. In his article "Why a Good Bishop Should Not Ignore but Obey His Unjust Deposition by a Pope" [see chapter 3 above—*Ed.*], José Antonio Ureta attempts to refute my position. While I understand the classic arguments he presents, I am not convinced he is in the right. First, throughout much of Church history, bishops were chosen in different ways than by direct papal appointment and functioned without his express grant of jurisdiction. Second, if the crisis of our times is of a qualitatively unique character, it is not clear to me that the right way forward is simply to emulate the past and to fall back on the thinking of the past. That is a paradox of traditionalism in general: there are many things we say and do that have no precedent. For example, we resist a liturgical rite published by two popes and intended for the whole Church, even if it was never technically *mandated*. Surely, the same people who defend papal primacy in jurisdiction would defend papal primacy in liturgical law; yet traditionalists (including Ureta) assert the rights of immemorial and venerable custom and the rights of the faithful against papal legislation. So we are obviously willing to push back against the pope when he does something egregiously harmful to the good of the Church. It seems to me, similarly, that allowing a heretic like Francis to remove orthodox bishops is exactly such a case, where the harm of submissive acceptance massively outweighs the harm of direct resistance. Third, could it not be the case that the hypertrophic expansion of the papacy, the absolutization of its monarchy to the denigration and destruction of other poles of authority in the Church (liturgy, episcopacy, tradition in general), is precisely what needs to be challenged and stymied in order for health to return to the body? In short: the Ultramontanes, like Ureta, assume that the one and only solution to every ecclesiastical difficulty is the absolute power of the pope (that is, as long as a saintly orthodox pope is someday elected, who can right all wrongs); yet it is exactly this Maistrean assumption that the anti-Ultramontanes call into question. Today's ultramontanists are looking for a conventional solution along nineteenth- and early twentieth-century lines. We are looking for a recalibration of the network of authorities and obediences.

Why a Bishop Should Ignore His Unjust Deposition by a Pope

of the bishop of San Luis in Argentina, Pedro Daniel Martínez Perea, who was removed by the Vatican at the age of 64, not long after he prohibited altar girls in the diocese.[276] Similarly, the seminary of San Rafael was shut down after its bishop refused to allow Communion only in the hand.[277] What do we do in situations like this? Is a bishop just supposed to pack up his bags and leave? Should such a seminary be shut down? I remember Bishop Schneider talking about what bishops and priests should do in light of the severe restrictions on the Latin Mass: he said it's wrong to follow these directions, and it's right to disobey them because they're unjust.

Paulinus: The most important principle to begin with—it's a principle of natural law, something that belongs to the structure of reality as God created it—is that all authority exists for a certain purpose. It doesn't exist as a free-floating, arbitrary imposition that can coerce people to do whatever it wants them to do. No; authority's purpose is to promote and foster the common good of the society over which a wielder of authority is placed. That common good is also something *definite*. For example, in a country it might be the peace of the country, good laws, good morality. These are the things that the ruler is supposed to see to. And if the ruler acts against the good of the people in an extreme way, they can either refuse to consent to what he's doing or even rise up against him. Now, in the Catholic Church, we don't rise up against popes and bishops—we don't take out pitchforks and run after them. Although in the Middle Ages some people might have done that . . .

Servideus: They probably did!

Paulinus: But it's still true that, as with any authority, the pope is placed by Christ in the Church to serve a given function, which is to promote the common good of the Church. He does that by preaching the true faith, teaching the deposit of faith revealed by Christ through the Apostles; by fostering good morals and good discipline; by appointing worthy bishops or at least bishops that he thinks are worthy. He might be mistaken, everyone can be mistaken at times. But what a pope wouldn't have the authority to do, even though he has supreme authority in the Church, is thwart Catholic doctrine, undermine Catholic morality, or appoint men as bishops wickedly, as occurred with nepotism or simony—when popes in the Renaissance were appointing

---

[276] See "El obispo de San Luis prohibió la presencia de mujeres en los altares," *Clarín*, November 1, 2019, www.clarin.com/sociedad/obispo-san-luis-prohibio-presencia-mujeres-altares_0_OSD-mgCY.html.
[277] See Andrea Zambrano, "Seminario cerrado y sombras sobre Roma: 'El obispo se ha equivocado,'" *Brújula Cotidiana*, August 3, 2020, https://brujulacotidiana.com/es/seminario-cerrado-y-sombras-sobre-roma-el-obispo-se-ha-equivocado.

their fourteen-year-old nephews as cardinals and so forth. When they do this kind of thing, they are acting *ultra vires*, outside their powers, outside their authority, contrary to the nature of what their authority was given for.

Servideus: That raises the really interesting ecclesiological question: Is it possible for a pope to act *so* contrary to the common good and to justice in a given situation that his act is invalid, that it has no force—it's not merely an imperfect law or command, but not a command *at all*, not a law *at all*? Is that possible?

Paulinus: The answer of the tradition of the Church is yes, that *is* possible. St. Thomas says an unjust law is no law at all, it doesn't have the rationale of a law. I would argue that if a pope removed a bishop arbitrarily, that is, for no good cause, without a due canonical process, with no reason given and no reason discoverable—and especially if there was evidence that the reason that bishop was removed is because he was conservative or traditional, teaching the faith, upholding good discipline and morals—then that act would be null and void, an act that should be ignored. The bishop in question should assume that he is still the bishop of that place, because he *is*. The pope can remove somebody only for just cause, he can't arbitrarily remove people. The papacy is not a tyranny, it's a monarchy. And we have to remember that.

Servideus: Bishop Strickland was a hero for American Catholics, for Catholics around the world. Even though there are a good number of bishops who are faithful and who every once in a while will make their voices heard, no one was doing that like Bishop Strickland. He ruffled feathers. His conscience urged him to proclaim the Faith, including its hard teachings that run against the modern secular consensus (shared by all too many of his fellow bishops), and a lot of the faithful rallied around him. So, let's say it's for that reason—for his being outspoken, for his going to Los Angeles to do the procession of reparation, his bold pro-life and pro-family stance, his taking to task Father James Martin for his homoheresy—it's for that reason that Bishop Strickland was targeted.

Paulinus: Exactly so. I want to address a point you've raised, because I think it's important. Is it legitimate for Bishop Strickland or for Bishop Schneider, an auxiliary bishop in Kazakhstan, to speak about issues all over the world, to address issues outside of their dioceses, to be teaching the Catholic faith to a very large audience, you might say a global audience? There are some people out there who want to say, no, every bishop should restrict himself to his own diocese and only concern himself with local affairs. You know I'm not the biggest fan of Vatican II who's ever lived, but that objection is completely contrary to what Vatican II says in *Lumen Gentium* section 20:

Why a Bishop Should Ignore His Unjust Deposition by a Pope

> Just as the office granted individually to Peter, the first among the apostles, is permanent and is to be transmitted to his successors, so also the apostles' office of *nurturing the Church* is permanent, and is to be exercised without interruption by the sacred order of bishops.

Then it goes on to say in section 23:

> The individual bishops, who are placed in charge of particular churches, exercise their pastoral government over the portion of the People of God committed to their care, and not over other churches nor over the universal Church. But *each of them, as a member of the episcopal college and legitimate successor of the apostles, is obliged by Christ's institution and command to be solicitous for the whole Church*, and this solicitude, though it is not exercised by an act of jurisdiction, contributes greatly to the advantage of the universal Church. For it is the *duty of all bishops* to promote and to safeguard the unity of faith and the discipline *common to the whole Church*, to instruct the faithful to love for the whole mystical body of Christ, especially for its poor and sorrowing members and for those who are suffering persecution for justice's sake, and finally to *promote every activity that is of interest to the whole Church*, especially that the faith may take increase and the light of full truth appear to *all men*.[278]

I mean, it's as if the Council Fathers are trying to double-underline this point: even though the bishop's proper territory over which he has immediate jurisdiction is his own diocese, he's still concerned with and should be promoting actively the good discipline and the faith of the entire Church in whatever ways are suitable for him.

Servideus: A good example of that would be the way Bishop Fulton Sheen preached over the radio and television to millions of people. Although I'm sure he ruffled some modernist feathers back then, most people were happy to have Bishop Sheen on primetime television preaching the gospel.

Paulinus: Well, this is what Bishop Schneider is doing, this is what Bishop Strickland was doing on Twitter, YouTube, and other such media pulpits. Such bishops look outrageous, not because of what they're saying, but because of how *few* are saying the things that they're saying. If you rewound the clock by fifty or a hundred years, what they're saying would be perfectly obvious: "Of course—that's what the *Baltimore Catechism* says." So

---

[278] Emphases added.

Unresolved Tensions in Papal-Episcopal Relations

we're not talking about outlandish opinions, as if these bishops are saying things from outer space. They're saying what's in the traditional catechisms.

Servideus: To get back to my main question, what if one day a bishop's just told: "That's enough. You're gone. As with Bishop Fernández Torres and Bishop Strickland, we're going to replace you with someone else. Pack your bags." If we assume that this is an unjust act, what do you think should happen next?

Paulinus: Unquestionably it would be an unjust act. I find it noteworthy that Bishop Daniel Fernández Torres published a statement saying: "I have done nothing wrong. They've never told me I've done anything wrong. And in fact, they offered me another position if I would resign my diocese." That shows that he hadn't done anything wrong, because if you're guilty of some wrongdoing, they're not going to say, okay, here's another plum position over here that we'll give you. Basically they were trying to bribe him to leave his diocese because the other bishops didn't like him. And it wasn't just about vaccinations. It was about him not wanting to send his seminarians to an iffy interdiocesan seminary. He didn't want to suppress the traditional Latin Mass. None of these things could be called *faults*, let alone delicts or any kind of serious cause for as grave a step as removal. Similarly, Bishop Strickland admitted that it was, in part, his refusal to implement the unjust demands of *Traditionis Custodes* that got him sacked. He said that he could not, in good conscience, "starve part of his flock." His rationale here is perfectly sound, based on divine and natural law.

Servideus: How, then, should a bishop respond in that situation?

Paulinus: He could say: "With all due respect, Holy Father, I pray for you, I want to be in communion with you. But although it was a pope who appointed me bishop, when I was consecrated a bishop it was *Jesus Christ Himself* who established me as a bishop. And that's also the teaching of the Church. It's not the pope who makes a bishop a successor of the apostles; it is Jesus Christ. Once someone is a bishop, he's a bishop forever, just like a priest is a priest forever. Since there are no suitable grounds for removing me, I remain the bishop of this diocese, and intend to continue my work here, for the benefit of my presbyterate and my people."

Servideus: But the pope is the one who named him the bishop of that place . . .

Paulinus: Yes, but since the pope is not the source of his episcopacy, the pope doesn't have complete arbitrary authority over a bishop's continuing to serve his flock, once he has been placed there. His power to rule and care for the flock comes from Christ,

Why a Bishop Should Ignore His Unjust Deposition by a Pope

not from the pope. The pope says, "you go to this diocese, I'm appointing you to this diocese"; but it's Christ who gives him the rights and duties of the episcopate. This is very important to grasp.

Servideus: Of course, these two spheres sort of collide, or better, overlap, don't they?

Paulinus: The pope has immediate and supreme universal jurisdiction in the Church, which means, in practice, he can do whatever is within his ambit of authority to do, and nobody can stop him and nobody's over him. But again, *within the ambit of his authority*, within the sphere of it.

Servideus: So, if a bishop dug in his heels, what would happen next?

Paulinus: Maybe the pope would excommunicate him and assign another bishop to the place. Then there would be, so to speak, two bishops in this area. But there would be only one true bishop, because there's *already* a bishop there—he's going to be there as long as he lives unless he's removed for just cause, is transferred to another See, retires, or dies. That means the new bishop will be a usurper or an imposter.

Servideus: What a mess!

Paulinus: Absolutely. Has Church history seen these kinds of messes before? Yes. If you read about the history of the Church of Constantinople, for example, patriarchs were deposed and reinstated, they went back and forth and there were conflicting patriarchs. We don't *desire* that situation. But we should be willing to tolerate such a messy situation rather than compromise on this point—namely, that the bishops are not the "vicars of the pope." Recall the strong words of *Lumen Gentium*, section 27:

> The pastoral office or the habitual and daily care of their sheep is entrusted to them [the bishops] completely; *nor are they to be regarded as vicars of the Roman Pontiffs*, for they exercise an authority that is proper to them, and are quite correctly called "prelates," heads of the people whom they govern. Their power, therefore, is not destroyed by the supreme and universal power, but on the contrary it is affirmed, strengthened, and vindicated by it, since the Holy Spirit unfailingly preserves the form of government established by Christ the Lord in His Church.

Could the Council have emphasized any more clearly that the power of the pope is for edification, not for destruction; that the Holy Spirit wants to preserve the dignity of the episcopacy rather than allowing it to be effectively absorbed into a singular autocracy;

Unresolved Tensions in Papal-Episcopal Relations

that the bishops are not delegates of the pope, as if they were all nuncios, but are proper authorities in their own right and, as the medievals saw it, wedded to their local church? Arbitrary removal would be an ecclesiastical "no-fault divorce," which is incoherent.

Servideus: Many nowadays *do* think of bishops as vicars of the pope. We have to recover the truth that their authority to govern comes from *Christ*. It helps to remember this when you have a dictator pope.

Paulinus: I think what happens is that, as long as a pope is exercising his monarchy in a reasonable way—a way that doesn't give cause for scandal or for alarm—most people are content to assume that he is completely in charge of everything. And if he doesn't do anything to make you *question* your understanding, maybe you will never find out that you have a false understanding. But Pope Francis is so extreme in his actions and in his teachings—his opinions on marriage and family, LGBTQ, the death penalty, sacraments, liturgy, I mean, there are so many alarm bells ringing, you're in danger of ear damage—that he makes us start to look at these issues more closely until we realize, oh, wait a minute, the papacy actually *has* limits.

Servideus: It's obvious once you *say* it, because it's a created authority and the only authority that is absolute is God's.

Paulinus: And, needless to say, any created authority can be resisted if he abuses his authority. This is something you can find in the whole canonical and theological tradition. Torquemada says this, Aquinas says it, Bellarmine, Suárez . . . They all say that when an authority abuses his office, he can be fraternally corrected and even resisted and disobeyed. These views were part of our tradition, but they tended to be forgotten in the wake of Vatican I and the ultramontanist spirit that swept through the Church.

Servideus: Tell me what you mean by "ultramontanist" here?

Paulinus: After the French Revolution, the Church was on the run in Europe—anticlericalism, Freemasonry, rising socialism, eventually communism . . . All of these ideologies were forcibly acting against the Church, trying to suppress it, trying to destroy Catholic schools, trying to obliterate the clergy. And in the face of that kind of pressure against Catholicism, Catholics had a very natural instinct to rally around the pope. The pope is our head, our father. He's our universal leader. He's our general, in a sense—the general of the Catholic armies. And we have to rally around him. A strong pope can lead us in this modern battle against all of these ideologies. That's legitimate. People needed the pope to be that way for them.

Why a Bishop Should Ignore His Unjust Deposition by a Pope

But the problem is, this attitude, born of peculiar historical circumstances and magnified by modern media, can morph into a cult of personality, with the pope as "the Great Leader": the faith *is* the pope; the faith is all about the pope. It's not. That's a caricature that Protestants play upon quite a bit, because they would *love* to be able to say, "oh, you Catholics don't follow Scripture, you just follow whatever the pope says." We know that that's false, but the ultramontanism that's looking over the mountains to the pope for everything all the time *suggests* this error—suggests that our faith is wrapped up in the person of the present pope and in what he's teaching right now, as opposed to being something that's been handed down by all of the popes and all of the bishops from the beginning until now.

Servideus: How does the issue of ultramontanism relate to the reduction of bishops to "vicars of the pope"?

Paulinus: As we saw earlier, *Lumen Gentium* 27 tells us that the church is not like a multinational corporation in which the bishops are branch managers and the pope is the CEO. In a corporation, the CEO could just ring up Daniel Fernández Torres or Joseph Strickland and say, "You know what, Daniel (or Joseph), it's been good having you on the team, but you're fired. Incompatible visions." And the CEO of Vatican, Inc. puts another manager in there.[279] No, it's not like that. The managers, the *prelates* of this Mystical Body, this Mystical Corporation (so to speak), are put in place by *Christ* and are permanently in place unless they actually do something to forfeit being in their place. They're like the professors who have tenure, whom you can't get rid of unless they burn down a building or murder a colleague.

Servideus: Well said!

Paulinus: I'll tell you a story that shows how seriously the episcopal dignity used to be taken. It has to do with Pius XII.

There was almost nobody who was more fiercely anti-Nazi than Pius XII, Eugenio Pacelli. Although he was engaged in diplomacy with the Third Reich, he quickly realized he was dealing with a liar and a psychopath. And that's why he drafted the text of one of the most passionate encyclicals ever, *Mit Brennender Sorge*, published by the pope at the time, Pius XI. So if you know your history, you can't justly accuse Pius XII of being sympathetic to Hitler or the Nazis, although some people have maliciously said that. Anyway, after World War II, a bunch of people in the French government—people who

---

[279] See Appendix 1.

Unresolved Tensions in Papal-Episcopal Relations

had been fighting for the Free French and had been against the Vichy regime—asked the pope to remove not only the papal nuncio, who had been sympathetic to Vichy, but also dozens of French bishops who had been in cahoots with the Vichy regime. They wanted the pope to remove *all* of them from office.

Well, how did the pope reply? Did he say, "Oh, I understand, it's just terrible. I'll remove them all." No! He sent word of his displeasure with the attitude of the French government, which he regarded as offensive, discourteous, and injurious. He agreed to change the nuncio, but not without misgivings. And as for purging the episcopacy, he declared that there can be *no question* of changing the bishops. That has never been done. That will not be done. That would be an injustice without precedent. Inadmissible. What his reaction shows is that for him, it was unthinkable to remove bishops, *even if* they had been in cahoots with the Nazis.

But we have Daniel Fernández Torres removed for not going along with highly debatable Covid protocols, choosing to send his seminarians elsewhere than an interdiocesan seminary, and allowing the venerable Latin Mass to continue. We have Joseph Strickland "relieved from pastoral governance" because he "did his duty in preaching and defending with *parrhesia* the immutable Catholic faith and morals and in promoting the sacredness of the liturgy, especially in the immemorial traditional rite of the Mass," as Bishop Schneider said.[280] Pius XII would be sickened.

Servideus: So far, we've been discussing a situation where a good bishop is removed unjustly from his flock. But it's even worse if the reason the pope removes a good bishop is to install a bad bishop, that is, a wolf, who will prey on the flock. Can a good shepherd abandon his sheep to the wolves? Could the sitting bishop, knowing or suspecting his replacement will be someone in the mold of Cardinal Cupich or Cardinal McElroy—could he leave his flock without sinning? Or must he remain at his post, no matter what?

Paulinus: I don't think that's a difficult question. It *seems* to us to be a difficult question because our hyperpapalist instincts or habits of thought make us never want to think about somebody disagreeing with the pope in such a major way, on such a major issue as the episcopacy. We also tend to downplay or underestimate the obligation that a bishop has to his own flock, *because* we have gotten used to thinking of them as branch managers who can be moved around. Eric Sammons has frequently made this point (but so have many others): ever since it's become customary to move bishops around, to advance them from a (so to speak) "lesser" diocese to a "greater" diocese, we've had

---

[280] "Bishop Strickland's Removal is a 'Blatant Injustice,' says Bishop Schneider," *LifeSiteNews*, November 11, 2023. See also chapter 8.

Why a Bishop Should Ignore His Unjust Deposition by a Pope

a terrible plague of ambition, of career climbing. It's like going up the corporate ladder, from lower management to higher management, with increasing perks and power. That mentality has crept into everybody's minds to such an extent that we don't think of a bishop anymore as a *father*. The medievals talked about the bishop as the *bridegroom* of the local church, just as Christ is the Bridegroom of the whole Church. What does it say when a bishop is then "promoted" to another local church? This is like ecclesiological polygamy, or divorce and remarriage.

Servideus: But it's not *impossible* to move a bishop . . .

Paulinus: I'm not saying that it's impossible; only that it's weird and unhealthy, seen against the backdrop of church history, where, for very sound reasons, theoretical and practical, that was never the custom. The bishop is the husband of the local church, and therefore the father of his faithful. They're his spiritual children, right? And isn't it beautiful to think about how, in pre-modern times, the image of a father was something that people thought of with the warmth of affection. Now, everybody attacks patriarchy, and fatherhood is dismissed or seen as an arbitrary social construct. But in reality, the fatherhood of God is the source of all authority: "For this cause I bow my knees to the Father of our Lord Jesus Christ, of whom all paternity in heaven and earth is named" (Eph 3:14–15). The *highest* title of a bishop, in a way, would be "father of his spiritual children" and then "shepherd of his flock," to use another metaphor. So, it's not difficult *in itself* to say that a bishop should be prepared to die rather than abandon his children and his flock, especially if he believed they were in danger of having sacraments, or the traditional liturgy they know and love, or sound doctrine and moral guidance, removed from them.

Servideus: For me, that says all the hassle, all the awkwardness, is worth it. Like the possible removal of buildings: a canceled bishop is going to have his residence and his chancery taken over by the usurpers. He will have to get a new place and have a new office.

Paulinus: That's right.

Servideus: It seems to me that your position rests on recognizing a crisis in the Church. Would you say that's true? I mean, if things were peaceful and stable, none of this would be happening.

Paulinus: Correct. We are living in times when a different gospel, a false gospel, is being preached. As St. Paul sternly taught us: "But though we, or an angel from heaven, preach a gospel to you besides that which we have preached to you, let him be anathema" (Gal 1:8), that is, accursed, condemned.

Unresolved Tensions in Papal-Episcopal Relations

Servideus: But Pope Francis and his supporters tell us that there isn't a new gospel, just a better, more developed understanding of the gospel, and so the bishops need to get behind this "fuller" gospel and not be stuck in the past. It's serious enough that apparently some bishops ought to be removed if they are not "on board" with the program!

Paulinus: That's their approach.

Servideus: What's wrong with it?

Paulinus: We can let one of the Fathers of the Church answer that question. St. Vincent of Lérins was the first to articulate the truth that the deposit of faith can never essentially change. Even if the way that we grasp it and formulate it develops over time, the essence of the faith, the substance of it, never changes. This Church Father is often misquoted by Pope Francis as if he's some kind of an evolutionist, so that, doctrinally speaking, you can start with a microbe and end with a mammoth. But that's not what Vincent teaches; he says there is growth (*profectus*), not a radical change (*mutatio*).

The verse I mentioned from St. Paul's Epistles to the Galatians is quoted again and again by Vincent, to drive home that the deposit of faith given by Christ our Lord to the Apostles is so rock-solid, so definite and definitive, that neither the Apostles nor even the angels who are above the Apostles—the angels in heaven, who see God face to face!—not even *they* have the authority to change it. Paul's assertion is a counterfactual: *even if* an angel from heaven were to come down (not that any of them would) and preach something other than the gospel you received, you shouldn't, you mustn't follow that angel. Follow the original, hold fast to the faith once delivered to the saints.

What I find most pertinent to our situation is that Paul emphasizes: if *we*—that is, the *Apostles*: himself, Peter, Andrew, James, John—if *we* should preach a gospel other than the one we originally preached, let us be accursed, and whatever you do, don't follow us. There's no verse in Scripture that more beautifully highlights the fact that the pope and the bishops are subordinate to the truth handed down, not superior to it. They're not in control of it, they can't mold it however they wish to fit it to a humanist, modernist, globalist, or whatever agenda. They have no authority to do that. Let them be accursed who try to do it.

Servideus: Unfortunately, it does seem that that's where we're at. So many teachings of this pope and his supporters contradict Scripture, Tradition, and the preceding Magisterium. This can't be from the Apostles; it's surely not from God.

Paulinus: Right. One of the themes I insist on over and over in my writing is that God gave us two powerful and precious gifts—John Paul II called them two wings with

Why a Bishop Should Ignore His Unjust Deposition by a Pope

which we rise up to the contemplation of truth: reason and faith. We can see with our reason that certain acts are contrary to the natural law. Even pagan philosophers like Plato and Aristotle saw that homosexuality was contrary to human nature. Aristotle unquestionably rejects it, classifying sodomy as a form of bestiality or subhuman vice.[281] And these men lived without any benefit of divine revelation! We have the gift of reason, we have the gift of faith. The gift of faith gives us access to the teaching of Christ and the teaching of the Church across all the ages. There's no question whatsoever about the uninterrupted, constant, universal ordinary magisterium on issues of sexual morality.

Modernity is characterized, in general, by irrationality, irrationalism, the exaltation of the ego, the exaltation of the will or voluntarism: *I want what I want*. Reality is what I want to make it. That kind of thinking has been around in the writings of philosophers for centuries now, long enough to have trickled down and permeated a vast number of minds. Reason, you might say, is having a terribly hard time right now. And as for faith, how many people really take pains to learn their faith? When you read the good old catechisms—hundreds of catechisms going back hundreds of years—they all taught the same thing about matters of importance. When we study them side by side, we can see very clearly what the Church teaches. We can see how Pope Francis is departing from the Faith; how somebody like Victor Manuel Fernández, Prefect of the Dicastery for the Doctrine of the Faith, departs from it.

Servideus: His being put in charge is like Pope Francis rubbing salt into the wounds that all of us have suffered for the past decade.

Paulinus: Absolutely. That appointment in and of itself—if that isn't a supreme wake-up call for all of the conservatives or all of the moderates who are still sitting on the fence, I'm afraid they're just going to die on the fence. They must be glued to it, because if you can't see that this man is totally unsuitable for the office he has, with his questionable morality, his record on clerical abuse, and his ideas that are contrary to Faith, can you see anything at all?

Servideus: So we are in a state of crisis. In a crisis or an emergency, certain steps are more defensible or more necessary than they would be in times of peace. This is an accepted moral principle.

---

[281] See *Nicomachean Ethics*, Bk. 7, ch. 5, where, after calling sodomy brutish, a "diseased state or habit," Aristotle notes that homosexual tendencies form in people who have been sexually abused since childhood.

Unresolved Tensions in Papal-Episcopal Relations

Paulinus: There are things we can do when a house is burning down—like break down a door, enter in uninvited, shoot water all over the place, remove people without consent—that we can't do when a house is not burning down.

Servideus: So, granting all the chaos that would ensue from a bishop not stepping down when told to do so, it is still better that he remain than for him to further enable the abuse of papal authority, lend support to the heretical faction in charge, and abandon the flock to the wolves.

Paulinus: Exactly.

Servideus: I'm curious: would you say this scenario could play out at the parish level as well? Let's say you have a dictatorial bishop who removes a priest in charge of a parish for doing good things, and that priest has reason to believe his successor at the parish will be a wolf. Could the priest refuse to leave his position?

Paulinus: To give a detailed answer we would have to make some canonical distinctions between a pastor and a parish administrator, but we can answer the question generally. It seems to me that it's much more grave when you're talking about the pope unjustly removing a bishop than when you're talking about a bishop moving a priest around. Because the priests are not equipped by Christ with a "pastorship" when they are ordained. They are simply given assignments by the bishop. Essentially, the way to think about the presbytery of a diocese is that all of the priests are an extension of the bishop because he can't be everywhere at the same time. That's certainly the way it developed in the ancient church. Early on, when the flock was small, it was the bishops who celebrated Mass and the other sacraments. As the Church grew and grew during the early centuries, and especially after the fourth century when Christianity was legalized and took off like wildfire, the bishops became overwhelmed. They couldn't possibly be everywhere they needed to be.

Servideus: If the priests are like an extension of the bishop, he can move them around as he pleases.

Paulinus: Yes. That doesn't mean, however, that he should move them with no consideration for their aptitudes, personalities, and gifts, as if they were unfeeling chess pieces, nor is it to say they shouldn't push back respectfully if they believe a big mistake has been made or seek canonical recourse if they are *unjustly* attacked, removed, or disciplined by their bishop. There's a lot of that kind of injustice going on nowadays, and it *is* injustice that should be identified publicly so that bishops can at least be shamed into acting better, or undoing some of the damage they've done.

Why a Bishop Should Ignore His Unjust Deposition by a Pope

Servideus: That's why something like the Coalition for Canceled Priests exists.

Paulinus: Quite so. Still, you couldn't ever say "I'm a pastor by Christ's divine institution." You can't say that. You are a pastor solely because your bishop made you one. The bishops, on the other hand, are not, as it were, an extension of the pope simply because the pope can't be everywhere in the world at once. For that to be true, Christ would need to have appointed only *one* apostle, Peter, who, after being bishop for a while, said, "I'm way too busy. I can't go to every city in Asia Minor, so I'm going to appoint other people who represent me." That would be the "vicars of the pope" or "nuncios" model of the episcopacy that we just rejected and that *Lumen Gentium* rejected. From the beginning, Christ said: I want there to be *many bishops*. That is by divine institution.

Servideus: It's amazing to think that there is a way forward. It might be messy, but there's a way forward amidst all the confusion. We just need to find those bishops who are willing to stand up. We really need to pray hard for God to raise them up.

Paulinus: Let me add one final point. In church history, the fourth century is extremely valuable to study. What a lot of people don't realize about the Arian crisis is that it spread so widely that in some dioceses there were two men claiming to be bishop: an Arian one and a Catholic one. Sometimes there was a Catholic bishop and an attempt was made to bump him out by appointing an Arian bishop; or a Catholic bishop died and an Arian bishop replaced him. Meanwhile, a Catholic bishop like St. Athanasius might pass through to minister to the orthodox (i.e., Catholic) faithful. There were wildly different scenarios in different places. The point is, it was extraordinarily messy. But St. Athanasius didn't ever say, "It's just too messy. Let's not do this. We'd better wait for better times." No, he just *dealt with the mess*, threw himself into it, because he could never abandon the Catholic flock. Even if it's a flock outside your proper diocese, you don't abandon the sheep of Christ. He didn't say, "Well, you know, the pope is letting it happen this way, so who are we to judge? The pope excommunicated me, so I'll stop saying divine liturgy and stop acting like a bishop." No! Even when he was excommunicated, he continued to act like a bishop and he continued to do the liturgy. God gave us St. Athanasius for a reason: He wants him to be a permanent example for other crisis periods in church history.

Servideus: The faithful laity will play a big role, too. You have to support your true bishop at a time when a lot of people will be saying: "He's not the bishop. He's been kicked out. Stop already. You're being so divisive. You're schismatics!"

Unresolved Tensions in Papal-Episcopal Relations

Paulinus: Exactly. Don't give in to their simplistic views. Reject what you know is wrong, and stick to what you know is right. As Newman said, the laity were the great supporters of the minority of orthodox bishops during the Arian crisis. We are seeing the same scenario in our times.

Servideus: Time to fast and pray.

Paulinus: Amen to that.

Appendix 3

Do Not Go Gentle into That Good Retirement

Peter A. Kwasniewski

On November 11, 2023, the feast of the great bishop St. Martin of Tours, the Vatican announced: "The Holy Father has relieved from the pastoral governance of the Diocese of Tyler H.E. Msgr. Joseph E. Strickland and appointed the Bishop of Austin, H.E. Msgr. Joe Vásquez as the Apostolic Administrator of the vacated diocese."

In last chapter's dialogue, "Paulinus" explained why a bishop should not only refuse to retire under pressure if he is guilty of no wrongdoing, but also refuse to acknowledge his deposition if Rome proceeds to that dire step. As we saw, the Second Vatican Council teaches that "the apostles' office of nurturing the Church is permanent and is to be exercised without interruption by the sacred order of bishops. Therefore, the Sacred Council teaches that bishops by divine institution have succeeded to the place of the apostles."[282] Moreover,

> The pastoral office or the habitual and daily care of their sheep is entrusted to them completely; nor are they to be regarded as vicars of the Roman Pontiffs, for they exercise an authority that is proper to them, and are quite correctly called "prelates," heads of the people whom they govern. Their power, therefore, is not destroyed by the supreme and universal power, but on the contrary it is affirmed, strengthened, and vindicated by it, since the Holy Spirit unfailingly preserves the form of government established by Christ the Lord in His Church.[283]

Finally, the Council affirms that a bishop, although governing only the portion of the flock of Christ entrusted to him, nevertheless has a responsibility to and for the whole Catholic Church.

Originally published at *Crisis Magazine* under the title "Resisting Papal Overreach: The Story of Bishop Isidore Borecky," and incorporated into Peter Kwasniewski, *Bound by Truth: Authority, Obedience, Tradition, and the Common Good* (Brooklyn, NY: Angelico Press, 2023), 194–99; reprinted here with minor edits.

[282] *Lumen Gentium*, no. 20.
[283] *Lumen Gentium*, no. 27.

Unresolved Tensions in Papal-Episcopal Relations

In short: a bishop is a bishop because Jesus Christ has made him a high priest of the Church and a successor of the apostles. He is not a "vicar of the pope," that is, one who stands in for the pope like a branch manager beholden to Vatican, Inc., but a vicar of Christ in his own diocese, receiving his episcopacy from God at the pope's delegation.[284] In the absence of a just cause for the grave step of deposition—historically used for cases of heresy or other notorious crimes—the bishop remains bishop of his see by divine authority. Nor can he be faulted for addressing and assisting the faithful who dwell beyond the borders of his own diocese even if he has no immediate pastoral care over them, for in bearing witness to Christ and the sacred deposit of faith, he is simply doing his job, according to his discernment of what the times demand.

The reader may well ask: "Is there any *precedent* for resisting a deposition?"

Let me tell you the story of Isidore Borecky (1911–2003). Born in Ukraine, he studied for the priesthood in Lviv and in Munich between the wars, and was ordained on July 17, 1938. He then worked in Canada for ten years until Pope Pius XII appointed him apostolic exarch of the Apostolic Exarchate of Eastern Canada. Ten years later, he was appointed eparchial bishop of the newly-created Ukrainian Catholic Eparchy of Toronto, an office he held until his retirement on June 16, 1998. He was a father at the Second Vatican Council, and, as the founding bishop of his eparchy, much beloved.[285]

So far, so good. But you see, he was *supposed* to stop being bishop when he reached the "mandatory retirement age" of 75. At least, that's what Rome thought. Bishop Borecky, however, refused to retire, saying that this rule applied to the Latin church and not to the Eastern churches, that he was exempt from it, and that he would remain in his office until he died. "We have, as the Ukrainian Catholic Church, to fight for our rights," the bishop told a reporter.[286] The Vatican eventually appointed a successor, Roman Danylak (1930–2012), but Borecky refused to acknowledge him as the new bishop.

The above-cited news article continued:

---

[284] [See Appendix 1; cf. chapters 4 and 6 above.—*Ed.*]

[285] It must be admitted, in the interests of fairness, that Bishop Borecky had his critics: those who said he was clinging to power as if the eparchy was his personal fiefdom, or that he was fixated on bringing married clergy into the eparchy and pushing a sort of "Ukrainian nationalist" agenda. My point here is not to argue that Borecky was entirely right in what he did, but simply to point out *what he did*, and that it may be time for such action on the part of faithful bishops vis-à-vis a faithless Rome. In general, it seems to me that if a significant number of laity, priests, and bishops in any given territory pushed hard against the wayward governance of their superiors, the superiors in turn would be compelled (or at least given adequate reasons) to back down and negotiate instead of assuming they can lord it over their subordinates.

[286] See Art Babych, "Ukrainian bishop fights to hold eparchy: he claims Vatican II rule does not apply," *National Catholic Reporter*, September 24, 1993.

Do Not Go Gentle into That Good Retirement

The dispute has immobilized and divided the eparchy, which has about 100,000 members as well as 125 priests, most of whom are married. Some laypeople and priests, along with Borecky, stayed away from Danylak's consecration as bishop.... For his part, Danylak did not attend the celebration of Borecky's 45th anniversary as bishop in June.... The dispute between the two bishops appeared to come to a head in a letter of June 28 from the Vatican. It affirmed that Danylak has "all rights and duties" in spiritual and temporal matters. It said Borecky "retains only the prerogative of a liturgical character," and that his decisions about the eparchy were "void of every judicial effect." The letter came at the request of Danylak after both he and Borecky issued letters to the eparchy claiming authority over its affairs.

The Vatican letter was from Cardinal Achille Silvestrini, prefect of the Congregation for Eastern Churches. He said the pope had given Danylak the authority over the eparchy and pointed out that Borecky "has already completed his 81st year of age." Borecky countered in an Aug. 5 letter to Silvestrini, "I have taken the position, based on advice, that there is some question" whether Vatican II's "resignation requirement" applied to bishops appointed before the council, especially an Eastern-rite bishop.... "Unfortunately, I did not have the courtesy of a direct communication from Your Eminence either advising me of the appointment of the apostolic administrator or outlining the specific reasons which would constitute the 'serious and special reasons' for the appointment," wrote Borecky.

I was told by an elderly gentleman living in that eparchy that a majority of the clergy supported Bishop Borecky.[287]

How did the story end? As an entry on Danylak notes, after six years of standoff Bishop Lubomyr Husar of Lviv "negotiated a resolution whereby Borecky retired and Danylak was reassigned to 'special responsibilities in Rome,' resulting in the vacancy of the Toronto eparchy effective June 24, 1998. Bishop Cornelius Pasichny of Saskatoon was appointed the new bishop on July 1 of that year."[288] Bishop Borecky stuck to his post till 87, and died five years later. Although he didn't die in office, he relinquished it of his own volition, as befits the dignity of a successor of the apostles.

---

[287] Those who are interested in reading some articles from the midst of the events may consult *The Ukrainian Weekly* of Sunday, January 3, 1993 (https://archive.ukrweekly.com/print-media/1993/The_Ukrainian_Weekly_1993-01.pdf) and Sunday, February 7, 1993 (https://archive.ukrweekly.com/print-media/1993/The_Ukrainian_Weekly_1993-06.pdf).

[288] See "Roman Danylak," *Wikipedia*, accessed March 14, 2024.

Unresolved Tensions in Papal-Episcopal Relations

"This is all very interesting," you may be thinking, "but after all, the Borecky case was a dispute between a prelate of an Eastern Church *sui iuris* and the bishop of Rome, so of course there was more room for such a protest. There isn't really any lesson here for us Latin Catholics, since the pope is the undisputed head of our own rite-church."

There's some truth to that point. Nevertheless, we mustn't forget the language of the magisterial text that hyperpapalists appeal to more frequently than to any other:

> Wherefore we teach and declare that, by divine ordinance, the Roman Church possesses a pre-eminence of ordinary power over *every other Church*, and that this jurisdictional power of the Roman Pontiff is both episcopal and immediate. Both clergy and faithful, *of whatever rite and dignity*, both singly and collectively, are bound to submit to this power by the duty of hierarchical subordination and true obedience, and this not only in matters concerning faith and morals, but also in those which regard the discipline and government of the Church throughout the world.[289]

What this Ukrainian bishop did was certainly contrary to a narrow or positivistic reading of this passage in Vatican I, and yet he did it nonetheless, convinced that he was defending prior and legitimate rights, rooted in apostolic succession, that papal authority is required to respect, *regardless* of its primacy. Is it not possible that the Church has, for a long time, been overlooking the inherent dignity of the episcopal office after two ecumenical councils (Vatican I and II) that *both* overemphasized the papal primacy at the expense of—or at least to the eclipse of—other elements of ecclesiastical life, or formulated it in a way that has allowed erroneous extrapolations?[290]

Many speak of "the spirit of Vatican II," but there is also a "spirit of Vatican I." Indeed, it may be argued that every influential council emanates or fosters a spirit, and this can be good, bad, or a mix of the two depending on whether or not it aligns with the letter of the Council's teaching and pastoral intentions. The spirit of the Council of Trent was overwhelmingly good, for it became the animating force of the Counter-Reformation that pushed back Protestantism and revitalized the Church in Europe and well beyond. The spirit of Vatican II was overwhelming bad, for it became the animating force of a Counter-Counter-Reformation that systematically undermined the handing-on of the Faith, a reversal exemplified in the attempt to replace (in an abuse of papal authority) the Roman Rite canonized after Trent—the *lex orandi* corresponding to the Roman

---

[289] *Pastor Aeternus*, ch. 3, emphases added.
[290] See Darrick Taylor, "Can We Learn Anything from the Critics of Vatican I?," in Kwasniewski, ed., *Ultramontanism and Tradition*, 341–52.

Do Not Go Gentle into That Good Retirement

Church's *lex credendi*—with a modern papal rite diluted by Protestant, modernist, and secular influences.

The spirit of Vatican I, however, was decidedly mixed: on the one hand, ultramontanism raised the dignity of the Apostolic See and recognized the authority of the common father of Christians at a time when the Catholic Church was everywhere under attack and the faithful needed a shining beacon to look to; on the other hand, a tendency to absolutize papal monarchy and infallibilize papal statements took hold throughout the Church, paving the way for an increasing pastoral passivity among bishops and a thoughtless, almost mechanical obedience in their flocks. This strange evisceration of hierarchy and infantilization of the faithful was, of course, unsustainable, and a tidal wave of opposing errors submerged the Church after Vatican II, in which bishops frequently ignored traditional teaching emanating from Rome (of the many examples that might be cited, recall John XXIII's *Veterum Sapientia*, Paul VI's *Humanae Vitae*, John Paul II's *Veritatis Splendor*, and Benedict XVI's *Summorum Pontificum*) and the laity, egged on by those renegade bishops, claimed exemptions of conscience from any teaching they preferred not to follow, if they still bothered to practice at all.

We have come full circle now, with a progressivist pope who nevertheless employs ultramontanist tactics and surrounds himself with curial and episcopal sycophants who have quite suddenly rediscovered, after decades of dormancy, an almost latreutic devotion to the supreme pontiff, while the orthodox are few in number and beleaguered. It is in this precise context that we must understand the possibility and indeed the necessity of some bishops digging in their heels to say (whether it be to politically-motivated demands for resignation, manifestly ideological depositions, the schismatic Synodal Way, the heretical rewriting of catechisms, or the ongoing demolition of matrimonial morality): *Non possumus. Non licet.* We cannot do it. It is not allowed.

The shameful treatment of Bishop Daniel Fernández Torres set a precedent for what happened to Bishop Joseph Strickland. Sadly, both bishops lost their opportunity to stand firm against papal overreach, as Bishop Borecky stood firm, and, indeed, as Cardinal Slipyj and Cardinal Wojtyła had done decades earlier.[291] It may seem as if allowing an injustice to be done to oneself and not resisting it is the more Christian path, but this is true only if "turning the other cheek" does not contradict one's God-given vocation and one's responsibilities to others. An individual may let himself be struck and not strike back, but a father of a family may not allow his wife or his children to be struck without striking back; he must defend them. A president may allow himself

---

[291] See "Clandestine Ordinations Against Church Law," in Kwasniewski, *Bound by Truth*, 167–77.

Unresolved Tensions in Papal-Episcopal Relations

to be inconvenienced by a personal antagonist but he may not allow his country to be unjustly assaulted by enemy troops. Emperor Charles I of Austria refused to lay aside his crown and took whatever steps he could to continue ruling, although he was unsuccessful (in earthly terms). So, too, with a bishop whom the Vatican "cancels" with neither due canonical process nor published evidence of grave wrongdoing: he has obligations to his people and his brother bishops that make it necessary to resist a papal tyranny that would deprive the flock of orthodox governance and violate the dignity of the apostolic college. Placid cooperation with a dictator pope and toleration of manifest grave injustice is not to the benefit of the Catholic Church.

Appendix 4

Latin and French Texts for Chapter 4

The Latin texts of Palmieri and Vitoria are provided here for ease of reference. They are somewhat more extensive than the translated passages in chapter 3. The text of Vitoria is not a critical one; there are significant textual difficulties with his works, because he did not publish anything in his lifetime and his surviving works are reconstructed from the notes taken by his enthusiastic auditors. Both authors sometimes paraphrase Scriptural texts when they quote them, rather than giving the exact wording of the Vulgate. Extensive citations from the original article from the *Dictionnaire de théologie catholique* article on the jurisdiction of bishops are also provided.

Domenico Palmieri S.J.
Tractatus de romano pontifice
Prato: Giachetti & Sons, 1891

[447] I. . . . Plenitudi potestatis, de qua loquimur, non absoluta est, sed relativa ad societatem quae regitur: est scilicet plenitudo potestatis in regno et pro regno. Hanc porro claritatis gratia dicimus duplex ratione concipi posse: positive tantum et exclusive. Positive tantum, si potestas princeps possit quidem atque ordinario iure omnia, quae necessaria et utilia sunt pro regimine totius regni omniumque subditorum: sint tamen alii qui simul cum ipso et sub ipso, quin tamen acceperint ab ipso, aliquid saltem [448] possint. Exclusive vero, si ita princeps possit omnia, ut omnis potestas qua regnum regitur vel sit sua ipsius potestas, vel sit ab ipsa, it ut eius potestas vel formaliter vel virtualiter contineat omnem potestatem aliam qua societas regitur. Talis est potestas absoluti monarchae in societate politica.

Plenitudem potestatis secundum priorem rationem competere Romano Pontifice facili negotio demonstratur. Ea enim hos postulat characteres: quod possit scilicet ordinario jure in iis quae pertinent ad regimen societatis omnia quoad omnes sive in ferendis legibus, sive in iudiciis instituendis, sive in tuenda coercitive exsecutione legum atque nihil legitime fieri possit contra eius voluntatem, ut omnis proinde potestas alia in regno sit directe ab eo dependens. . . . Atqui talis est potesta Romani Pontificis in Ecclesia. Qui enim habet claves regni omniaque et omnes potest ligare et solvere et idcirco subiectum est unicum potestatis supremae et universalis in Ecclesia omnesque

Unresolved Tensions in Papal-Episcopal Relations

tum singillatim tum coniuctim immediate regit, is potest profecto ordinario iure omnia quoad omnes sive in ferendis legibus sive in iudiciis instituendis sive in tuenda coercitive observatione legum omnes que in regno auctoritatem habentes, quoad eorum functiones regiminis, directe regit; haec enim sunt propria auctoritatis supremae in societate. Nullus propterea valere potest actus, qui contra voluntatem eius ab aliquo fiat qui sit in regno; ad potestatem enim ligandi et solvendi spectat vis efficiendi ut actus subditi, si ea velit, nihil legitime valeat: hac autem vi exsistente, iam est irritum et inane quidquid fit dissentiente eo, qui illa potestate in universum regnum potitur. Certum proinde est quod ait S. Pius V in Bulla excommunicationis reginae Elisabeth. "Regnans in excelsis, cui data est in caelo et in terra potesta, unam sanctam et apostolicam Ecclesiam, extra quam nulla est salus, uni soli in terris, videlicet Apostolorum Principi Petro Petrique successori Romano Pontifici in potestatis plenitudine tradidit gubernandam." . . .

[449–450] II. Sed difficultas potissimum est quoad aliam rationem plenitudinis potestatis. Haec autem quaestio huc redit: an iuridiction Episcoporum in suis ecclesiis sit a Christo immediate, an sit a Christo mediante Romano Pontifici, h. e. immediate a Romano Pontifice. Neque enim ullus negat eam esse a Christo, a quo omnis est in Ecclesia potestas atque esse etiam immediate a Deo immediatione actionis, Deus enim in omnibus cum omnibus causis immediate operatur; sed quaestio est de immediato principio, immediatione scilicet suppositi, quae causam secundam inter primam aut principalem et effectum excludit.

Sunt igitur qui censeant iurisdictionem ordinariam Episcoporum esse immediate a Christo, iisque argumentis utuntur, quibus iam (Prolog. §17), demonstravimus divinam institutionem Episcopatus. Hanc vero immediatam a Christo derivationem potestatis ita generatim explicant, ut ea a Christo conferatur in ipsa ordinatione episcopali, sit tamen tantum in actu primo et quoad exercitium ligata nec ad actum reducibilis nisi cum Summus Pontifex, approbans Episcopum, territorium et subditos assignat. Sic putant manere in tuto subordinationem Episcoporum erga Rom. Pontificem; nam licet utrique immediate a Deo obtineant iurisdictionem, illi tamen subordinatam eam habent potestati Rom. Pontificis; nec enim opus est ut quaevis iurisdiction procedens immediate a Deo, sit independens. Censent e contrario alii plures, instituisse quidem Christum Episcopatum voluisseque Episcopis regi Ecclesiam suam, ita tamen ut Episcopis singulis iurisdictio ordinaria a Papa conferretur, adeo ut ante hanc Papae collationem nulla vi ordinis sit Episcopi jurisdictio vel in actu primo, se solum aptitudo ex Christi institutione, et iurisdictio obtineatur.

In priore hypothesi dici nequit Romanum Pontificum posse absque iusta causa licite et valide iurisdictionem Episcopis adimere vel restringere: posita enim conditione

Latin and French Texts for Chapter 4

a Romano Pontifice assignationis subditorum, se exerit in Episcopis iurisdictio divinitus accepta; ipsa est enim quae exercetur: ea vero a Romano Pontifice poterit quidem ratione dependentiae iustis de causis modificari, temperari, imo ex iure interpretandi ius divinum declarare licebit Romano Pontifici quod certis in casibus sit amissa, at directe auferre ab ipsis non poterit; quia in subiecto hoc non exsistit per ipsum, sed iure divino et ius divinum praevalet iuri Pontificis. In altera autem hypothesi nequit quidem id licite Papa, sed potest certe valide, ut actus eius vim per se habeat, nec sibi iurisdictionem asserere possit Episcopus ob praetextum defectus iustae causae. Ex quo iam incipit apparere, quaestionem hanc non esse de nomine, quod manifestius in sequentibus liquebit; attingit enim quaestio naturam Primatus totamque oeceonomiam iurisdictionis ecclesiasticae. Loquimur de iurisdictione Episcoporum in suis ecclesiis: quid de iurisdictione in synodis oecumenicis erga universam Ecclesiam tenendum sit, docebimus deinceps suo loco. Quaestio praesens agitur inter Theologos catholicos.

III. Defendimus itaque plenitudinem potestatis Romani Pontificis in universam Ecclesiam esse talem, ut vel formaliter vel virtualiter complectatur omnem potestatem qua Ecclesia regenda est et regitur, ut idcirco sit immediatus fons a quo est iurisdictio Episcoporum....

Itaque id primo dicimus exigi a natura Primatus quem Christus instituit: cuius proinde verba accurata analysi considerandi sunt. Sane Romanus Pontifex habet sub Christo claves huius regni caelorum quod est Ecclesia: iam vero, cellatis iis, quae dedimus in 1a thesi, functio et potestas habentis claves ita repraesentatur, ut ipse aperiat et nemo claudere possit, ut ipse claudat et nemo possite aperire; qui vero talem potestatem aperiendi et claudendi puta domum habet, eo ipso tali etiam potestate est instructus, ut nemo alius aperire aut claudere possit nisi ipso simul aperiante aut claudente, vel faciente potestatem aperiendi aut claudendi. [451] Si enim quis sine ipso aut citra potestatem ab eo factam possit aperire et claudere, fieri quoque poterit ut eo aperiente aliquis claudat, et eo claudente aliquis aperiat. Propria ergo vis huius imaginis clavium, quas habens aperit et nemo claudit, claudit et nemo aperit, eo spectat quoque, ut significetur, quod sine eius cooperatione aut sine potestate ab eo facta nemo possit claudere et aperire. Porro si haec ad rem significatam transferantur quae est potesta in regno nempe in Ecclesia: manifestum est, talem significare potestatem Petri, ut non nisi ipso cooperante aut facultatem tribuente valeat quivis alius in hoc regno potestatem aliquam exercere quod metaphorice dicitur aperire et claudere. Ergo iurisdictio episcoporum immediate a Romano Pontifice dependet non quidem quatenus cum illis cooperetur; id enim excluditur a dignitate Episcoporum qui ex Christi institutione debent esse in

Unresolved Tensions in Papal-Episcopal Relations

Ecclesia ordinarii Pastores, sed quatenus iurisdictionem accipiant ab eo, qui claves solus accepiant ab eo, qui claves solus accepit communicandas ceteris.

Et re quidem vera Romanus Pontifex potest in hoc regno omnia solvere et ligare. Si per se res spectatur, actus huius potestatis hic quoque esse potest, ut iurisdictio cuiuslibet Episcopi valide etiam citra certam causam vel sine reddidat ratione auferatur. Bonum quidem Ecclesiae, sicut nec alterius societatis, non exigit ut suprema potestas ex arbitrio exerceatur; sed bonum Ecclesiae postulare potest, ut talis sit potestas suprema quae, etsi identidem (frequentiam enim casuum ipsa natura societatis ac supremi rectoris utilitas, spectatis legibus moralibus, ac divina providentia certe impedient) sine iusta cause exerceatur, eius tamen actus valeat. Id certe exigitur quoad plura quae auctoritati politicae subduntur, cum in civili societate suprema potestas se exercet idque finis ipse socialis h. e. tranquillitas ordinis exigit. Igitur potuit Christus hanc auctoritatem conferre Romano Pontifici, ut valeat enim sine iusta causa auferre ab Episcopo iurisdictionem. Iam vero si ita est, oportet verba Christi: *quodcumque solveris* etc. ita interpretari, ut hanc quoque potestatem contineant. Nam Christus nullum iurisdictionis supremae actum excipit, imo omnem includit; limes proinde si quis figendus est, peti debet ex fine qui est bonum Ecclesiae. Sed ne erretur in usu huius normae, ea caute adhibenda est. Scilicet non ita est adhibenda, ut ea tantum auctoritas asseratur collata a Christo Petro, quae necessaria et sufficiens est, aut nobis videtur; nam fieri potest quod Christum aliquid amplius dare voluerit et amplitudo verborum Christi quantum fieri potest servanda est: sed ita est ea norma adhibenda, ut illud solum excludatur quod nequit componi cum utili regimine huius regni vel quod ab alia aliunde nota Christi institutione [452] excludatur. Atqui regimen Ecclesiae tantam potestatem a iurisdicione Romani Pontificis non excludit, sicut nec societates politicae eam excludunt a suprema auctoritate; alia vero instituto Christi, quae est institutio episcoporum, huic potestati Romani Pontificis non adversatur; cum eo enim quod Christus voluit esse episcopos, apte componitur quod voluerit ipsorum iurisdictione ex toto pendere a suo Vicario. Ergo verba Christi dicta Petro hanc quoque potestatem continent. Atqui non haberet hanc potestatem Romanus Pontifex, si ipse non conferret Episcopis iurisdictionem, ut iam monuimus: ergo.

Et sane iurisdictio Romani Pontificis est iurisdictio vicaria Christi, est scilicet ipsa iurisdictio Christi communicata Romano Pontifici: est autem iurisdictio universalis pro toto regno. Atqui institutio talis potestatis vicariae exigit ut quam libet iurisdictionem, quam Christus in Ecclesia exercet, exerceat per suum vicarium: porro conferre iurisdictionem est actus iurisdictionis: ergo.

Talem certe potestatem intellexerunt tum Optatus. [etc.]. . . . [453]

Latin and French Texts for Chapter 4

Alia demonstratio, qua efficiatur iurisdictionem episcoporum conferri immediate a Romano Pontifice, deducitur ex analysis sententiae oppositae, quae continet contradictionem.

Nam affirmatur, Episcopum consecratum habere iurisdictionem et simul affirmatur, oportere a Rom. Pontifice subditos assignari ut ea ad actum procedat. Ergo ante assignationem factam a Rom. Pontifice nulli sunt subditi Episcopo consecrato nullique fideles designari possunt, in quos ius habeat Episcopus quique teneantur illi parere. Atqui contradictoria haec sunt; nam iurisdictio est essentialiter aliquid relativum postulans terminum nempe subditos. Fieri quidem potest, ut iurisdictio sit tantum in habitu, quemadmodum in rege vi exacto a Regno: at in hoc quoque casu ideo iurisdictio manet habitualiter; quia exstant et possunt designari illi qui per se tenentur ei parere, puta cives illius regni, licet ex accidenti suspendatur haec obligatio; quod si nusquam illi exstent qui dici possunt subditi sui, nec ulla est amplius in eo Rege expulso iurisdictio. Atqui par huic regi est in hypothesi adversariorum episcopus solum consecratus; nulli enim adhuc sunt aut designari possunt qui subditi sint Episcopi solum consecrati: nam ad eos designandos non sufficit postulatio populi vel nominatio Principis aut electio capituli ad aliquam ecclesiam; certum est enim his nullam conferri iurisdictionem electis aut postulatis, nec ullam obligationem imponi fidelibus parendi illis. Ergo Episcopus antequam R.P. ipsi assignat subditos, habet et non habet iurisdictionem, quod implicat: ergo.

Idem evinci potest ex defectu rationis sufficientis eorum, quae in opposita sententia affirmantur. Dicitur enim conferri iurisdictio consecratione: quaeritur an possit nec ne conferri ante consecrationem a Romano Pontifice? Si affirmas, negare debes talem esse ex institutione Christi hanc iurisdictionem ut sit immediate a Deo; quo posito deest ratio cur contendas eam a Deo immediate conferri. Si vero negas, adversaris praxi Romanae Sedis Ecclesiaeque sensui, quae eos habet ut vere instructos iurisdicitone episcopali quos R. P. elegit et confirmavit licet nondum consecratos. Oportet ergo, ut dicas aliam esse iurisdictionem, seu aliam esse eius vim vel stabilitatem, eo quod alio modo conferatur. Verum huius affirmationis quoad vim iurisdictionis quaenam est ratio? cum constet reapse idem posse non consecratum ac qui est consecratus, quod spectat ad iurisdictionem. Quoad stabilitatem vero ratio cur non adeo stabilis sit [454] in non consecrato iurisdiction haec potest afferri, quia ex Christi institutione Episcopi sunt ii quibus cura Ecclesiarum demandata est generatim; id autem probat quidem ex Christi institutione Episcopos debere praeesse Ecclesiis; non vero ipsos a Christo immedate obtinere iurisdictionem: ergo.

Tandem sic licet arguere cum Bellarmino l. c. ex inaequalitate iurisdictionis. Nam si Deus conferret per ordinationem episcopis iurisdictionem, omnes episcopi haberent

Unresolved Tensions in Papal-Episcopal Relations

aequalem iurisdictionem sicut habent aequaliter ordinis potestatem; Deus enim non determinavit unquam εν άτομω[iota subscript] episcoporum iurisdictionem: at episcopi omnes non eadem habent iurisdictionem sive quod extensionem sive quod intensitatem; ergo.

Talis igitur est plenitudo potestatis Romani Pontificis, ut in ipsa tanquam in fonte sit omnis iurisdictio, qua Ecclesia regitur.

Haec est profectio sententia S. Thomae. . . .

[456] IV. Quae pro contraria sententia proferentur argumenta, petuntur vel ex iis testimoniis Scripturae, quibus docemur auctore Christo aut Spiritu S. esse in Ecclesia Episcopos, ut Act. 20:28 (perperam provocari ad Act. 13:1–2, ostendimus Th. 6), evl ex eo quod Episcopi sunt successores Apostolorum, quos immediate Christus misit, sicut Romani Pontifices sunt Petri successores, vel ex eo quod in nostra sententia Episcopi forent vicarii papae, qualis reapse non sunt, vel eo quod e sententia theologorum regimen Ecclesiae sit monarchicum aristocratia temperatum, vel eo quod olim Episcopi citra consensum Romani Pontifics instituebantur sive ad Apostolis sive deinde ab Metropolitanis aut Patriarchis.

Verum 1° iis Scripturae testimoniis efficitur quidem divina institution Episcopatus; at non efficitur immediate a Deo collatio potestatis. 2° Episcopi a) non sunt successores Apostolorum presse accepta successione; quia Episcopi exstiterunt viventibus Apostolis, qui eos constituebant" nec sunt b) successores quoad aequalitatem; quia potestas apostolica qua talis desiit in Apostolis: sed c) sunt successores quoad similitudinem, quia continuatur in ipsis potestas quaedam Apostolorum, potestas scilicet ligandi et solvere, docendi et sacramenta administrandi sacrosque ministros et episcopos consecrandi, quam potestatem voluit Christus ordinariam esse in Ecclesia in aliis praeter successores Petri. Haec autem non postulant eadem missione mitti Episcopos qua missi sunt Apostoli. Quemadmodum ratione potestatis sacrificandi et remittendi peccata presbyteri [457] quoque dicitur successores Apostolorum (Trid. Syn. Sess. 23 c. 1); quin exinde liceat inferre quod habeant a Deo immediate iurisdictionem in foro conscientiae, vel quod licite valeant celebrare sine licentia Episcopi. Quocirca d) falsum est esse Episcopos successores Apostolorum sicut Romanus Pontifex est successor Petri; nam hic succedit in universa iurisdictione Petri quae maior erat quam in ceteris Apostolis, et ordinaria: deinde Romanus Pontifex sedet in cathedra episcopali Petri quae iure divino saltem consequente evecta est ad dignitatem Primatus; nullius vero Episcopi sedes iure ullo divino exstitit.

3° Falsum est, esse in nostra sententia Episcopos Vicarios Papae. Nam non iure Papae sed Christi sunt Episcopi in Ecclesia nec eorum dignitatem aut auctoritatem potest Papam abolere: exinde duplex est potestas et tribunal Papae et Episcopi; quia Christus praeter cathedram Petri voluit esse cathedras Episcoporum. Nec sunt Episcopi delegati Papae, quia iurisdictionem habent ordinariam vi muneris a Christo instituti. Regunt scilicet Episcopi oves ut suas, quoniam ex Christi institutione Pastores esse debent portionis gregis, in quam potestatem ligandi et solvandi exerceant. Et licet possit Romanus Pontifex valde a singulis et ab omnibus quoque iurisdictionem auferre, tenetur tamen alios subsistere, ut semper sit Episcopi in Ecclesia; nequit enim ipse episcopalem auctoritatem abolere.

Francisco de Vitoria O.P.
"Relectiones," in Arbor magna iurisductionis ecclesiasticae
Venice, 1640

Relectio I de potestate ecclesiae (1532)

[12] Duplex igitur est potestas Ecclesiastica, potestas ordinis, et iurisdictionis. Potestas ordinis est in ordine ad corpus Christi verum, scilicet Eucharistia; iurisdictionis in ordine ad corpus Christi mysticum, id est, ad gubernandum populum Christianum in ordine ad beatudine supernaturalem. Sed in potestate ordinis non solum intelligitur potestas consecrandi Eucharisticum, sed disponendi, et idoneos reddendi hominis ad Eucharistiam, ut est consecrandi presybteros, et alios ordines conferendi, et universim omnia sacramenta administrandi, remittendi quoque peccata, et tandem omnia faciendi, quae alicui ratione alicuius consecrationis conveniunt; Unde etiam potestas ordinis, potestas consecrationis plerumque vocatur. Ad potestatem autem iurisdictionem spectat gubernatio populi Christiani extra Sacramentum, vel consecrationem vel administrationem: ut eius leges ferre, et tollere, excommunicare, dicere ius extra forum poenitentiae, et id genus alia facere....

[24] Quarto propositio: Tota potestas Ecclesiastica, et spiritualis, quae nunc residet in Ecclesia, est de iure Divino positivo mediate vel immediate. Probatur haec conclusio: Nam, ut infra disputantur, tota potestas Ecclesiastica derivata est ab Apostolis, sed Apostoli habuerunt potestatem a Christo vero Deo, et Domino, ergo tota potesta Ecclesiastica est de iure Divino positivo. Dixi autem mediate vel immediate, non solum, quia primo habuerunt Apostoli et inde derivata sit in in successores: sed quia non nego, quin in Ecclesia [25] sit aliqua potestas Ecclesiastica solum de iure positivo, ut dicam non ita multo post, sed ea ortum habuit a potestate Ecclesiastica, quae est de iure divino, qualis est potestas minorum ordinum, et fortasse aliqua alia de qua statim. Et confirmatur authoritate Apostoli ad Ephes. 4. *Unicuique nostrum data est gratia secundum mensuram donationis Christi, et ipse dedit quosdam quidem Apostolos, quosdam autem Prophetas,*

Unresolved Tensions in Papal-Episcopal Relations

alios vero Evangelistas, alios autem Pastores, et Doctores ad confirmationem Sanctorum in opus ministerii, in aedificationem corporis Christi. Sed omnes potestas Ecclesiastica, vel est aliqua illarum ab Apostolo enumeratum, vel pendet ab illos: ergo, etc.

Relectio II de potestate ecclesiae (1533)

[82] Restat ut iam dicamus in quibus inveniatur huiusmodi potestas: Et ut ad originam suam totam rem revocemus, sit prima Conclusio. Tota potestas Ecclesiastica, et ordinis, et iurisdictionis fuit in Petro Apostolo [83] Haec conclusio nota est ex Evangelio Matt. 16 *Tibi dabo claves regni caelorum, et super hanc petram aedificabo Ecclesiam meam.* Et Ioan. ultimo, *Pasce oves meas.* Secunda conclusio: In omnibus Apostolis fuit potestas Ecclesiastica ordinis, et iurisdictionis. Haec enim nota est. Dictum est enim omnibus simul, *Hoc facite in meam commemorationem: etc: Quorum remiseritis peccata, et, Quodcumque solveritis, etc.* Luc. 22. Luc. 18. Io. 20.

Sed est circa quaestionem hanc primum dubium: An omnes Apostoli habuerint potestatem immediate a Christo, an solus Petro a Christ, et alii a Petro. Et de potestate quidem ordinis, de qua minus dubitandum videbatur, non omnino videtur esse certum. Nam et Iacobus ordinatus fuit Episcopus Hierosolymitanus post Ascenscionem Domini a Petro, Iacobo, et Ioanne, ut habetur in cap. Porro dist. 66 et Paulus, ac Barnabas ordinate etiam ab aliis fuerunt. Legitur enim Actuum 13, *Segregate mihi Paulum, et Barnabam.* Et subiunigitur, Imponentes illis manus, dimiserunt: ubi glo. *In modem ordinatorum,* et tamen non est dubitandum, quin Paulus tantam potestatem acceperit a Christo, quantam alii Apostoli acceperunt: Non ergo certum videtur, quod omnes Apostoli habuerint totam potestatem ordinis a Christo, quanquam de hac potestate satis Doctores conveniunt. Sed de potestate iurisdictionis bona pars scriptorum, et quidem gravissimorum, contendunt, solum Petrum habuisse a Christo eam potestatem, caeteros autem omnes a Petro.

Quod probant primo magnorum quidem virorum authoritate; ut Anacleti, Cypriani, August., Leonis, Alexand. Quorum ego verba recitare supersedeo, eo quod re vera non significant id, quod authores huius sententiae volunt. Si quis cupit videre, legat apud Cardinalem Turrecrematam lib. Secundo de Ecclesia, c. 54. sed eorum sanctorum testimonia eo tendent, ut asseverent solum, omnem authoritatem post Petro, a Petrum habuisse originem, ab eoque pendere ipsumque Petrum principe fuisse, tum aliorum Apostolorum, tum autem totius Ecclesiae Christi: quod tantum abest, ut nos negemus, ut pro intolerando contrariam sententiam habeamus. Sed si testimoniis non efficiunt quod volunt, rationibus hoc evincere conantur. Et prima ratio eorum est, Nam Apostoli non habuerunt subditos [84] ab ipso Christo: ergo nec iurisdictionem, quae nisi in subditos esse non potest. Antecedens probatur, Quia vel omnes homines, vel certos. Non secundum quia voluntarie diceremus hos potius quam illis, cum in Evangelio non habeatur, nec omnes dedisse videtur: fuissent enim multi Pastores, et ex aequo habentes plenitudinem potestatis in Ecclesia quod in omni principatu vitiosum est.

Multorem enim principum est pernitiosa, ut Arist. etiam dicit, 12. Metaphys. Et, *Omne regnum divisum desolabitur.* Praeterea, non esset unum ovile et unus pastor gregis Christi, si essent multi pastores ex aequo, praeterea non videtur quo modo Petrus fuisset princeps, et caput supra alios Apostolos, si alii similem cum Petro a Christo potestatem accepissent.

Verum quia in contrarium videtur stare Evangelium, pono talem conclusionem, omnem potestatem, quam Apostoli habuerunt, receperunt immediate a Christo. Probatur primo, Omnibus dictum est Matthei 18, *Quaecunque solvueritis super terram,* etc. Item omnibus, *Hoc facite in meam commemorationem,* Lucae 22. Item, *Quorum remiseritis peccata* Ioan. 20 et Matth. ultimo, *Euntes in mundum universum, predicate Evangelium omni creatura,* et Ioan. 20, *Sicut misit me Pater, et ego mitto vos.* Item, *Christum fecit eos omnes Apostolos*: ut patet Matthei 10 et Marci 3. et Lucae 6 et Corinth. 1–2 et ad Ephes. 4 sed ad officium Apostolatus spectat potestas ordinis, et iurisdictionis: ergo utranque habuerunt Apostoli a Christo. Unde est considerandum, quod tria spectant ad dignitatem Apostolatus. Primum authoritas gubernandi populum fidelem: secundum, facultas docendi: tertium, potestas miraculorum. Haec ostenduntur primo, Lucae 9. scribitur: *convocatis Iesus duodecim Apostolis, dedit eis potestatem super omnia daemonia, et ut languores curarent, et misit eos predicare regnum Dei, et sanare infirmos.* Matthei quoque ultimo, Dominus dicit eis, *Euntes in mundum universum, docete omnes gentes baptizantes, et docentes servare omnia, qua mandavi vobis.* In prima quoque Epistola ad Cor. cap. 12 *Ipse posuit quidem Apostolos* glo. dicit, *omnium ordinatores, et iudices.* Itaque si Christus eos Apostolos fecit, nec Apostoli esse poterant sine potestate ordinis, et iurisdictiones, ergo utranque a Christo acceperunt. Item non videntur minorem potestatem alii Apostoli recepisse a Christo, quam Paulus: sed Paulus [85] omnem potestatem, quam habuit, habuit a Christo, ipse enim dicit ad Galathas 1 quod non ab homine, nec per hominem habuit potestatem. Et ad Galathas 2 differte dicit, se nihil accepisse ab aliis Apostolis et nominatim a Petro. *Qui videbantur,* inquit, *aliquid esse, nihil mihi contulerunt, qui enim operatus est Petro in Apostolatu circuncisionis, operatus est, et mihi inter Gentes.* Pro certo ergo mihi videtur pronuntiandum, et tenendum, Apostolos omnes accepisse utranque potestatem a Christo.

Sed superest dubium, An aequalem acceperint cum Petro: nam haec etiam quaestio in utranque partem habet asserores. Sed quia maiora festinanti non vacat utriusque

Unresolved Tensions in Papal-Episcopal Relations

partis fundamenta tradere, pro sententia, quam veriorem puto, pono conclusionem: Apostoli omnes habuerunt aequalem potestatem cum Petro. Quam sic intelligo, quod quilibet Apostolorum habuit potestatem Ecclesiasticam in toto orbe, et ad omnes actus quos Petrus habuit: Non tamen loquor de illis actibus, qui spectat ad solum Summum Pontificem, ut est congregatio generalis Concilii. Haec probatur primo quo ad primam partem ex loco iam citato Matthei ultimo. *Euntes in mundum universum*, etc. Et sine exceptione: *Quaecunque solveritis*, etc. *Et quorum remiseritis peccata*. Matthei 18 etc. et Ioann. 20. Sicut misit me pater, etc. Christus autem missus fuerat in totum orbem: ergo, et in totum orbem ipse misit Apostolos. Secunda vero pars, quod ad omnes actus, videtur posse probari ex eo, quod (ut dictum est) authoritas gubernandi est de ratione Apostolatus: et non videtur quod sit limitata, quia nulla ratione diceretur, quod extendat se ad certos actus et non ad alios, sed potius probatur ex gestis Apostolorum ipsorum, qui ubique terrarum constituebant Ecclesias, et Episcopos, et leges ferebant potestate: nec apparet quid Petrus posset, dimissis iis, quae ad solum Pontificem attinent, quod non, et alii. Et Paulus ad Galathas 1 & 2, satis defendet, se parem potestatem cum Petro habere. Haec est aperte sententia Cypriani in Epistola de unitate Ecclesiae ad Novatianarum: et habetur 14 quaest. 1. *Ego dico tibi hoc: Utique erant ceteri Apostoli, quod Petrus, pari consortio praediti, et honoris et potestatis*. Nec audienda est glos. dicens, hoc debere intelligi in ordine, et dignitate consecrationis, non in potestatis plenitudine: ut patere potest ipsam Epistolam [86] Divi Cypriani legendi.

Et ne quisquam suspicetur, me velle quicquam derogare dignitati, aut praerogativae, aut primatui Petri, quem non solum cum Catholica Ecclesia confitemur, sed etiam pro virili defendimus: pono aliquam Conclusionem, Petrus inter omnes Apostolus fuit authoritatem et potestate primus, et princeps cum summa supra totam Ecclesiam potestate. De hac conclusione a doctissimis viris non iusti solum: sed praegrandes libri confecti sunt, et editi, atque ideo ego brevi me hoc loco nunc expediam paucis modo contentus Evangelii testimoniis. Primus locus est Matthei 10. *Duodecim autem Apostolorum nomina sunt haec. Primus Simon, qui dicitur Petrus*. Et Lucae 6. *vocavit Dominus discipulos suos, et elegit duodeciim ex ipsis, quos et Apostolos nominavis, Simonem, quem cognominavis Petrum, et Andream fratrem eius*, etc. Et eodem ordine nominantur, et numerantur a Marc. cap. 3, et tamen nulla ratione Petrus potuit dici primus, nisi dignitate Apostolatus, vel Pontificatus. Nam ordine quidem vocationis, primus fuit Andreas frater petri, ut patet ex primo cap, Ioann. Imo Andreas iam vocatus a Christo, ut refert Ioann. *invenit Simonem fratrum suum, et dixit ei, Invenimus Messiam: et adduxit eum ad Iesum*. Est praeterea insigne testimonium, et omnino non refractario, et obstinato intellectui apertissimum Matthei 16. ubi ad quaestionem Domini musantibus, et cunctantibus aliis

Latin and French Texts for Chapter 4

Discipulis, respondet Petrus, *Tu es Christus filius Dei vivi.* Cui Dominus, *Beatus es Simon Bariona, quia caro et sanguis non etc. sed Pater meus, etc.*, et ego dico tibi quod tu es Petrus, et super hance Petram aedificabo Ecclesiam meam, et tibi dabo claves regni caelorum. Certe vel caeco notum esse potest, pro tam praeclara Confessione aliquid promissum Petro prae ceteris Apostolis. Item *Ego orabo pro te, et tu aliquandeo conversus confirma fratres, etc.* Lucae 22. Nec obscurior locus est ille Ioann. ultimo, ubi cum bis Dominus rogasset petrum; an se diligere plus aliis Apostolis, illo respondente, se quidem amate, subiunxit bis, *Pasce oves meas, pasce oves meas.* Prorsus est hominis praeposteri, et perverse alioqui apertum testimonium interpretantis, negare Christum eo loco voluisse Petro, pro maiori erga se amore, maiorem etiam authoritatem praestare: at que vel ex his duobus [87] locis liquido constat, Petro integram authoritatem in Ecclesia commissam. Cui enim data est, si Petro est negata? Licet etiam, ut dictum est, alii Apostoli habuerint aequalem potestatem cum Petro ad sensum supra positum, tamen potestas Petro erat eminentior. Primo quia potestas Petri fuit ordinaria, Apostolorum autem extraordinaria. Secundo quae sequitur ex hac, potestas Petri erat perseveratura in Ecclesia, non autem aliorum. Tertio, aliorum potesta nec supra Petrum, nec supra se invicem, Petri autem super omnes alios. Quarto, aliorum potestate subordinate fuit Petri authoritati. Praevaluisset enim authoritas Petro contra authoritatem aliorum.

Sed ut aliquando illum locum, *Pasce agnos meos,* absolvam (nam difficilior alius restat) fit in hoc argumento haec ultima conclusio, Praeter Sanctos Apostolos nullus alius a Christo potestatem Ecclesiasticam aliquam videtur accepisse. Haec probatur etiam, quia in omnibus locis, ubi data est potestas, non erant discipuli. Haec probatur, Nam si quisquam alius accepisset: maxime fuisset ex numero seputaginta duobus autem probatur, quia in omnibus locis, ubi data est potestas, non erant discipuli isti, ergo. Et praeterea, quia Ioseph, qui congnominatus est Barnabas, erat unus ex discipulis, ut patet Act. 1 et tamen Actuum 4 dicitur post ascenscionem Domini quod erat levites. Non est autem credendum, si Christus potestatem aliquam Ecclesiasticarum dedisset ei, quod fecisset solum Levitam, quia Dei perfecta sunt opera, et Philippus, qui praedicavit Samaritanis, Actuum 8 et baptizavit eunuchum Candacis reginae, non fuit Philippus Apostolus, ut multi putant, nec sine causa quod ad baptismum ipsius Samaritani non receperant Spiritum sanctum: Sed dicunt esse Philippum unum ex septem diaconis, de quo Actor. 6 et 21. Ita dicit Sanctus Thomas in 4 dis, 2 q. 2 ar. 4 ad 1. Et quodlibet 11 ar. 7 livet oppositum videatur dicere super Ioann. Cap. 12 lect. 3. Hic igitur Philippus, non videtur dubitandum, quin esset de numero septuaginta duorum, cum post. Apostolos non temere legatur alius Praestantior praedicator, aut minister Evangelii, ad quod opus delect fuerunt 72. Discipuli, et tamen non erat presbyter, sed tantum Diaconus. [88]

Unresolved Tensions in Papal-Episcopal Relations

Imo septem illi diaconi, qui Act. 6 fuerunt administrandum mensis, creduntur fuisse de numero discipulorum. Non enim ex Neophytis fuissent assumpti ad tale ministerium, et tamen non erant praesbyteri, ut pro certo constat: imo re vera nullam habent spiritualem potestatem. Ergo septuaginta duo Discipuli, nec fuerunt a Christo ordinati, nec habuerunt potestatem aliquam Ecclesiasticam; quae sine ordine non est. Restat ergo conclusio vera, quod praeter Apostolos nullus alius accepit a Christo potestatem Ecclesiasticam: atque ita habemus primam originem potestatis Ecclesiasticae: fuerunt enim, et primi, et soli: qui a Christo Domino et Redemptore nostro hanc potestatem acceperunt duodecim Apostoli.

Superest nunc tractare, qua ratione haec potestas derivata est usque ad nos, et perseverat in Ecclesia, et sic erit absolutum totum negotio, quod suscepimus de subiecto potestatis Ecclesiasticae.

Sit ergo de hac quaestione prima propositio, Potestas Ecclesiastica non solum fuit in Apostolis, sed etiam in aliis. Haec est nota ex scripturis. Nam Paulus constituit Episcopum Titum, et Timotheum. . . .

Secunda propositio, Defunctis Apostolis Christi perseveravit in Ecclesia omnis potestas ordinis, et iurisdictionis, quae prius erat in Apostolis. Probatur, gradus potestatis Ecclesiae sunt instituti a Christo, non solum pro tempore Apostolorum, sed in totum tempus, quo perseveratura erat Ecclesia: ergo perseveraverunt in Ecclesia post decessum Apostolorum. . . .

[89] Tertia propositio, Tota potestas ordinis in Ecclesia derivata est, et pendet immediate ab Episcopis. Volo dicere, quod sicut Apostoli, et illi soli habuerunt iure Divino ordinare, et consecrare presbyteros, et alios inferiores ministros, ita omnes, et soli Episcopi hoc habent etiam iure Divino . . . nec inter Catholicos est dubitatio, Episcopis hanc habere potestatem. Et quod soli Episcopi habeant, videtur, quia nunquam legimus ordinationes factas nisi ab Apostolis, vel ab Episcopis aliis. . . . [90] Item potestas ordinis est iuris Divini: ergo non est usurpanda, nisi ab eis, quibus constat iure Divino commissam, tales sunt solu Episcopi: ergo etc. . . .

Quarta propositio, Defuncto Petro principe Apostolorum, aliquis successit Petro cum simile authoritate, et potestate iurisdictiones in totum orbem. Probatur a sancto Thom. 4. contra Gen. Cap. 76. Christus sic instituit Ecclesiam, [91] ut esset usque in saeculum duratura, Unde Esa. 9 Super solium David, et super regum eius sedebit, ut confirmet illud, et corroboret in iudicio, et iustitia amodo, et usque in sempiternum. Sed Christus aedivicavit Ecclesiam super Petrum, ut ipse dicit Matth. 16 opus fuit, ut eo a medio sublato, alius loco ipsius subrogaretur. Item inveteri lege a Deo instituta semper fuit unus summus Sacerdotes. Patet Deutero. 17 et aliis locis. Hoc est quod Augustin.

Latin and French Texts for Chapter 4

24 Quaestion, 1. cap. *quodcunque*, dicit, quod cum Petrus accepit claves, accepit non tanquam privatus, sed nomine Ecclesias: hoc data est ei potestas, quae esset duratura in Ecclesia, in cuius aedificationem Christus dedit. Unde sicut Adam quaedam dona habuit personalia, quae in posteros transfundere non potuit, ut plenitudinem omnium scientiarum, quaedam autem communia statui innocentiae, ut institutam, gratiam, immortalitatem: sicut et Petrus privata dona habuit, quaedam in quibus successorum non habuit (nec erat necesse) ut gratiam miraculorum, donum linguarum: quaedam vero accepit, in posteros translaturus, ut potestatem clavium, quam non sibi, sed Ecclesiae accepit. Item ille ordo, a principio constitutus a Christo in Ecclesia, ut scilicet, esset unum caput, et unus princeps super omnia in tota Ecclesia, erat convenientissimus ad administrationem Ecclesiae. Quod constat non solum facto ipso Christo, cuius est summa sapientia, et providentia, sed etiam consensu meliorum Philosophorum, quod Monarchiam aliis principatus praeferunt, ut constat ex Aristotel. in Politicorum, et Ethicorum libris, et Metaphysicorum. Sed Christus non minus diligit nunc Ecclesiam suam, quam tunc diligebat, cum etiam promisit se nobis adfuturum usque ad consummationem saeculi, Matth. ultimo. ergo nullo modo verisimile, quod voluerit, defuncto Petro, mutare rationem, et formam administrationis ab ipso Petro institutam, ut scilicet esset unus princeps totius potestatis Ecclesiasticae. Nec enim Petrus principatum in suum commodum acceperat, sed in utilitatem, et aedificationem Ecclesiae. . . .

[95] Superest ut agamus de successoribus aliorum Apostolorum. De quo sit prima propositio, Nemo succedit aliis Apostolis cum aequali potestate, et authoritate iurisdictionis: hoc est, ut in toto orbe haberet plenitudinem potestatis, sicut quilibet Apostolorum habuisset, ut supra ostensum est. Haec probatur primo ipso facto. De nullo enim legimus, quod se gesserit pro Episcopo universalis Ecclesiae, praeter Romanum Pontificem, sed proximi quique Apostolorum vel Hierosolitanus, vel Antiochenus, vel alterius urbis dictus est. Secundo, quia illa potestas universalis in aliis Apostolis fuit extraordinaria, et personalis, ut dictum est (et sic non potuerunt eam successoribus reliquere), et sola potestat Petri erat ordinaria, et in perpetuum duratura, ab Ecclesia autem nullus recipit tam amplem potestatem, quae etiam sine suo capite [96] nihil potest: nec a Summo Sacerdote, hoc est, vel Petro, vel Clemente, legimus quemquam subrogatam cuiquam Apostolorum cum illa potestatis amplitudine. Tertio, fuisset maxima occasio schismatis, et dissensionum in successoribus, qui non erant in gratia confirmati, si provincias non habuissent distinctas.

Secunda propositio, Quilibet aliorum Apostolorum a Petro potuit relinquere successorum, licet non universalem, saltem in quacunque provincia voluisset, qui esset verus Episcopus illius provinciae. Hanc propositionem, scio non placituram omnibus

Unresolved Tensions in Papal-Episcopal Relations

doctoribus, tum Theologis, tum iure consultis, quae nec ipsis Cardinalibus, Turrecremata et Caiet. placeret. Omnes enim illa persuasio semel invasit, omnem potestatis iurisdictionis ita dependere a Romano Pontifice, ut nullus possit habere, nec minimam quidem spiritualem potestatem, nisi ex mandato, vel lege ipsius: post Apostolos quidem, qui ex singulari privilegio habuerunt a Christo, quod nullus alius potest habere, nisi a Petro. Sed probo primo hanc propositionem aperte, Quilibet Apostolorum potuit vivens creare Episcopum in quacunque provincia, et ille non amitteret potestatem defuncto Apostolo: ergo potuit reliquere successorum. Antecedens est notum, quia Paulus constituit Titum, et Timotheum, et idem iuris habuit alii Apostoli: et in hoc sensu propositio a nemine negare potest. Sed dico, eam esse verum in sensu, in quo diximus, Petrum potuisse nominare successorum: id est qui re vera non haberet potestatem, nisi post obitum Apostoli: ita inquam potuit Ioannes in Asia nominare Ignatium, ut post se Episcopus esset in ea provincia. Hoc probatur, Nam, ut supra abundam probatum est, nec alli diffitentur, caeteri Apostoli viventes aequalem habuerunt potestatem cum Petro: ergo potuerunt condere legum, ut vivens Apostolus eligeret sibi successorum: ergo potuit illa lege ipse primus eligere. Certe de antecedente non videtur dubitandum esse, quin concedunt aequalem authoritatem aliis Apostolis cum Petro. Et si Petrus poterat talem legem ferre in provinciis, quare Paulus non potuisset? Imo certum est non indigere alios Apostolos, expectasse mandatum Petri ad omnia, quaecunque opus erant in provinciis. Atque adeo videtur mihi propositio non solum probabilis, sed de qua dubitari non potest.

[98] Tertia propositio, Non solum Apostoli hoc potuerunt, sed quilibet successorum similiter potuit relinquere sibi successorum. Haec probatur aperte ex secunda, Nam lata lege a Ioanne, vel Paulo, ut vivens Episcopus nominaret successorum, potuisset Titus nominare alium. Sed ultra addo (quod difficilius videtur, sed puto non minus verum) quod etiam si de hoc nulla lex esset lata a Paulo, potuit Titus, et Thimotheus nominare sibi successorum, inconsulto etiam successorum Petri: et simile de omnibus aliis Episcopis. Probatur, quia Episcopus est pastor, et gubernator provinciae iure Divino: ergo si maiore potestate non impediatur, potest facere omnia, quae expediunt ad salutem suae provinciae: sed hoc potuit maxime eo tempore esse expediens, ut vivens Episcopus nominarem successorum: ergo potuit hoc facere, imo, et legem ferre, ut hoc modo perpetuo fieret. Unde enim habemus, quod Episcopus possit legem condere de electione Abbatis, vel Parochi, vel de quacunque alia re, et non de de electione Episcopi? Et confirmatur, Quia certe non solum hoc videbatur possibile, et conveniens, sed omnino eo tempore necessarium. Quomodo enim defuncto in ultima India Episcopo potuisset expectare mandatum Petri ad sufficiendum novum Episcopum? Et haec omnia dicta sunt quantum ad potestatem iurisdictionis. Nam quo ad potestatem ordinis, si Episcopatus

Latin and French Texts for Chapter 4

dicit ordinem, vel potestatem distinctam a prebyteratu, et a iurisdictione, sicut video placere pene omnibus: oportuit praeter electionem concurrere aliquam consecrationem tam ad institutionem Papae, quam Episcoporum: sed illam potuit facere quilibet Episcopus vivens, sacrando successorum, vel etiam uno defuncto Episcopus alterius provinciae potuit ordinare successorum prius electum, et nominatum.

Ultima proposition, Quilibet Episcopus in sua provincia potuit condere legem, ut presbyteri eligerent Episcopum, vel aliam formam institutionis dare, etiam inconsulta sede Petri. Haec sequitur ex aliis. Nam potuit leges convenientes provinciae facere de hac re, sicut de aliis. Ecce rationem, quomodo authoritas, et dignitas Episcopalis potuit derivari successive ad uno in alterum usque ad nos, et per Episcopos omnis alia potestas inferior.

Sed his non obstantibus (ne quis putet me velle derogare [98] Romane Sedi, et dignitati) pono aliam Conclusionem: Successores Petri potuerunt, et possunt pro suo arbitrio Episcopos creare in singulis provincias, et quascunque leges de hac re prius latas tollere, et novas condere, et provincias distinguere, et omnia ad haec spectantia pro suo iudicio, et potestate facere. Omnia, enim quae dicta sunt, intelligenda sunt, nisi a Sedi Petri aliter provideatur. Haec propositio probatur clare: Quia Petro dictum est absolute, *Pasce oves meas*, sine aliqua exceptione. Ergo ad Petrum spectat omnis administratio sine exceptione, et per consequens etiam creatio Episcoporum. Si enim quicunque aliorum Apostolorum hoc poterat, et secerunt, ut constat, multo magis ad Petrum, et successores Petri. Ex quo patet corollarium, quod nunc non potest Episcopus fieri, nisi secundum forma traditam a Summis Pontificibus: et si secus tentatum fuerit, nihil efficiatur ratum, sed totum erit irritum, et inane. Dico vero quantum ad authoritatem iurisdictionis: nam quod ad consecrantionem spectat, secus est. Secundo sequitur, quod tota potestas Ecclesiastica, sive ordinis, sive iurisdictionis, mediate, vel immediate pendet a sede Petri. Patet, quia ab illa sede pendent Episcopi: ab eis presbyteri, et omnes inferiores ordinis, et potestates.

E. Valton
"Évêques: questions théologiques et canoniques"
Dictionnaire de théologie catholique 5:1701–25[292]
Paris: Letouzey & Ané, 1912

Les évêques sont institués de droit divin. C'est un dogme de foi défini par le concile de Trente, sess. XXIII, can. 6: "Si quis dixerit in Ecclesia catholica non esse hierarchiam

---

[292] Ed. A. Vacant and E. Mangenot; the first selection below is cols. 1702–3; the second, col. 1708.

Unresolved Tensions in Papal-Episcopal Relations

divina ordinatione institutam quae constat ex episcopis, presbyteris et ministris, anathema sit." Mais s'il est hors de doute que le pouvoir d'ordre est conféré immédiatement par Dieu aux évêques, de manière que l'Église ne saurait y rien modifier, la chose n'apparaît pas aussi certaine s'il s'agit du pouvoir de juridiction. En effet, l'origine divine de la juridiction épiscopale est-elle immédiate, ou seulement médiate, de sorte que, s'appuyant sur le droit divin, elle découle immédiatement du souverain pontife? La question est controversée entre catholiques, comme on peut le voir dans Bellarmin, *De romano pontifice*, 1. IV, c. XXII sq. Les uns soutiennent que la juridiction est conférée immédiatement par le Christ aux évêques dans l'acte même de la consécration épiscopale, quoique cette juridiction reste liée, quant à son exercice, jusqu'à ce que le souverain pontife ait assigné au nouvel évêque un territoire et des sujets. Parmi les théologiens qui défendent cette opinion, il faut citer, d'après Bouix, *De episcopo*, Paris, 1873, part. I, p. 61, François de Victoria, Alphonse de Castro, Vasquez, Tournely. D'autres pensent plus communément, avec saint Thomas, *Sum. theol.*, IIa IIae, q. xxxix, a. 3; *Contra gentes*, l. IV, c. 76; Suarez, *De legibus*, l. I, n. 12 seq.; *Defensio fidei*, l. IV, c. ix; Benoît XIV, *De synodo dioecesana*, l. I, c. iv, n. 2, que la juridiction des évêques se rattache immédiatement à celle du vicaire du Christ, auquel a été confiée non seulement une portion, mais la plénitude du pouvoir ecclésiastique. Cf. const. Pastor aeternus du concile du Vatican, c. III. D'où il faut conclure avec saint Thomas, *Contra gentes*, loc. cit., qu'à Pierre seul ont été promises les clefs du royaume des cieux, afin de montrer que, pour conserver l'unité de l'Église, le pouvoir des aux autres par son intermédiaire: "Petro soli promisit : Tibi dabo claves regni caelorum, ut ostenderetur potestas clavium per eum ad alios derivanda, ad conservandam Ecclesae unitalem." Reiffenstuel, *Jus canonicum universum*, Paris, 1889, 1. I, tit. xxxi, n. 69 sq., précise d'une manière très juste la thèse en question la juridiction épiscopale, considérée en elle-même et en général, a été instituée immédiatement par le Christ, en sorte que le pouvoir des évêques revêt un caractère qui n'est pas purement temporel, mais spirituel et divin; cf. Matth., xxvii, 19; Marc, xvi, 15; toutefois, si cette juridiction est examinée d'une manière concrète, par rapport à tels sujets et à tel diocèse, elle émane immédiatement du pontife romain, comme vicaire du Christ et pasteur suprême de l'Église universelle, ainsi qu'il appert des can. *Qui se scit, Decreto, Multum*, q. vi, et *Sacrosancta*, dist. XXII. Cf. Pirhing, *Jus canonicum*, Dilingen, 1722, 1. I, tit. XXXI, n. 39 sq. D'ailleurs, cette discussion n'a pas toute l'importance qu'elle paraît tenir. Car si les uns prétendent que l'autorité des évêques descend immédiatement de Dieu, ils ne nient pas qu'elle soit limitée et dépendante de l'autorité du souverain pontife; et si les autres soutiennent que la juridiction épiscopal dérive immédiatement du souverain pontife, ils accordent pleinement qu'elle s'appuie

Latin and French Texts for Chapter 4

sur le droit divin et qu'elle reste une juridiction ordinaire que les évêques exercent en leur propre nom. On doit, en effet, reconnaître que, quoique les évêques dépendent du souverain pontife, dont le primat est universel, ils ne sont point ses simples vicaires; mais leur pouvoir est ordinaire, en raison de l'office même, *ratione muneris*, qui leur a été confié, c'est-à-dire en raison de la charge pastorale par laquelle le Saint-Esprit les a constitués évêques, avec mission de gouverner l'Église de Dieu. En outre, les évêques sont les successeurs des apôtres, comme le proclame encore le concile de Trente, loc. cit., c. IV: *in locum apostolorum successerunt.*

Or le pouvoir de l'évêque est de deux sortes: le pouvoir d'ordre, qui découle de la consécration épiscopale, et le pouvoir de juridiction qui dépend de l'institution canonique, auxquels il faut ajouter certains droits honorifiques et privilèges spéciaux. Les pouvoirs d'ordre et de juridiction sont incontestablement séparables; et, de même que la juridiction épiscopale peut exister sans le pouvoir d'ordre, par exemple, dans l'évêque élu et confirmé, mais non encore consacré, ainsi le pouvoir d'ordre peut exister sans la juridiction épiscopale, au moins exercible en fait, par exemple, dans l'évêque qui a déjà reçu la consécration épiscopale, mais auquel le souverain pontife n'a pas encore assigné un diocèse propre ni des sujets déterminés. Le pouvoir d'ordre peut-il exister sans un certain pouvoir de juridiction, au moins lié dans son exercice, mais constitué dans sa racine et en principe? Cette dernière question est intimement liée à celle que nous avons signalée précédemment, voir col. 1702, à savoir, si l'évêque reçoit immédiatement de droit divin la juridiction épiscopale au moment de la consécration, ou bien si cette juridiction lui est conférée immédiatement par le souverain pontife.

Works Cited

Magisterial documents

Benedict XIV. *De synodo diocesana*. Venice: Typographia Bassanensi, Sumptibus Remondinianis, 1767.

Catechism of the Catholic Church. Second edition. English translation. Washington, DC: USCCB, 1997.

Congregation for Bishops. Directory *Apostolorum Successores*. February 22, 2004.

Congregation for the Doctrine of the Faith. Letter *Communionis Notio*. May 28, 1992.

———. Declaration *Dominus Iesus*. August 6, 2000.

Council of Constantinople III. *Exposition of Faith*. AD 680–681.

Council of Trent. Session XXIII. AD 1563.

Council of Vatican I. *Acta et decreta sacrosancti oecumenici concilii Vaticani*. Vol. VII. Freiburg, 1892.

———. Dogmatic Constitution on the Church of Christ *Pastor Aeternus*. July 18, 1870.

Council of Vatican II. Congregatio Generalis XLIII, *Relatio circa emendationes propositas*. *Acta Synodalia*. Volumen II, Periodus secunda, Pars II. Vatican City: Typis Polyglottis Vaticanis, 1972.

———. Constitution on the Sacred Liturgy *Sacrosanctum Concilium*. December 4, 1963.

———. Dogmatic Constitution on the Church *Lumen Gentium*. November 21, 1964.

———. Dogmatic Constitution on Divine Revelation *Dei Verbum*. November 18, 1965.

———. Decree *Christus Dominus*. October 28, 1965.

Denzinger, Heinrich. *The Sources of Catholic Dogma*. Trans. Roy J. Deferrari. Fitzwilliam, NH: Loreto Publications, n.d.

Jaffé, Philip, ed. *Regesta Pontificum Romanorum*. Leipzig: Veit, 1885.

John Paul II. Apostolic Constitution *Sacrae Disciplinae Leges*. January 25, 1983.

———. Apostolic Letter *Apostolos Suos*. May 21, 1998.

———. Encyclical *Ecclesia de Eucharistia*. April 17, 2003.

———. Post-Synodal Apostolic Exhortation *Pastores Gregis*. October 16, 2003.

John XXII, *Lettres communes*, vol. VI, ed. G. Mollat (Paris, 1912), 483; letter of March 18, 1327.

Leo XIII. Encyclical *Libertas Praestantissimum*. June 20, 1888.

Works Cited

Paul VI. Closing Speech at Second Vatican Council. December 7, 1965.

Peters, Edward N., ed. *The 1917 Pio-Benedictine Code of Canon Law: In English Translation with Extensive Scholarly Apparatus.* San Francisco: Ignatius Press, 2001.

Pius XII. Encyclical *Ad Apostolorum Principis.* June 29, 1958.

———. Encyclical *Ad Sinarum Gentem.* October 7, 1954.

———. Encyclical *Humani Generis.* August 12, 1950.

———. Encyclical *Mystici Corporis.* June 29, 1943.

Pontificium Consilium de Legum Textibus Interpretandis. *Congregatio Plenaria diebus 20–29 octobris 1981 habita.* Vatican City, 1991.

Other works

Arocho Esteves, Junno. "All of Chile's bishops offer resignations after meeting pope on abuse." *National Catholic Reporter,* May 18, 2018.

Augustine of Hippo. *De civitate Dei contra paganos.* CCL 48. Edited by B. Dombard and A. Kalb. Turnhout: Brepols, 1955.

Augustine of Hippo. *Enarrationes in Psalmos.* Edited by V. Tarulli. Rome, 1977.

Babych, Art. "Ukrainian bishop fights to hold eparchy: he claims Vatican II rule does not apply." *National Catholic Reporter,* September 24, 1993.

Baucher, J. "Juridiction." *Dictionnaire de théologie catholique* 8/2, ed. A. Vacant and E. Mangenot, cols. 1976–1996. Paris: Letouzey et Ané, 1925.

Beltrán de Heredia, Vicente. "Vitoria (François de)." *Dictionnaire de théologie catholique* 15/2, cols. 3118–33. Paris: Letouzey et Ané, 1950.

"Bishop Joseph Strickland Must Resist Pope Francis if Told to Step Down." *John-Henry Westen Show, LifeSiteNews,* July 12, 2023.

"Bishop O'Donoghue: I was baffled by lack of support from fellow bishops." *Catholic Herald,* April 2, 2015.

"Bishop Strickland relieved of pastoral governance of US diocese." *Vatican News,* November 11, 2023.

Boulay de la Meurthe, Alfred. *Histoire du rétablissement du culte en France (1802–1805).* Tours: Maison Alfred Mame et Fils, 1925.

Cajetan, Thomas. *Conciliarism and Papalism.* Edited by J.H. Burns and Thomas Izbicki. Cambridge: Cambridge University Press, 1998.

Campbell, Phillip. "The Context of Cajetan's Comments on Praying for a Pope's Death." *Unam Sanctam Ecclesiam,* March 29, 2024.

———. "Strict Consistency with the Past." *Unam Sanctam Catholicam,* November 12, 2023.

———. "The Church as a Barnacle Encrusted Ship." *Unam Sanctam Catholicam*, March 5, 2023.

Chiron, Yves. *Paul VI: The Divided Pope*. Translated by James Walther. Brooklyn, NY: Angelico Press, 2022.

Cicognani, Amleto. *Canon Law*. Second edition. Translated by Joseph M. O'Hara and Francis Brennan. Philadelphia, PA: Dolphin Press, 1935.

Congar, Yves. "De la communion des Églises a une ecclésiologie de l'Église universelle." In *L'Episcopat et L'Eglise universelle*. Paris: Cerf, 1962.

———. *Tradition and Traditions: An Historical and a Theological Essay*. New York: The MacMillan Company, 1966.

da Silveira, Arnaldo Vidigal Xavier. *Can Documents of the Magisterium of the Church Contain Errors?* Spring Grove, PA: The American Society for the Defense of Tradition, Family, and Property, 2015.

"Declaración del Obispo Daniel Fernández Torres." www.diocesisdearecibo.org/2022/03/09/declaracion-del-obispo-daniel-fernandez-torres/, accessed March 21, 2022.

de la Soujeole, Benoît-Dominique. *Introduction to the Mystery of the Church*. Washington, DC: The Catholic University of America Press, 2014.

de Mattei, Roberto. *The Second Vatican Council: An Unwritten Story*. Translated by Patrick T. Brannan, Michael J. Miller, and Kenneth D. Whitehead. Fitzwilliam, NH: Loreto Publications, 2010.

Demos II [pseudonym]. "A profile of the next Pope, writes Cardinal." *Daily Compass*. February 29, 2024.

de Muralt, André. *Néoplatonisme et aristotélisme dans la métaphysique médiévale: Analogie, causalité, participation*. Paris: J. Vrin, 1995.

Ertelt, Steven. "Catholic Bishop: Pope Francis Ousted Me Because I Spoke Truth to Power." *LifeNews*, November 13, 2023.

Fenton, Joseph Clifford. "Cardinal Ottaviani and the Council." *American Ecclesiastical Review*, vol. 148 (January–June 1963): 44–53.

———. "Episcopal Jurisdiction and the Roman See." *American Ecclesiastical Review*, vol. 120, no. 4 (April 1949): 337–42.

Fuchs, Josef. "Origines d'une trilogie ecclésiologique à l'époque rationaliste de la théologie." In *Revue de sciences philosophiques et théologiques*, no. 53 (1969): 185–211.

Ghirlanda, Gianfranco. "Cessazione dall'ufficio di Romano Pontefice." *Civiltà Cattolica*, Quaderno 3905, 2013, vol. 1, pp. 445–62, n15, www.laciviltacattolica.it/articolo/cessazione-dallufficio-di-romano-pontefice/.

Works Cited

———. "Conferenza Stampa di presentazione della Costituzione Apostolica 'Praedicate Evangelium' sulla Curia Romana e il suo servizio alla Chiesa nel mondo. Intervento del Prof. Gianfranco Ghirlanda, S.I." March 21, 2022. https://press.vatican.va/content/salastampa/it/bollettino/pubblico/2022/03/21/0192/00417.html#ghirlanda.

Gregory I. *Liber Regulae Pastoralis*. Translated by James Barmby. In *Nicene and Post-Nicene Fathers, Second Series*, vol. 12, ed. by Philip Schaff and Henry Wace. Buffalo, NY: Christian Literature Publishing Co., 1895. Revised and edited for New Advent by Kevin Knight.

Huit, Charles. "Les éléments platoniques de la doctrine de Saint Thomas." *Revue thomiste*, no. 19 (1911): 724–66.

Hunwicke, John. "Peter Says No." *First Things* online, February 7, 2017.

Journet, Charles. *The Apostolic Hierarchy*. Volume 1 of *The Church of the Word Incarnate*. Translated by A.H.C. Downes. London: Sheed & Ward, 1955.

Kallio, Albert. "Collegialità nel Vaticano II: una nuova dottrina?" *Chiesa e post concilio*, June 23, 2018, https://chiesaepostconcilio.blogspot.com/2018/06/collegialita-nel-vaticano-ii-una-nuova.html.

Kwasniewski, Peter. *Bound by Truth: Authority, Obedience, Tradition, and the Common Good*. Brooklyn, NY: Angelico Press, 2023.

———."Can We Legitimately Pray for a Pope's Death." *Tradition and Sanity*, April 8, 2024.

———, ed. *From Benedict's Peace to Francis's War: Catholics Respond to the Motu Proprio* Traditionis Custodes *on the Latin Mass*. Brooklyn, NY: Angelico Press, 2021.

———. *The Road from Hyperpapalism to Catholicism: Rethinking the Papacy in a Time of Ecclesial Disintegration*. Volume 2: *Chronological Responses to an Unfolding Pontificate*. Waterloo, ON: Arouca Press, 2022.

———, ed. *Ultramontanism and Tradition: The Role of Papal Authority in the Catholic Faith*. Lincoln, NE: Os Justi Press, 2024.

Lawler, Phil. "The Pope's arbitrary actions belie his call for 'synodal' governance." *CatholicCulture.org*, March 9, 2022.

Mangenot, E. "Anticoncordataires." *Dictionnaire de théologie catholique* 1/1, cols. 1372–1378.

Margelidon, Philippe-Marie, and Yves Floucat. *Dictionnaire de philosophie et de théologie thomistes*. 3rd revised edition. Paris: Parole et Silence, 2023.

Marmor, Andrei, and Alexander Sarch. "The Nature of Law." *The Stanford Encyclopedia of Philosophy* (Fall 2019 edition), ed. Edward N. Zalta, https://plato.stanford.edu/archives/fall2019/entries/lawphil-nature/.

Unresolved Tensions in Papal-Episcopal Relations

Montagne, H.-A. "Notre programme." *Revue thomiste*, vol. 17 (1909): 5–37.

Muggeridge, Anne Roche. *The Desolate City: Revolution in the City of God*. Revised and expanded ed. New York: HarperCollins, 1990.

Newman, John Henry. *The Church of the Fathers*. London and New York: John Cane, 1900.

The New Raccolta, or Collection of Prayers and Good Works to which the Sovereign Pontiffs Have Attached Holy Indulgences. From the third Italian ed. Philadelphia, PA: Peter F. Cunningham & Son, 1903.

"El obispo de San Luis prohibió la presencia de mujeres en los altares." *Clarín*, November 1, 2019, www.clarin.com/sociedad/obispo-san-luis-prohibio-presencia-mujeres-altares_0_OSD-mgCY.html.

Origen. *Homilies on Numbers*. Translated Thomas P. Scheck. Downers Grove, IL: IVP Academic, 2009.

Ottaviani, Alfredo. *Institutiones juris publici ecclesiastici*. Rome, 1947.

Packwood, Joshua. "Everything Is Flat: The Transcendence of the One in Neoplatonic Ontology." Doctoral Thesis, University of Arkansas, 2013.

Palmieri, Domenico. *Tractatus de romano pontifice*. Prato, 1891.

"Petite Église." *Wikipedia*, accessed September 26, 2023.

Plotinus. *The Six Enneads*. Translated by Stephen MacKenna and B.S. Page. Grand Rapids, MI: Christian Classics Ethereal Library.

"Pope removes Puerto Rican bishop from office." *National Catholic Reporter*, March 9, 2022.

Quasten, Johannes. *Patrology*, vol. 2: *The Ante-Nicene Literature after Irenaeus*. Westminster, MD: Christian Classics, 1983.

Reid, Alcuin, ed. *A Bitter Trial: Evelyn Waugh and John Carmel Cardinal Heenan on the Liturgical Changes*. San Francisco: Ignatius Press, 2011.

Rivoire, Réginald-Marie. *Does* Traditionis Custodes *Pass the Juridical Rationality Test?* Lincoln, NE: Os Justi Press, 2022.

"Roman Danylak." *Wikipedia*, accessed March 14, 2024.

San Martín, Inés. "Pope removes Puerto Rican bishop from office after he refused to resign." *Crux*, March 9, 2022.

Schneider, Athanasius. "Bishop Strickland's Removal is a 'Blatant Injustice,' says Bishop Schneider." *LifeSiteNews*, November 11, 2023.

Sforza Pallavicini, P. *Histoire du concile de Trente*. Montrouge: Migne, 1844.

Shaw, Joseph, ed. *The Intellectuals and the Latin Mass: Petitions to Save the Ancient Mass from 1966 to 2007*. Waterloo, ON: Arouca Press, 2023.

Works Cited

Strickland, Joseph E. "A Brief Update from Bishop Strickland." BishopStrickland.com, September 20, 2023.

Tissier de Mallerais, Bernard. *Marcel Lefebvre: The Biography*. Kansas City, MO: Angelus Press, 2004.

"Twelve Notable Decretists of the Middle Ages." *Unam Sanctam Catholicam*, March 5, 2023.

Valton, E. "Évêques: questions théologiques et canoniques." *Dictionnaire de théologie catholique* 5, ed. A. Vacant and E. Mangenot, cols. 1701–25. Paris: Letouzey et Ané, 1928.

van Noort, G. *Dogmatic Theology*. Vol. II: *Christ's Church*. Translated and revised by John J. Castelot and William R. Murphy. Westminster, MD: Newman Press, 1957; repr. Waterloo, ON: Arouca Press, n.d.

Vazquez, Gabriel. *In primam secundae Sancti Thomae*. Lyons, 1631.

Vitoria, Francisco de. *Relectiones*. In *Arbor magna iurisdictionis ecclesiasticae*. Venice, 1640.

von Hefele, Karl Joseph, et al. *Histoire des conciles d'après les documents originaux*. Paris: Letouzey et Ané, 1907ff.

The World Over with Raymond Arroyo, November 16, 2023: "Bishop Strickland Speaks and the Strickland Dismissal."

Zambrano, Andrea. "Seminario cerrado y sombras sobre Roma: 'El obispo se ha equivocado.'" *Brújula Cotidiana*, August 3, 2020, https://brujulacotidiana.com/es/seminario-cerrado-y-sombras-sobre-roma-el-obispo-se-ha-equivocado.

Zuhlsdorf, John. "What the mighty Jesuit Karl Rahner would say, said, about suppressing *Summorum Pontificum*." *Fr. Z's Blog*, July 1, 2021.

You might enjoy some other titles published by Os Justi Press:

Dogmatic Theology

Lattey (ed.), *The Incarnation*
Lattey (ed.), *St Thomas Aquinas*
Pohle, *God: His Knowability, Essence, and Attributes*
Pohle, *The Author of Nature and the Supernatural*
Scheeben, *A Manual of Catholic Theology* (2 vols.)
Scheeben, *Nature and Grace*

Spiritual Theology

Doyle, *Vocations*
Guardini, *Sacred Signs*
Leen, *The True Vine and Its Branches*
Swizdor, *God in Me*

Liturgy

A Benedictine Martyrology
The Life of Worship
The Roman Martyrology (Pocket Edition)
Chaignon, *The Sacrifice of the Mass Worthily Offered*
Croegaert, *The Mass: A Liturgical Commentary* (2 vols.)
Kwasniewski (ed.), *John Henry Newman on Worship, Reverence, and Ritual*
Parsch, *The Breviary Explained*
Pothier, *Cantus Mariales*
Shaw, *Sacred and Great*

Language & Literature

The Little Flowers of Saint Francis (illustrated)
Brittain, *Latin in Church*
Farrow, *Pageant of the Popes*
Kilmer, *Anthology of Catholic Poets*
Lazu Kmita, *The Island Without Seasons*
Papini, *Gog*
Walsh, *The Catholic Anthology*

www.ingramcontent.com/pod-product-compliance
Lightning Source LLC
Chambersburg PA
CBHW030243010526
44107CB00030B/1312/J